PEN~GUIN~

HADRIAN'S WALL

Brian Dobson was born in 1931 at Hartlepool, educated at Stockton Grammar School and Durham University. He stayed firmly at Durham (as Staff Tutor, later Reader, in Archaeology in the Department of Adult and Continuing Education) apart from National Service and two years at Birmingham University, concentrating on the Roman army and on Hadrian's Wall. He has now retired.

David Breeze, born in 1944, was educated at Blackpool Grammar School and at University College, Durham, and is now Chief Inspector of Ancient Monuments in Scotland. He has excavated extensively in North Britain and written books and articles on Roman archaeology and the Roman army. He is married with two sons and lives in Edinburgh.

DAVID J. BREEZE AND BRIAN DOBSON

HADRIAN'S WALL

Fourth Edition

PENGUIN BOOKS

To Pamela and Anne

PENGUIN BOOKS

Published by the Penguin Group
Penguin Books Ltd, 27 Wrights Lane, London W8 5TZ, England
Penguin Putnam Inc., 375 Hudson Street, New York, New York 10014, USA
Penguin Books Australia Ltd, Ringwood, Victoria, Australia
Penguin Books Canada Ltd, 10 Alcorn Avenue, Toronto, Ontario, Canada M4V 3B2
Penguin Books (NZ) Ltd, Private Bag 102902, NSMC, Auckland, New Zealand

Penguin Books Ltd, Registered Offices: Harmondsworth, Middlesex, England

First published by Allen Lane 1976
Second edition published in Pelican Books 1978
Third edition 1987
Fourth edition 2000
13

Set in 9.75/12.25 pt Monotype Van Dijck
Typeset by Rowland Phototypesetting Ltd, Bury St Edmunds, Suffolk

Printed and bound in Great Britain by
Antony Rowe Ltd, Chippenham, Wiltshire

ISBN-13: 978-0-14027-182-9

CONTENTS

LIST OF PLATES

vii

The authors and publishers would like to thank the following for supplying photographs for use in this volume:

Committee for Aerial Photography, Cambridge University, Plates 8, 34;
Mr P. Connolly, Plates 19, 20;
English Heritage, Plates 4, 10, 11, 26, 27, 30, 31, 33;
Historic Scotland, Plates 15, 16;
Dr V. A. Maxfield, Plates 17, 24, 25;
Newcastle upon Tyne Museum of Antiquities, Plates 3, 6, 12, 21, 22, 32, 35;
Turners Ltd, Newcastle upon Tyne, Plate 9;
Tyne and Wear Museums Service, Plate 18.

LIST OF TEXT FIGURES
AND MAPS

Figures 2, 5, 9, 20 and 21 have been drawn by Mr T. Borthwick. All other line drawings have been prepared by D. J. Breeze. They have been produced at uniform scales for comparative purposes. North usually lies at, or towards, the top of the page. As far as possible stone has been produced as a solid line, while turf is hatched. Thanks are also due to Mr D. B. Gallagher for assistance in revising Figures 10, 25 and 29.

N.B. 'Small forts' in the figures and text mean forts too small to hold a complete unit; 'fortlets' denote forts too small to hold more than a century. This can only be a rough classification.

LIST OF TABLES

NOTE ON
MEASUREMENTS

All measurements are given in modern miles and feet, with metric equivalents, except where Roman measurements are specified. The Roman foot was half an inch shorter than the modern foot:

1 Roman foot = 11½ modern inches (292 mm)
1 Roman mile = 1686 modern yards (1.54 km)

PREFACE

The number of books on Hadrian's Wall has multiplied disconcertingly of late. Nevertheless there still seems a place for a book concerned above all with the history of the Wall. This book therefore is not a guide to the Wall nor is it a description in detail of the actual physical remains. It is an attempt to review the evidence for the best-known and best-preserved of all Rome's artificial frontiers in order to explain why it was built at a particular time on a particular line across Britain, and to follow its history till the end of Roman control in Britain.

The book starts therefore with a condensed history of Roman Britain and the Empire up to the decision to build Hadrian's Wall, concentrating on Roman thought about frontiers in general and Rome's aims and objectives in Britain in particular. Next the building of the Wall is examined in detail, using a variety of evidence which allows some reconstruction of the planning and timetabling of the project. The following chapter deals with the abandonment of Hadrian's Wall, still in process of modification, for a new Wall in Scotland. This, the Antonine Wall, is examined in depth to see the differences and similarities between the two Walls. In the next chapter the later history of these Walls till the final abandonment of the Antonine Wall and the return to Hadrian's Wall is discussed and the new arrangements for controlling the northern frontier considered.

There is a natural pause at this point in the story. In the third century the northern frontier saw an era of peace broken by the first appearance of the Picts (under that name at least) and the Scots at the end of the century. These new dangers of the fourth century lead to a completely different situation from that of the first and second centuries. The fourth century also sees a complete reorganization, civil and military, of the administration of the Empire, and a complete change in the organization of the army. The tranquil interlude of the third century and the turbulent fourth century are therefore discussed after two general chapters on the organization of the army and life in the forts, which apply to the first, second and third centuries A.D., and to some extent to the fourth.

These two chapters are divided rather arbitrarily, but the first, 'The Army of the Wall', is intended to give the basic organization of the units in the Roman army and the layout of the Roman fort. It also acts as a glossary for some of the discussion in the historical chapters which involves unit organization and the internal buildings in forts, such as the suggested garrisons for the Wall forts. The second of these chapters, 'Life on the Wall', is an attempt to show what life on Hadrian's Wall was like, concentrating on the soldiers but not ignoring their dependants who created the *vici*, the villages outside the forts where soldiers' families and traders lived. Some notes on the later developments in the army are appended here.

There follows a chapter on the third and fourth centuries, and a conclusion. Some matters have been relegated to appendices. A list of emperors and governors is given, for reference purposes, which supplements chronological tables in the text. The units which at one time or another were stationed in the forts of the Wall, its outposts and its Cumbrian coast flank, are listed by names of unit and by fort. There is a rather longer treatment of the gods worshipped on the Wall than would be possible in the main text without over-extending the chapter on 'Life on the Wall'. Finally the places on the Wall are singled out where some of the features referred to in the text, details of construction or types of buildings in forts, may be most clearly seen.

It has already been said that this book is not a guide nor a gazetteer, nor can it be an exhaustive account of every aspect of the Wall. The purpose is to show how the Wall came to be, what it was and how it developed, how it influenced and was influenced by its alternative, the Antonine Wall, and what happened during its later history. Life on the Wall for the soldiers garrisoned there, and, as far as the evidence allows, for their dependants, is described in the light of evidence from the Wall and elsewhere. The bias is military, for the Wall was built and garrisoned by soldiers, though paradoxically its own purpose was bureaucratic rather than military, the establishment of a tidy method of controlling movement into and out of the Empire. The full effects of the Wall on the native peoples north and south of it, the full story of the civil settlements under its shadow, still remain to be discovered and recorded. Till these are known the story must be incomplete.

The views here presented are of course personal ones, and there can be no pretence that they represent the final solution or even the 'official' agreed one. For convenience the writing of this book has been divided between us, David Breeze taking the chapters on 'The Building of Hadrian's Wall', 'The Antonine Wall', 'The Two Walls', and the 'The Third and Fourth Centuries', Brian Dobson the Preface, Conclusion and those on 'The Concept of a Frontier', 'The Army of the Wall' and 'Life on the Wall'. The appendices are mostly Brian Dobson's work, apart from that on 'The Evidence on the Ground'. But the separation is purely one of convenience; the book is in every way a joint product.

The citation of evidence has presented a problem. This has been met by giving references rather than full texts for the evidence, citing where possible J. C. Mann's valuable collection of relevant literary, epigraphic and numismatic evidence in addition to standard works. A running bibliography has been preferred to footnotes. There is no attempt to provide a bibliography for the Wall. Attention is drawn simply to the major books or articles bearing on the points under discussion.

Our views are personal ones, but many of them have been formed in active discussion with other scholars, from whom we have learnt much. We should like to mention with special gratitude Eric Birley, who introduced us both to Wall studies, and who has done so much to make Hadrian's Wall more intelligible, and John Gillam, whose deep knowledge of Hadrian's Wall has been a continual source of stimulation. We are grateful also to the many others whose names appear in the following pages. We owe a particular debt of gratitude to Dr John Mann and Dr Valerie Maxfield, who were kind enough to read through our typescript and make constructive comments and criticism, and to Mr H. Russell Robinson, who looked through the section on armour and equipment. We have learnt much from all of these, but the responsibility for the views here put forward remains our own.

Finally we should like to thank our wives, who have perhaps suffered most throughout this partnership, in this volume and in others, for their long patience and forbearance with us over our Wall fever. We dedicate this book to them.

Edinburgh and Durham   August 1974

PREFACE TO THE PAPERBACK EDITION

We have been able to take account of some of the newly published work since the original manuscript left our hands. As a result of this, a number of minor changes have been made in the text and the most important publications on Hadrian's Wall have been added to the bibliography. We are grateful to several colleagues for their help in correcting inaccuracies in the text and in particular Professor Eric Birley for his detailed scrutiny of the text and constructive criticism and Mr C. M. Daniels for making plans of Wallsend available to us in advance of publication.

Edinburgh and Durham   May 1977

PREFACE TO THE THIRD EDITION

The last twelve years have seen a considerable amount of work on Hadrian's Wall, both in the field and in the study. We are grateful to Penguin Books, through Mrs Eleo Gordon, for agreeing to publish a third edition so that we can take account of this new work. We are also grateful to Messrs P. Austen, P. Bidwell and J. Crow for providing information on their excavations in advance of publication.

Two points merit particular comment. We have accepted that on present evidence the earlier dates for Agricola's governorship, 77–83, seem more likely than 78–84. We have also decided to commit ourselves to reversing the normal attribution of milecastle and turret types to legions VI and XX. Further, our doubts on the Stanegate 'system' grow, while we have accepted recent suggestions regarding the building of the Antonine Wall and the location of units on Hadrian's Wall according to the *Notitia Dignitatum*.

Edinburgh and Durham   1987

PREFACE TO FOURTH EDITION

We welcome the opportunity to take account of over a decade of work on the two Walls. Our thinking has changed to some extent as a result. In Chapter 1 we have tried to allow for the possibility that Domitian was already shifting the emphasis to the Tyne–Solway isthmus before Trajan. In Chapter 2 we have accepted the argument that the inscriptions from milecastles do not necessarily indicate the original legionary builders, and so we have become even more cautious over attributing the different work on Hadrian's Wall to specific legions. On the Antonine Wall the great change is the disappearance of the second period, following N. Hodgson's discussion in his article in *Britannia* 26 (1995), which suggests the possibility of shifting the beginning of its abandonment firmly into the later 150s. This has affected Chapter 4, as has the ability to attribute all references to Ulpius Marcellus to one governor of that name. Difficulties remain, but the new evidence allows for rather different conclusions. Chapters 5 and 6, on the army of the Wall and life on the Wall, have some important modifications in detail on the basis of new work. Here we may highlight the importance of further writing tablets from Vindolanda, now supplemented by those from Carlisle. The broad similarity between so many of these writing tablets and military documents from the eastern provinces validates the use of the eastern material to illuminate life in the northern provinces. Finally Chapter 7, on the third and fourth centuries, has had to be largely rewritten in the light of recent work, in particular at South Shields, Vindolanda and Birdoswald.

We are grateful to Lindsay Allason-Jones, Paul Bidwell, Peter Connolly, Peter Hill and Margaret Roxan for assistance on specific points.

We mourn the passing of three great Wall scholars, to whom we owe so much, Eric Birley, Charles Daniels and John Gillam.

Edinburgh and Durham 1999

1

THE CONCEPT OF A FRONTIER

(Hadrianus) murumque per octoginta milia passuum primus duxit, qui barbaros Romanosque divideret.

(Hadrian) was the first to build a wall, eighty miles long, to separate the Romans from the barbarians.

(Scriptores Historiae Augustae, Vita Hadriani, 11 2)

Such is the sole surviving Roman comment on the reason for the building of Hadrian's Wall. Why, almost eighty years after the invasion of Britain under the emperor Claudius in A.D. 43, should his tenth successor as emperor, Hadrian, decide in A.D. 122 that the Empire should be given artificial boundaries where no natural ones existed; and that in Britain the boundary should take the form of a wall, effectively to divide the inhabitants, willing or unwilling, of the Empire, from the barbarians outside? To understand why, the history of the province must be examined in the wider context of the Roman Empire.

THE EARLY EMPIRE

Rome in A.D. 43 already had eight centuries of history behind her. The literary tradition points to the middle of the eighth century B.C. for the foundation of the city, though archaeological evidence suggests the beginnings of a settled community by the tenth century B.C. During that time defeat in war had been virtually unknown to her since the sack of the city by the Gauls in 390 B.C. She had not even lost the war against Hannibal of Carthage, the second Punic War, and since her victory in that war at Zama in 202 B.C. no power had been capable of challenging her. This run of success, unparalleled in world history, was founded on an army which was unbeatable on its chosen battle ground, the open field. This single fact meant that even when Rome was reluctant to assume the role of supreme power after the victory over Hannibal the role was hers. As J. C. Mann has said, 'Roman history is essentially the virtually unique story of a nation trying to catch up with the situations produced by the incredible success of its army.' The idea of a more or less permanent boundary between Roman and barbarian was unthinkable, for it would set a limit to Rome's ability to conquer.

Rome saw her ability in terms of government and war. The remaining arts could be left to others:

Tu regere imperio populos, Romane, memento
(Hae tibi erunt artes) pacisque imponere morem
Parcere subiectis et debellare superbos

'Do you, O Roman, be mindful to rule the nations at your command (these will be your skills) and impose the law of peace; show mercy to those who have submitted and crush the proud in war'

(*Aeneid* VI 851–3)

So wrote Vergil, court poet to Augustus, the first emperor. Peace was to be achieved by force. Those who submitted would certainly receive merciful terms, that was true, but the *superbi*, those who resisted, must be crushed; then would the *pax Romana* be world-wide.

World conquest did not seem so remote a possibility. The world was not a big place to the Roman of the first century A.D.; according to the best theories, it was perhaps 10,000 miles east–west by 4000 miles north–south. Augustus already claimed its conquest in his account of his achievements, the great monument known as the *Res Gestae divi Augusti*; that it was not quite complete was a matter of detail. His trusted lieutenant, Agrippa, kept a map of the world in his portico; he presumably thought on similar lines.

Such concepts could not embrace the idea of frontiers as permanent boundaries, still less armies strung out along frontier lines in forts and fortresses. The Roman army operated in groups of legions, under the command of the emperor, his lieutenants, or the governors of provinces. Their essential task was to seek out the enemy forces and destroy them in battle, to inflict so crushing a defeat that the enemy would sue for peace. Occupation of ground was unimportant, so that Roman wars often take on the aspect of wrestling bouts, to be settled by falls or submissions, with a number of rounds separated by regular retirement to winter quarters in friendly territory – rather than a succession of lines on a map, representing territory gained in each year's campaign.

The dispositions of the legions were related to these aims. In the first century A.D. great army groups lay around Cologne and Mainz, ready to strike into Germany, or if need be intervene in already-conquered Gaul. In the East three or four legions were concentrated at Antioch, astride the main east–west route from Parthia. Elsewhere internal problems bulked larger than the enemy beyond the limit of Roman territory; in Spain, Dalmatia, Judaea, Egypt, the threat to security arose from within the province. Even the great river 'frontiers', the Rhine and Danube, on closer inspection prove to have been convenient stopping-places before another leap forward (which in the event never came in quite the form expected) and useful clear boundaries for the control of unauthorized movement; militarily they had limited value. In fact rivers are rarely if ever cultural boundaries dividing one people from another; they are routes along which people, goods and ideas flow, affecting both banks. They only become important as frontiers because they provide clearly visible lines for bureaucracies wishing to invent frontiers and control movement across them.

The military dispositions of the first period with which we have to deal, up to the late 80s A.D., consisted then of legions in bases chosen with an eye to swift assembly of mobile striking forces. The auxiliary forces, infantry and cavalry support troops gradually acquiring stature and importance, were often grouped around the legions. When they were not, their forts were for the most part winter quarters, placed with an eye to their convenience when assembling the summer task force, and for ease of winter provisioning. They could well be situated also with an eye to controlling and protecting newly conquered tribes, so in some areas the Roman dispositions might take the form of a network of forts, linked by strategic all-weather roads. In such a network there would be an outer strand of Roman troops posted nearest to the border of Roman territory, but there would be no special emphasis on it. More important still, only a small minority of forts would be garrisoned when the army was on campaign. The verdict was sought on the field of battle, with only the minimum number of troops on the lines of communication.

What attention was paid to the frontier, then, and what reality had it? Rome had found early that after an enemy had been defeated in war occupation of at least some of his territory became necessary. So the overseas empire had been reluctantly born after the first war against Carthage. Rome took over the boundaries of the state that had submitted to her, voluntarily or after defeat, and the responsibility for the defence of that state's territory. But she saw no military advantage in stringing her forces along those boundaries, nor any advantage in emphasizing their position by erecting barriers. Boundaries would set limits to her own expansion, without warding off encroachment or infiltration from without.

This situation obtained from the accession to sole power of the first Roman emperor, Augustus, in 31 B.C. to the 80s A.D. It was inherited from the late Republic, but there was one important difference. Under the Republic expansion was largely the work of individual generals and governors, who sought in conquest military glory in the form of triumphs or ovations, and the booty to recoup the money spent on past elections to magistracies and to fill their purses for the next ones, with little restraint from the Senate. Under the Empire, even though the emperor inherited the destiny of Rome to conquer the world, and could take on necessary but unattractive tasks like the subduing of the Alpine tribes and the extension of Dalmatia, even the full conquest of Spain, he could not and would not authorize a general advance. If the emperor was to control he had to limit the scope of his governors. Only the most trusted general could be allowed military success. Thus only the most secure of emperors with good and trustworthy lieutenants would conduct advances on more than one front at a time; worse still, the caution or weariness of an emperor might bring all expansion to a premature halt. Thus the shock the aged Augustus received from the loss of three legions in Germany in A.D. 9 seems to have inspired his advice to his successor Tiberius to keep the Empire within its limits — advice which he had never followed himself till the reverses of the revolt in Illyricum, beginning in A.D. 6, were followed by the disaster of A.D. 9. His successor, Tiberius, was already old, tired and disillusioned, and the advice was found acceptable and acted upon. For nearly thirty years there was no expansion.

JULIUS CAESAR IN BRITAIN

The invasion of Britain by Julius Caesar in 55 B.C. is typical of the way Rome expanded under the late Republic. From his base in Gallia Narbonensis (Provence) Caesar had already conquered the rest of Gaul (France and Belgium) with the necessary protestations that he was safeguarding his province and the interests of Rome. The reality of the dangers he claimed to be eliminating need not be discussed here, but it is abundantly clear that Caesar would have sought glory and booty whatever the situation, as part of the normal career of an ambitious nobleman in the late Republic. His initial success was so great that he was in danger, so it seemed, of running out of tribes to conquer, and so risking recall. The invasion of Britain justified the retention of his command for a further five years; he needed this justification so much that in 55 he took tremendous risks, invading too late in the campaigning season to make more than a reconnaissance in force, and nearly met with complete disaster. The glamour of crossing the ocean to an island that till then Romans had hardly believed to exist was sufficient to gain him a record number of days of public thanksgiving in Rome, exceeding what he had been given for the conquest of Gaul.

Caesar returned in 54 B.C., and won the formal submission of the British tribes opposed to him, but he did not winter there, although that seems to have been his original intention. Uncertainty about the security of the so recently conquered Gaul and about the political situation in Rome may have persuaded him not to risk being isolated beyond the Channel. Seneca asserts that he heard while still in Britain of the death of Julia, his daughter and Pompey's wife; if this was so it would be sufficient to bring Caesar back to Gaul to see its effects on his alliance with Pompey. Events in Gaul, which proved not to have been finally subdued, kept him from returning to Britain before the outbreak of civil war; significantly when he was sole master of the Roman world and seeking new worlds to conquer he did not think of Britain. For the governor of Gaul it had been the best place to conquer, a far easier one than Germany. For the master of Rome it was of peripheral interest; the East was the place to win military glory, now that his choice was unrestricted. The point is worth making, as it has a great influence on the history of Roman Britain, and of the Wall: Britain was never a number one priority. Also, whatever Caesar had written in his commentaries in order to justify the invasion, Gaul could be held down without conquering Britain.

For nearly a hundred years after Caesar no Roman military action was initiated against Britain. Although Britain in one sense was embarrassingly unfinished business (it should have been created a province after its submission to Caesar) and there are odd references to Augustus' intention to do something about it, he found much more important things to do; Tiberius' acceptance of Augustus' advice meant the shelving of the British venture for another quarter of a century. As was the way of Rome, diplomatic relations with the rising British kingdoms continued, and the successor to Tiberius, the young Caligula, had thoughts of invading Britain, with the usual fugitive princeling at hand to supply a pretext, just as he had thoughts of invading Germany. It was a natural return to expansion after the unnatural check imposed by the aged Augustus and Tiberius. Both enterprises were abandoned, probably because of the uncertain loyalty of Caligula's commanders on the Rhine, and his insecurity in Rome.

THE INVASION OF BRITAIN

Caligula's successor, Claudius, dragged from behind a curtain after the murder of his nephew to be made emperor because of the troops' loyalty to his dynasty, was also insecure. Created emperor in A.D. 41, he faced a serious rebellion in A.D. 42, only thwarted by the continuing loyalty of the troops. His situation was precarious; he lacked the glory of military success, the imperial virtue. A triumph must be obtained; the easiest place to win one, Britain. It was not so much the glory of defeating the dominant tribal kingdom in southern England, ruled by Togodumnus and Caratacus, the sons of the great Cunobelinus, lately dead, that mattered. It was once more the glory of crossing Ocean, the feat that had so impressed Caesar's contemporaries. This done, and the neighbouring tribes to the Catuvellauni defeated or made allies of Rome, Claudius could leave Britain after his stage-managed victory, telling his governor Plautius to conquer 'the rest'. Britain still retained the interest of Claudius while Caratacus was at liberty; his capture was an appropriate occasion to bore everybody with reminders of Claudius' one great success. The capture also marked a change of tempo in Britain – as the emperor loses interest the pace of conquest slows. Claudius ordered one of the leading generals of the day, Domitius Corbulo, to withdraw across the Rhine when he had crossed it on a punitive expedition. Corbulo wryly commented on the greater good fortune of those who had been generals under the Republic. Now only the emperor could initiate expansion.

A new youthful emperor, Nero, marked a change of tempo once more. Rid of his advisers, who had controlled policy during his early years, he launched out at both ends of the Empire. Ostorius Scapula, the captor of Caratacus, had died in office and been replaced as governor of Britain by Didius Gallus, who had kept things quiet. His successors were two special-ists in mountain warfare, Veranius and Suetonius Paullinus. Their activities were directed towards the conquest of the tribes of the Welsh hills, the north being temporarily tranquillized under a client (dependent) queen supported by Roman arms. It was again characteristic of Roman priorities that the governor Paullinus was away campaigning when another client kingdom, that of Prasutagus, king of the Iceni of East Anglia, was being absorbed into the Roman province. The rebellion led by the widow of Prasutagus, Boudica, showed how casual the approach to pacification had been. Plans for advance were shelved, and three successive governors concentrated on keeping things quiet. One of the four legions in Britain was withdrawn in A.D. 67, indicating that no advance was expected in the near future, and in A.D. 69 civil war broke out. Vettius Bolanus, the last of the three, appointed as governor during the civil war, could not keep the client kingdom of Brigantia, covering the greater part of northern England, under Roman domination. Queen Cartimandua, who had strength-ened her claim on Roman support by delivering Caratacus to them, quarrelled with her consort Venutius. Venutius won, although the queen was rescued by Roman troops, and with a civil war raging no more could be done. Clearly, however, Brigantia could not be left in the hands of the fiercely anti-Roman Venutius.

When the civil war was over the new emperor, Vespasian, was one of the relatively few senators who knew Britain, where he had served during the invasion and first campaigns. The governors he sent in succession were faithful adherents and competent soldiers – two of whom, Petillius Cerialis and Iulius Agricola, also had previous experience in Britain. Cerialis, the first, conquered or fought over a great part of Brigantia. His successor, Iulius Frontinus, conquered the Silures of south Wales. Both may have done rather more than this, as Agricola, the third of Vespasian's governors, in his first season put down the Ordovices of north Wales, but described them as rebels, men presumably then already conquered by Frontinus, or even by Paullinus. In his second he forced tribes to submit who had been independent, and may have been already fighting Rome. Tacitus does not say where these tribes lived, but they were presumably beyond and north of the Brigantes. So far he may only have been dealing with tribes that Cerialis had previously encountered, but in his third season he met hitherto unknown tribes and penetrated to the Tay, though without fighting a battle. The conquest of the Welsh peninsula, northern England and southern Scotland in a decade (A.D. 71–80) suggests strongly that the real hindrance to earlier conquest had been the lack of personal involvement on the part of the emperor; Nero's enthusiasm had been quenched by the Boudican rebellion.

Did this conquest of the north reflect a change of policy, forced on Rome by the collapse of the northern client kingdom? Many have thought so, and some have even suggested that lowland England, largely won in the first hectic years after 43, was the original limit of Rome's objectives. Naturally there is no way of demonstrating whether this view is correct. There seems, however, no need to interpret the military dispositions in the early period as representing successive frontier lines. They suggest rather an overall distribution of troops in winter quarters, and perhaps the occupation of some key points to hold down the conquered, protect the provincials against raids, and pass the winter quietly before the summer campaign took the army into enemy territory. They contrast markedly with the forts strung out along linear earthworks and rivers of the Empire in the second and succeeding centuries. The Fosse Way, the great road that runs from Lincoln to Exeter, both legionary bases in the early years, is not a frontier line. Roads were not to be used in this way for another forty years. The other 'evidence' for a linear frontier in the years before A.D. 80, Ostorius Scapula's intention to control everything 'this side' (south) of Trent and Severn (if that is really what Tacitus said originally), seems rather to indicate the area of the province which in Scapula's view should be regarded as pacified. To make pacification effective disarmament was necessary (provincials were not allowed to carry arms except on journeys or for hunting); the first to object were the Iceni, a client kingdom well within the province. This consolidation before advance, characteristic of Scapula, as Tacitus remarks, does not justify any conclusion that he was establishing a permanent frontier. There is no convenient stopping-line, like the Rhine or Danube, in Britain south of the Forth–Clyde isthmus, and no evidence that the Romans thought that they had reached one. The frontier at any time would be the boundaries of the tribes allied to or subject to Rome, with perhaps a few forts pushed forward to hold important river-crossings or passes.

There is no way of demonstrating that the client kingdom of Brigantia was to be a permanent arrangement; the history of other client kingdoms makes this seem highly unlikely. The agreement reached with Cartimandua, like that with Prasutagus of the Iceni, could have been part of the diplomatic offensive at the time of the invasion in 43, with the immediate objective of isolating the Catuvellauni. Alternatively it may have been part of the arrangements made by Claudius or his governor to control the largest of the British tribes on the vulnerable northern flank of the new province. It would lapse at her death, unless Rome chose to renew it. If she had died when Prasutagus did, her kingdom would presumably also have been absorbed into the province. In the event the success of Venutius and the eviction of Rome's nominee Cartimandua meant that Rome had a war on her hands.

MONS GRAUPIUS – THE INCOMPLETE VICTORY

By A.D. 79 then, not yet forty years from the invasion, the Roman governor Agricola had carried Roman arms to the Tay. How far his predecessor Petillius Cerialis had come in his operations against the Brigantes and consequently how far Agricola's advance was into new territory does not matter for our purposes. What does is that at this point his son-in-law and biographer, the great Roman historian Tacitus, puts in an interesting thought: 'If the courage of our army and the glory of the name of Rome would have allowed it, a halting-place could have been found inside Britain, for Forth and Clyde . . . are separated only by a narrow neck of land', i.e. an alternative was conceivable to the straightforward advance till the northernmost coast was reached. The year, as determined by the dating of Agricola's governorship accepted here, would, significantly, be 80; Vespasian had died on 23 June 79, as Agricola's army was moving up towards the Tay. Agricola now halted his advance, presumably to await the orders of the new emperor, Titus. Agricola was in his fourth season and had already served a term as long as the average for a governor; he might well be replaced. A year passed, and Agricola was still in Britain. He drew up his troops on the coast facing Ireland, and he told Tacitus in later years that a conquest of Ireland would have been perfectly feasible. We do not know if he suggested this to the emperor, and he could hardly have invaded Ireland without permission. It would have given him the possibility of more conquest if further advance in Britain was deemed unnecessary. The Forth–Clyde isthmus is in fact the most sensible *terminus* (stopping-point) within Britain, as it offers the shortest line and the country beyond is so difficult. Perhaps it was at this time that the forts on the road up to the Tay were built, screening Fife.

Advance was resumed in A.D. 82, again on the dates accepted here, and it is tempting to link it with the death of Titus on 1 September 81. It was probably the new emperor Domitian, frustrated of military glory so far, who gave the word 'Forward'. Tacitus says merely that 'the courage of our army and the glory of the name of Rome' would not allow a permanent halt on the Forth–Clyde isthmus, but it was the emperor who determined what was allowed. Tacitus approved of the forward policy, but disliked Domitian. If the credit for the advance had been Agricola's, he would have said so. Agricola crossed the Forth in his sixth season, had a frustrating year marked by a near-disaster to the legion IX Hispana, and in his seventh season (A.D. 83) brought the enemy to battle in the classic Roman style at Mons Graupius.

This victory seemed decisive, to Agricola at least, but it was not pursued. Agricola himself was recalled but he had already served twice the average term of a governor. Forts were built at the mouths of the glens; a legionary fortress was begun at Inchtuthil. Whether these forts represented an earnest attempt to contain the Highlanders rather than to conquer them must remain uncertain; they could have been merely a pause for breath. In the 140s Lollius Urbicus did not reoccupy these advanced positions though he

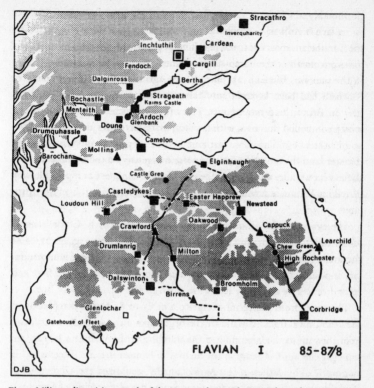

Fig. 1 Military dispositions north of the Tyne–Solway isthmus in the mid 80s. Forts are distinguished by large and small squares, small forts by triangles, fortlets by circles and the watch-towers along the road from Ardoch to Bertha by dots. The open square indicates a site possibly occupied at this time.

did reoccupy sites to their rear, on the road running up Strathmore, which suggests that the glen forts were more than purely defensive in intent. The legionary fortress at Inchtuthil also seems a springboard for further advance, in the tradition of Gloucester, York, Caerleon and Chester, rather than a legionary base in the front line of a purely defensive system, for which there would be no good precedent.

Decisive in the abandonment of further conquest seems to have been the withdrawal of one of the four legions of Britain, II Adiutrix, in order to meet a crisis on the Danube. The legion intended for Inchtuthil,

presumably XX Valeria Victrix, had to go to the new fortress at Chester
to replace II Adiutrix. Auxiliaries may also have gone with II Adiutrix to
the Danube; in any event it was not thought practicable to maintain auxiliary
garrisons north of the Forth–Clyde isthmus. It must be remembered that
in the previous fifteen years all of Wales, northern England and southern
Scotland had been brought into the province. Virtually every auxiliary
unit in Britain had moved into a newly constructed fort in a network
which controlled this area, with new legionary fortresses at York, Caerleon
and Chester. Holding more without a fourth legion would have courted
disaster, and the fourth legion was needed urgently on the Danube. Nevertheless its withdrawal marked the end of total conquest as a possible way
of making Britain secure until Severus attempted to revive it over a century
later.

The evacuation of all on and to the north of the Forth–Clyde isthmus
seems to have been within a few years of 86 – the coins suggest by 88 at
the latest. How long the Romans remained in southern Scotland is uncertain,
but it would appear that by somewhere about the turn of the first and
second centuries A.D. they had withdrawn to the Tyne–Solway line.

The years from the recall of Agricola in 83 or 84 to the completion of
the withdrawal from Scotland by the beginning of the second century, and
from then up to the beginning of the building of the Wall in A.D. 122, are
amongst the most obscure in the history of Roman Britain. Tacitus in his
biography of his father-in-law Agricola had summarized the achievements
of all the previous governors, and given a more detailed account of Agricola's
campaigns; this information is supplemented by other literary sources, for
Caratacus and Boudica by Tacitus' own accounts in the *Annals*.

The pattern is reasonably clear. An attack on Britain, lying on the edge
of the Roman world and across Ocean, had a certain glamour that had
commended itself at critical stages to Caesar, Caligula and Claudius. The
initial impetus from Claudius died away after the capture of Caratacus;
the renewed efforts of the young Nero foundered on the Boudica rebellion.
Vespasian, with his personal interest, initiated the renewed drive that
almost conquered the whole island, a policy continued by his two sons.

The rule of his younger son, Domitian, was a turning-point in the history
not only of Roman Britain, but of the Empire as a whole. He began with
advance in Britain, in Germany, and on the Danube. But defeat on the
Danube stopped the advance in Britain, and rebellion on the Rhine compro-

mised recovery on the Danube. In Germany the advance simply came to an end, but it was not immediately obvious that the arrangements then made were to have permanence. In Britain there was clearly a retreat, but the details are obscure. Tacitus, in the *Agricola* writing in 98, does not mention an abandonment of the idea of conquest. Of course his interest was in Agricola back in Rome, no longer in Britain, and there is no evidence that the recall of Agricola in itself vitally affected Roman policy in Britain. As events were to turn out, the halt was fatal, as Tacitus saw when he was writing the *Histories* about 105, when he used the phrase 'Britain was totally conquered, and then immediately let go'. If the reconstruction of events above is correct, all on and to the north of the Forth–Clyde isthmus was given up shortly after 86, as a result of the transfer of II Adiutrix to the Danube. The more difficult question remains whether the final withdrawal to the Tyne–Solway isthmus was the work of Domitian, murdered in 96, his successor Nerva, who died in 98, or the great warrior-emperor Trajan, who ruled from 98 to 117.

TRAJAN

It seems common ground that Trajan was responsible for or accepted this final withdrawal to the Tyne–Solway isthmus. How is this to be reconciled with the picture of Trajan as the great conqueror and extender of the boundaries of the Empire to their furthest extent? He was of course ambitious for military glory, like a true Roman, and despite the favourable picture given by our sources there is little clear evidence that his great wars of conquest against Dacia and particularly against Parthia were motivated solely, if at all, by considerations of the needs of the Empire. There is nothing, however, to suggest that he had any interest in Britain, except perhaps as a source of reinforcements for the wars elsewhere. He was not personally committed to conquest in Britain, and might accept a withdrawal from some territory to gain stability in Britain while he was engaged personally elsewhere.

By some such speculation must be found a reason why Trajan authorized a final withdrawal to the Tyne–Solway line, in what seems to have been an orderly evacuation of sites, with timber structures fired by the retreating Roman army, or accepted an earlier one by Domitian. The forts north of

Forth–Clyde had already been evacuated and the number of forts occupied between Forth–Clyde and Tyne–Solway considerably reduced at least under Domitian: if there was any further withdrawal to make it would have allowed units to be transferred from Britain to the Dacian wars. There is no need to postulate disaster – that would have to be avenged – and a Roman decision is more likely. This policy of reduced commitments to produce stability is reflected in the rebuilding in stone of the new legionary fortresses at York, Caerleon and Chester; the old fortress sites had been handed over, to colonies of veteran legionaries at Gloucester and Lincoln, and to *civitates* (civil authorities) at Wroxeter and Exeter. Rebuilding in stone implies that the legionary bases were not to be moved in the foreseeable future, and that the fourth legion, withdrawn under Domitian, was not to return and make total conquest possible. The abandonment of conquest did raise the problem of frontier control in a new form, for it was beginning to be clear that there would be a more-or-less permanent frontier.

It must be pointed out, though, that Trajan's objectives – if correctly interpreted – were not entirely achieved. In 117, when Hadrian succeeded Trajan, we are told that the Britons could not be kept under Roman control. An officer commanding the *cohors II Asturum*, in Germany in 89 but in Britain by 105, was decorated in a British war before becoming tribune of a legion, III Cyrenaica, in Egypt, a province that the legion had left by 128. This war may have been under Domitian or Nerva rather than Trajan. A unit, the *cohors I Cugernorum*, won the military distinction of the emperor's names, *Ulpia Traiana*, and a grant of citizenship to all its non-citizen soldiers concerned in a particular exploit, probably in Britain, between 103 and 122. The attribution of a recently discovered inscription at Vindolanda to a British war at about this time is uncertain as to its dating, whether the war was a British one, and whether the officer commemorated was a legionary centurion in command of the unit or simply an auxiliary centurion. A further complication is the possibility that Trajan had reduced the garrison of Britain to two legions by transferring the legion IX Hispana to the legionary base at Nijmegen in Holland in compensation for legions transferred from the Rhine to wars further east. It is not surprising, however, that there should be fighting in Britain when Trajan was perhaps attempting to make the military situation there stable and permanent. There was periodic serious fighting in Britain till the early third century. Oddly, though, the mass of information from the Vindolanda tablets for the period 90s to 120s, otherwise so poorly attested, nowhere suggests serious trouble on the frontier.

But did Trajan have a frontier system in Britain, whether or not it was partly inherited from Domitian? Thought had been changing since the dreams of world conquest of the age of Augustus. The world was now bigger than had been believed. The terrain beyond the Mediterranean world was increasingly alien and unattractive. Domitian's conquests in Germany had been real enough, but advance had stopped on the Taunus ridge and in the Wetterau. It can be argued that there was a logic to the frontier thus created, but it was a second best after the abandonment of original and far-reaching plans of conquest. Positions were linked under Domitian by a series of watch-towers on a path. A similar series of watch-towers has been discovered along the road running north from Ardoch to the Tay. Pottery dating to the late first century has been found in association with them; the fortlets which seem to be part of this line are, however, undated. These towers might have been erected as part of the arrangements in connection with the establishment of the Forth–Clyde line as a frontier in Agricola's fourth season. This would make them earlier than those in Germany. However, as several towers appear to have two phases, the history of the towers on the Ardoch–Tay road may be more complicated than we have supposed.

There seems to be similar thinking in Britain and in Germany. What had originally perhaps been no more than temporary limits of advance were acquiring the characteristics of permanence; static observation towers were supplementing normal patrols. It reflects the possibility of a final frontier between Rome and Barbary. Significantly it was under Domitian that the army groups which had waited so long on the Rhine to conquer Germany had their base areas made into provinces, Upper and Lower Germany. That was the only Germany they would ever conquer, although still in 98 Tacitus was hoping for that final conquest of free Germany: '*tam diu Germania vincitur*' ('the conquest of Germany is taking such a long time'). Domitian knew better – the legions on the Rhine were reduced from eight to six; soon there would be only four. H. Schönberger sees the years 89–90 as 'a historical turning-point and the final abandonment of the offensive against free Germany'.

Watch-towers appear on the south bank of the Danube on Trajan's Column in Rome, the great pillar adorned with a frieze showing scenes from his Dacian wars which Trajan set up in Rome. It is likely that frontier control, the observation of movement into and out of the Empire, had started early on these great rivers of Rhine and Danube, so convenient as boundaries. As early as 70 a German tribe, the Tencteri, had complained that they only had access to the *colonia Agrippinensis* (Cologne) if they were unarmed and practically naked, under guard and after paying a fee. In 98 Tacitus describes how the Hermunduri, on the upper Danube, had the privilege, unique to them among the German tribes, of trading not on the bank of the Danube but deep in the province and even inside a Roman colony; they could enter and leave without guards. To enforce rigid controls the rivers must be watched; the towers on the Taunus and in the Wetterau and in Scotland represented the first extension of such controls to frontiers without rivers.

Also under Trajan there is evidence for the stationing of *numeri* in Upper Germany. These contingents of troops retained the characteristics of irregulars, unlike the normal auxiliary cavalry (*alae*) and infantry (*cohortes*) regular units, standardized in organization and to some extent in equipment, with a fixed term of service. *Numeri* were to see much employment on frontier lines, particularly those with no great river barrier. Finally under Trajan appear small forts in Upper Germany, similar to those built on or near the Stanegate. There were fortlets, as yet undated, on the Gask frontier.

THE STANEGATE 'SYSTEM' (SEE FIG. 2)

If, then, Trajan meant to stabilize the situation in Britain, and accept that in Britain as on the Taunus and in the Wetterau installations on the furthest line of foreseeable advance were necessary to control movement, these were the devices to his hand: watch-towers; *numeri*; small forts; fortlets; and a road in default of a major river as a convenient boundary to the Empire. The Forth–Clyde isthmus had been abandoned; the next obvious, indeed only possible line, was the Tyne–Solway. There was a road already here, built under Agricola or his successors; what survives today reflects in its alignment its later history. It linked two forts which guarded important river crossings on routes into Scotland, Corbridge on the east and Carlisle on the west. It is probably best to reserve the term

'Stanegate' for the road between these two sites, and exclude extensions which may be postulated but are not proven. The Stanegate ran through a natural gap formed by the valleys of the Tyne and Irthing. It has been assumed for some time that Trajan did in fact base a frontier system on this road, the Stanegate, but the evidence is inadequate. It seems that at some point before or during his reign withdrawal to this line had taken place. On pottery evidence forts at Corbridge, Vindolanda, Nether Denton and Carlisle had been in existence since the Flavian period. Carvoran has been generally assumed to be of similar date, though what evidence there is is Trajanic, and Brampton Old Church is thought to have had a short occupation of about the time of Trajan. Newbrough has yielded pottery of the fourth century alone, but an earlier fort on this site is generally postulated as it fits a regular spacing of forts along the Stanegate. Finally Haltwhistle Burn and Throp have yielded pottery now thought to be Trajanic. Various schemes for the Stanegate have been put forward, generally tied to alternating large and small forts. What follows is one more attempt to reconstruct what happened between the evacuation of the land north of the Tyne–Solway isthmus and the building of Hadrian's Wall. It is written on the basis that the existence of a 'system' has to be demonstrated, not assumed.

The Stanegate was first built as a strategic road, not as a frontier. As such it would normally be provided with forts at one-day marching intervals (c. 14 Roman miles, 13 modern, or 21 km) to protect the movement of troops and convoys of supplies, who thus could always sleep under a fort's walls. These forts should be Vindolanda and Nether Denton, and the dating given to the samian pottery from these sites is consonant with their construction as forts on this strategic road under Agricola's successors. So far these forts were only part of the network of roads and forts which was the norm for the disposition of units. The forts that have been investigated, Corbridge, Vindolanda and Carlisle, show evidence for a number of changes in size and unit in the years between their construction in the 70s and 80s and the building of Hadrian's Wall. Aerial photographs indicate that Carvoran and Nether Denton had at one time a larger phase than the visible forts, as did Corbridge and Vindolanda. It has been suggested that the large forts may all belong to the 90s, but the dating evidence is insufficient. The final stage in development, it is often argued, is the building of forts in the gaps between the existing forts; forts would then be at a half-day's marching interval – the spacing on Hadrian's Wall when forts were built on its line.

Unfortunately two of the three forts at the heart of the discussion regarding the Stanegate – Newbrough and Carvoran – are of very uncertain date. A Trajanic Newbrough is inferred purely on spacing grounds, as only a small fort apparently associated with fourth-century pottery has been found; the fort at Carvoran is uninvestigated, though Trajanic pottery was observed in a fort ditch during building work. Excavation of Brampton suggested a short occupation at about this time, corresponding to that at Throp and Haltwhistle Burn. This evidence, for what it is worth, supports the idea that extra forts were built on the Stanegate under Trajan, but falls short of proof that this was done systematically. Brampton is the only unusual addition to the normally spaced forts of Vindolanda and Nether Denton that needs to be accounted for, as Carvoran can be explained in a different way. The latter is related to another road, the Maiden Way coming over from Kirkby Thore; it may have been built at the road junction before the Stanegate became a frontier road.

The placing of forts at a half-day's interval on the strand of the network nearest the enemy would be a military measure, to bring more troops into the crucial area. Stationing troops in more forts rather than in larger forts would provide local patrolling and a close military presence to any point on the frontier road.

The next element to be examined has little to do with military problems but a lot to do with control of movement across a frontier: the building of small forts (see p. x) between the normal-sized forts. This has still to be proven as a consistent feature along the Stanegate, for only two sites seem certain though another four have been suggested. The certain forts are at Haltwhistle Burn and Throp, 210 by 170 feet (64 by 52 m) and 200 by 195 feet (61 by 59.4 m) respectively, with areas of rather under one acre (0.4 of a hectare) overall. Haltwhistle Burn, with its stone internal buildings, has a curious plan. There seems to be one barrack, a possible granary, and other buildings that may be for administration. The most likely interpretation is that the fort is the base for a unit, most of which was out-stationed. However, all that can be said with certainty is that this small fort is Trajanic, that it could not accommodate a regular *ala* or cohort, and that unlike the Trajanic small forts in Germany or the Hadrianic milecastles it is not mainly taken up by accommodation.

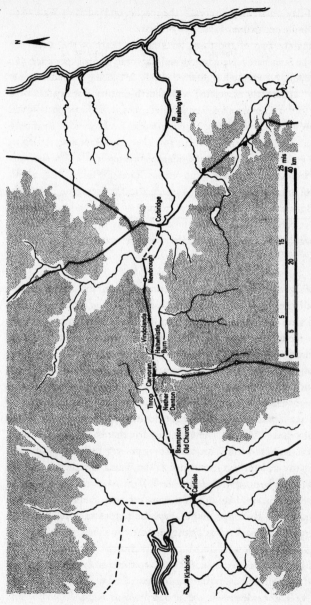

Fig. 2 Military dispositions upon the Tyne–Solway isthmus in the early second century. The open squares indicate forts probably occupied at this time.

Table 1   The distances between forts on the Stanegate

Fort	Distance in miles	(km)	Distance in miles	(km)
Carlisle				
Brampton Old Church			7½	(12.0)
Nether Denton	13½	(21.7)	6	(9.6)
Carvoran			4½ (or road junction)	(7.2)
Vindolanda	11	(17.7)	6½	(10.4)
(Newbrough)			6	(9.6)
Corbridge	13½	(21.7)	7½	(12.0)

The first column shows the distance in miles between the original forts, the third the distances when the 'half-day' forts were added.

Whether small forts similar to Haltwhistle Burn and Throp existed between all the forts suggested as 'half-day' forts on the Stanegate is uncertain. Only excavation can confirm the likely sites that have been suggested. Small forts may have been built only where local conditions justified them; presumably they are related to control by patrol and observation of the passage of natives across the frontier. If there were out-stationed troops from Haltwhistle Burn they must have been accommodated somewhere, but where is difficult to say. It would be dangerous to argue that it was in the observation towers which have been linked with the Stanegate 'system'. There are only five that have been suggested, one of which, on Walltown Crags, is dated by pottery to early in Hadrian's reign. This tower, later incorporated into the Wall as turret 45a, and the tower on Pike Hill, incorporated into the Wall as an extra turret, must be accepted as preceding Hadrian's Wall, as that wall simply abuts on to them. Suggestions that they might have been part of a long-distance signalling system, linked to the Stanegate or even to Hadrian's Wall, do not seem to carry weight, given that the practicability and advantage of such signalling are alike doubtful. Recourse to the nearest fort if there was trouble too hot to handle for observing and patrolling frontier guards seems more likely. The evidence for the undated Mains Rigg, Barcombe and

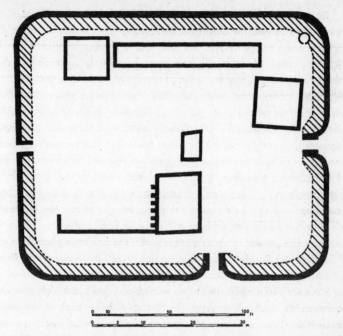

Fig. 3 The small fort at Haltwhistle Burn on the Stanegate. Scale 1 in. = 66 ft (1:792).

Birdoswald towers is unsatisfactory. All the towers can be explained as built singly to solve local problems, not as part of a chain. There are certainly nowhere near enough identified towers to form a closely spaced system, such as that on the Gask Ridge, in Germany, or later on Hadrian's Wall.

Fig. 4 Towers. a. Pike Hill; b. 45a (Walltown). Scale 1 in. = 40 ft (1:480).

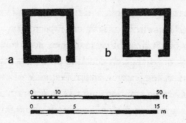

What happened west of Carlisle and east of Corbridge? There is no warrant to extend the Stanegate from sea to sea. West of Carlisle the Solway was a visible though not uncrossable boundary, better than the Stanegate road. Forts in this area were part of the network covering the military zone. There was a fort at Kirkbride, at the mouth of the river Wampool, overlooking Moricambe Bay, from Flavian times. Two forts have been discovered from the air at Burgh-by-Sands roughly halfway between Carlisle and Kirkbride. Pottery points to occupation in the period 90 to 130, and it is possible that one or both forts date to the first scheme for Hadrian's Wall (see below p. 39), though one may be earlier. One fort was apparently preceded by a timber tower, which produced pottery of the same period. This, and a second tower at Easton, may have been associated with a palisade and ditch running between the marshes. However, these features have not yet been published in detail and further comment is impossible. A road has been observed from the air in two places between Kirkbride and Burgh-by-Sands South, but even if it were precisely dated it would not necessarily be an integral part of the Stanegate, as a road or as a 'system'. In the east, the Tyne, unbridged below Corbridge, provided a convenient visible boundary. The fort at Washing Well, on the south bank of the Tyne, may have been part of the network in the east; it is still uninvestigated. The fort at South Shields was not yet built, on the known site at least. The area south of the Tyne and east of the Pennines has few fort sites, sufficient, it seems, only to provide shelter a day's march apart on the great Dere Street route. In contrast, forts west of the Pennines and on Stainmore are often less than a day's march apart..

Clearly much is uncertain about Trajan's 'frontier' in Britain. It is too easy to postulate without real evidence forts, small forts, towers, even an extension of a fort and small fort system west of Carlisle and east of Corbridge. A few suggestions only may be made. Rebuilding the legionary fortresses in stone, in itself perhaps no more than was necessary some thirty years after their construction in timber, may have been the occasion for a decision that Britain, like Germany, was to stay as it was, without significant expansion. Such stability made necessary some system of border control. Observation towers had been used as early as the time of Augustus. They are pictured on the Danube under Trajan. Fortlets of milecastle size appeared on the German frontier under Domitian; small forts, containing *numeri*, may have appeared under Trajan. In the light of these the two certain small forts, almost as big as those in Germany, and the use of observation towers, may indicate some extension of the German type of frontier control to Britain, but not (on present evidence) in a systematic way. At the same time there may have been some strengthening of the numbers of fighting troops on what now had become the frontier road by stationing them at closer intervals, which gave the road a special military importance and made possible more intensive patrolling. Most of the evidence, such as it is, comes from the sector between Vindolanda and the Irthing crossing near Brampton, which may or may not be significant.

The military control of north Britannia was still a network, but the outer strand had been thickened, intentionally or otherwise. At the same time the military forces, mobile units designed to fight the enemy in the field, began to be drawn into the paralysing role of frontier guards. But this development is still in its infancy. The situation is still extremely fluid – between about 85 and about 125 at least four structural phases have been identified at Corbridge and Vindolanda.

Can the process be dated? The legionary fortresses were being rebuilt from early in the reign. Caerleon in 99–100, Chester perhaps after 102, York in 107–8. On the Stanegate Brampton and Throp, together with Haltwhistle Burn, with its stone wall which seems to point to an imagined permanence, appear to be built in the reign of Trajan, and they must presumably belong to a time after the evacuation of southern Scotland, as they presuppose that the Stanegate is now the frontier, or, to be more precise, the point at which frontier control is exercised. It was no more a tribal or cultural boundary than the later Hadrian's Wall, and some area to the north must have remained Rome's responsibility as the outpost forts built under Hadrian are more likely to reflect a continuing responsibility than an advance by Hadrian. The evacuation is conventionally dated to 105 at latest. There is now evidence from Vindolanda and Carlisle for rebuilding about 105 to add to that suggesting that the second fort at Corbridge was built in 103 or later, so a date in the early years of the second century seems very likely.

How much of all this may have been anticipated under Domitian? In the absence of clear dating for many of the sites this can only be a matter for speculation. The situation discussed appears to be that in operation at the end of Trajan's reign, whatever its origins and development. Trajan would thus have acted in much the same way in Britain and Upper Germany:

he recognized, like Domitian when he turned from expansion after the Saturninus rebellion of 89, that Rome would not expand on these two frontiers. In Britain and in Upper Germany there was no river to act as a convenient administrative boundary. In both similar expedients seem to have been used, though the detailed arrangements in Britain will be unknown until further excavation takes place. The Forth–Clyde isthmus and much if not all of what lay between it and the Tyne–Solway isthmus had already been abandoned before Trajan's reign. Perhaps reoccupying the more northerly isthmus in force and holding some forts to the north of it (as was necessary in the 140s) was more than was feasible or desirable, if it meant drawing troops away from Trajan's own wars.

Stabilization of frontiers in Upper Germany and Britain, perhaps even retreat from territory occupied in Britain: how are these to be reconciled with Trajan the conqueror? The different roles played by the personality of the emperor and the inexorable underlying trends of imperial history must be recognized. Trajan desired military glory; he may or may not have been mistaken in identifying his search for glory with the true interests of Rome. He was not the last emperor to do so or to seek expansion. But the logic of the realization that Rome was not going to conquer the world was working itself out. Even if Rome promptly concluded that the rest of the world was not worth conquering she would need frontiers, clear boundaries, as a fluid situation became static. As has been seen, this was already happening where a river formed the boundary, even before hopes of advance were given up.

The new system of frontier control required a visible boundary, such as was provided by a river. The concept of a permanent artificial barrier to supply this boundary seems to be the work of Hadrian, and to him and his work we must now turn. But despite his different personality Hadrian did not set the Empire on a new path. He merely provided the logical culmination to the process of developing a frontier that had begun with Domitian.

2

THE BUILDING OF HADRIAN'S WALL

Hadrian's Wall is the concept of Hadrian much more than the Stanegate system is of Trajan; it is an accurate reflection of the man and his policies. Hadrian had gone through the normal career of a Roman senator, as Trajan had done. He had served with distinction as a legionary tribune, as a legionary commander, as a provincial governor. He had served Trajan faithfully, and probably had always been intended to be his successor (despite the doubts surrounding the adoption and the inevitable tensions between 'king' and 'heir-presumptive'); yet Hadrian and Trajan were far apart in thought. Hadrian intended to give the Empire permanent frontiers. His first act was to abandon the untenable conquests of Trajan in the East. Thereafter in two great journeys he visited all the armies of the Empire, inspecting them rigorously to ensure that they were kept in training and good discipline while winning their favour by his interest in their welfare and abolition of abuses. His policy was clear and decided: peace, stable, controlled frontiers, a well-trained and disciplined army, all under the vigilant eye of an itinerant emperor.

It has already been mentioned that when Hadrian came to power in 117 he found trouble in Britain. His biographer states simply that 'the Britons could not be kept under Roman control'. There is a coin showing BRITANNIA issued in 119 which is usually taken to imply a victory in Britain. This could mean either trouble within the province or attack from outside. Cornelius Fronto writing in 162 to his former pupil, the emperor Marcus Aurelius, refers to a large number of soldiers killed under Hadrian by the

Jews and by the Britons. The Jewish war was in the 130s but the British war, or wars, could have been at any time in the reign. The losses were clearly serious and may have been occasioned by the disorders at the beginning of the reign. A fragmentary tombstone found at Vindolanda in 1997 is of a centurion in a unit based there during the reigns of Trajan and Hadrian and killed in a war, but unfortunately the war is not named. It is, however, clear that the Ninth Legion was not destroyed in Britain at this time, as used to be thought. The legion was certainly still in existence in the 130s and recent theories suggest that it was transferred to Lower Germany from Britain by Trajan or Hadrian and moved thence to one of the eastern provinces, possibly being destroyed in Armenia by the Parthians in 161.

It may have been in response to the disorders at the beginning of his reign that Hadrian decided to deal effectively with the northern frontier in Britain. His inclinations were to conserve rather than expand, and so he chose to improve the existing frontier on the Tyne–Solway line rather than conquer the whole of the island of Britain or move forward to the much shorter Forth–Clyde isthmus. Hadrian visited Britain himself in 122 and, among other matters, concerned himself with the problem of the frontier. The other frontiers of the Empire were usually formed by natural boundaries: a sea, or a great river such as the Rhine or Danube, or a desert as in North Africa. In north Britain there was no such clear demarcation line and therefore Hadrian decided to create an effective frontier by the construction of a wall from sea to sea, a wall which would, as his biographer put it, divide the Romans from the barbarians.

THE POSITION OF THE WALL

The construction of Hadrian's Wall would appear to suggest that the existing frontier arrangements were insufficient. The only really effective method of control was a running barrier, a wall, which would allow the army to supervise small-scale movement of people, prevent petty raiding, hinder large-scale attacks and so encourage the peaceful development of the province right up to the frontier line (see Fig. 5).

The Wall was, however, planned with the existence of the vital east–west line of communication, the Stanegate, running through the Tyne–

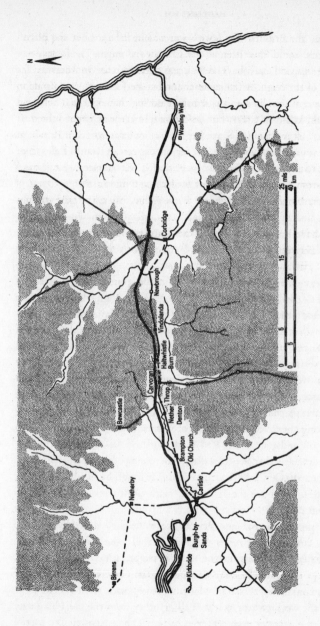

Fig. 5 Hadrian's Wall as planned, with the forts behind. The open squares indicate forts probably occupied at this time.

Solway gap, in mind. Its very position proclaimed that, for it was placed on the north side of the isthmus, remaining north of the rivers that run through the gap till Carlisle. The Wall was planned to be 76 Roman miles long (just over 70 modern miles or about 113 km) from Newcastle upon Tyne, where a new bridge was constructed and named Pons Aelius in honour of the emperor, to Bowness-on-Solway, so in the east and in the west it extended further than the Stanegate road as we have defined it. It was to be a stone wall, 10 Roman feet wide, for the eastern 45 Roman miles from Newcastle to the river Irthing, and a turf wall, 20 Roman feet wide at base, for the western 31 Roman miles from the Irthing to the Solway.

In the centre the Wall made use of the Whin Sill, a volcanic outcrop forming a line of north-facing crags. This, the best-known and most-photographed section of the Wall, forms only a part of the central sector which lies between the rivers North Tyne and Irthing (it stretches from Wall mile 33b to mile 46). East and west of the crags the Wall passes through very different terrain. In the east the Wall runs from the crags to Limestone Corner, the most northerly point on the Wall, where it changes direction and heads for the bridge at Newcastle. There are only minor deviations *en route*, as the Wall surveyors plotted its course from height to height. The line runs at an angle to the north side of the Tyne valley. The North Tyne is crossed at Chollerford opposite Chesters (the North Tyne and South Tyne unite just above Hexham). West of the crags the Wall runs towards the river Irthing. For some distance after crossing it at Willowford it perches rather uncomfortably on the north side of the Irthing gorge looking out towards the wastes of Spadeadam. With the change from limestone to sandstone at the Red Rock Fault the landscape softens, but the really dramatic change occurs after the crossing of the Eden at Stanwix, when the marshes of the Solway are reached at Burgh-by-Sands. From here the Wall lies just above the high-water mark till it runs down to the sea just beyond Bowness.

Across the whole isthmus the Wall ran through a relatively open landscape, farmed for centuries. Support for this comes from several sites on the Wall, particularly in the eastern sector, which have produced evidence for ploughing below the earliest Roman levels. In some cases it can be demonstrated that final ploughing took place shortly before the arrival of the work parties for the Wall; in other cases the ploughing may have occurred years or even centuries earlier. The construction of part of

Plate 1 The Wall at Cuddy's Crags looking east.

the Wall in turf also points to the existence of open countryside, though it is interesting to note that there is more evidence for woodland in the immediate pre-Roman period in the western part of the Wall than the eastern.

Throughout much of its length the view to the north from the Wall is reasonable – in many places it is impressively wide. There are places, however, where it is restricted, for example from Great Chesters westwards. Here no attempt was made to take a more advantageous line. The Wall followed the most convenient direct route, even if this left dead ground to the north. This was acceptable since the Wall was not to be defended as a city or fort wall is defended.

THE WALL AND DITCH (FIG. 19)

In front of the wall ran a ditch, except where the terrain rendered it superfluous, as on the Whin Sill – though here the ditch always reappears in the dips between the crags – or where, as at Limestone Corner, the effort to dig it through solid rock was unjustified. The ditch was separated from the wall by an open flat space or berm. This berm was usually 20 feet (6 m) wide on the stone wall, perhaps because of the pressure on the south lip of the ditch from the weight of the wall. On the turf wall it was only 6 feet (1.8 m) wide. The width of the ditch varied from 26 to 40 feet (8 to 12 m), usually about 27 feet (8.2 m), the depth was 9 to 10 feet (2.7 to 3 m), and the profile was V-shaped with a square-cut drainage or cleaning-out channel at the bottom. The material dug out of the ditch was thrown on to the north side and smoothed out so as to heighten the outer scarp of the ditch. In certain places small irregular mounds can be seen on the north side of the ditch. These may be the original spoil dumps which the ditch-diggers did not spread out, or they may have resulted from later cleaning-out of the ditch. Certainly the ditch was not always completed. This is vividly seen at Limestone Corner, where large blocks of whinstone lie tumbled out on the north side of the ditch while a huge block still remains in the ditch with wedge-holes visible on its upper side. A little to the east the overburden appears to have been removed but no effort has been made to dig out the rock. Elsewhere, on Cockmount Hill and at Allolee, the ditch was only partially completed or not even started.

The stone wall was erected on a foundation of slabs set in puddled clay. In some cases the foundations are known to have failed in their purpose, for example at the north gate of milecastle 37 (Housesteads). On this base the stone wall was built of squared rubble, the two outer faces of roughly dressed stones retaining a core of rubble usually bonded with clay though occasionally perhaps with mortar (Plates 11 and 14). The stone used in the construction of the wall was mainly sandstone, quarried locally. It seems that one or two courses of facing stones were laid, then the rubble and clay or mortar core added, then a couple more courses, more core, and so on. Today some of the quarries can be recognized from the inscriptions, usually mere doodles, that the Roman masons left on the rock face.

In some places traces of plaster surviving on the surface of the facing stones together with the discovery of decayed mortar lying beside the wall have led to the suggestion that the stone wall was completed with a lime-wash render. Evidence from elsewhere indicates that fort walls could be similarly plastered, with, in one known case, red lines painted to represent stone-work. It is a reasonable possibility that Hadrian's Wall was treated in like manner at some stage in its history.

Where water was likely to collect behind the wall drains were laid

THE BUILDING OF HADRIAN'S WALL

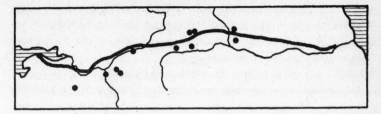

Fig. 6 Roman quarries near Hadrian's Wall, not all necessarily of Hadrianic date.

through the foundation. At first insufficient drains appear to have been provided, for more drains were inserted, at regular 20-foot (6-m), intervals, when the turf wall was later rebuilt in stone. Streams were culverted through the stone wall. At the two major river crossings, the North Tyne at Chesters and the Irthing by Willowford, bridges were provided. These were carried on stone piers and were wide enough to take a walk only. The wall itself was not carried by the bridge, that was pointless, but a boom may have prevented passage through the arches of the bridge.

It is impossible to be certain how high the wall was, or indeed how it was finished off at the top. The remains of the flight of steps at milecastle 48 (Poltross Burn) if projected upwards give a height of about 12 feet (3.6 m) for the wall top on the inside of the milecastle – 14 feet (4.2 m) on the outside – while the north gate of milecastle 37 (Housesteads) was 13 feet 8 inches (4.16 m) high. A recent study of the evidence, including the height of milecastle gate arches, suggests that it was designed to be 15 Roman feet (4.4 m) high. Roman fort walls may well have stood as high as 15 feet (4.5 m). This was the height of the wall of the fort at Wörth in Germany, which had collapsed complete into the ditch. It is possible that when the wall was later narrowed from 10 Roman feet wide to 6 to 8 feet the height of the wall was also lowered, but there is no clear evidence or necessity of this.

The turf wall was constructed of laid turves. A later military manual specifies the size of such turves, 18 by 12 by 6 Roman inches, but it is not known if the builders of Hadrian's Wall observed this rule. The dark lines caused by the grass of the turves can still be seen when a section is cut through the turf wall. What little survives suggests that the front of the wall had a steep batter, while the back, at first vertical, continued at a more gentle slope. The most recent discussion of the turf wall by R. L.

31

Bellhouse suggests that it was about 14 feet (4.2 m) high, similar in height to the stone wall. The turf wall was normally erected on a turf base, but in the area of milecastle 72 and at the milecastle itself this was replaced by a foundation of rounded cobbles.

It is difficult to answer the question why Hadrian's Wall was partly constructed in turf and not completed throughout in stone. The later rebuilding of the turf wall in stone demonstrates that this was not impossible, and if it was possible why was the whole wall not originally built in stone? Indeed this is closely linked to a second question, why was the stone wall so wide? It did not have to be 10 feet (3 m) wide, for the later parts of the wall were built 6 feet (1.8 m) wide. The massive nature of the stone wall has even led to the suggestion that Hadrian may have been influenced by travellers' accounts of the Great Wall of China, built some two hundred years before, though it now seems that the massive form of the Great Wall as we see it today is the product of much later work.

The purpose of the building in stone, apparently to excessive width and height, might have been to impress the local people, or to provide sufficient width for a parapet walk; it might even have been to erect an enduring monument to Hadrian, very necessary to an emperor who had eschewed military glory. Hadrian's biographer was duly impressed. But if so, constructing part of the Wall in turf is even more inexplicable. It may be that building in stone west of the Red Rock Fault, where limestone for mortar ran out, would take longer, and so the turf wall was a temporary expedient, but clearer evidence is needed. Certainly it cannot be argued, as has been done, that there is no good building stone in this area; this was manifestly disproved when the turf wall was rebuilt in stone. It also seems unlikely that the turf wall was constructed in a hurry as protection against a threat from the north; such a threat, if it existed, would have been dealt with by the army independently of the Wall. The provision of three outpost forts just to the north of the western end of the Wall has been taken to indicate a threat to the Wall from the south-west of Scotland, but it seems equally possible to consider these forts as protection for a part of the province, presumably Brigantian tribal territory, isolated by the construction of the Wall.

MILECASTLES AND TURRETS

This Wall, be it of stone or turf, was not a closed frontier. Regularly spaced along it at intervals of one Roman mile were fortified gateways, conventionally called milecastles, though the term is misleading, for the milecastle was simply an adaption of the normal fortlet constructed throughout Britain by the army since the earliest days of the conquest. The milecastles provided a way through the Wall with double gates at front and rear. Most of the earlier stone wall milecastles seem to measure about 60 by 50 Roman feet with a wall often the same width as Hadrian's Wall itself, while many of the turf wall milecastles appear to have been about 70 by 60 Roman feet internally. The milecastle walls were of stone on the stone wall and turf on the turf wall. One or two are known to have been surrounded by a ditch, but this seems to be unusual. Each milecastle contained one or two small buildings, presumably barrack-blocks for the soldiers, though at one milecastle a rather less substantial building was interpreted as a storehouse. These buildings were either stone or timber on the stone wall but were always of timber on the turf wall. They seem to come in two sizes – 20 to 32 feet by 12 (6 to 9.8 by 3.6 m), and 52 feet by 12 (15.8 by 3.6 m). The smaller building, divided into two rooms, is always found singly but the larger buildings, which are divided into four rooms, are in pairs in the two known examples. The milecastle also contained an oven, usually in the north-west corner, and in the opposite north corner a staircase to allow access to a tower over the north gate, and perhaps to the wall top. The existence of this tower is normally assumed since it would complete the chain of regularly spaced observation towers along the Wall. The plan of milecastle 50 on the turf wall has been taken as corroborative evidence for this; there the north gate was constructed of ten upright timbers, the south gate of six, suggesting a more substantial structure over the north gate. C. M. Daniels, however, has pointed out that supports for a tower require six timbers only and the other four probably served another purpose, possibly in connection with the revetting on the side walls of the gate passage. He emphasizes that, apart from this feature found only at one milecastle, the plans of the north and south gates of the milecastles were the same and he therefore suggests that both gates were surmounted by a tower.

Plate 2 Milecastle 42 (Cawfields). Nothing is known of the internal arrangements.

At two points main roads passed through the Wall. Nothing is known of the gate on the road passing through north of Carlisle, but excavations at the Portgate on Dere Street have demonstrated the existence of a gateway projecting to the north of the Wall here, though little is known of its plan.

The mile-long gap between fortlets was broken by two observation towers usually called turrets. The turrets were therefore one-third of a Roman mile apart, but unlike the milecastles they were of stone whether on the stone or the turf wall. They were about 20 feet (6 m) square and recessed about 6 feet (1.8 m) into the thickness of the stone wall. The turret was entered by a door in the south wall and to one side of this door, in the stone-wall turret, is usually found a stone platform, though these were not provided originally. Four or five steps, where they survive, led on to the platform, which may have formed the base or support for a means of access to the first floor and above, perhaps to the wall top. It was long considered that access was by a timber ladder, but a timber stair seems more probable. In the turf-wall turrets no precisely comparable platforms have been found but most of these turrets contain a low stone dais, similar to the platforms but without any steps, beside the north wall. This platform could also have served as the base for a stair. It has been suggested, however, that it served as a raised bench where the soldier could eat his food and unroll his bedding clear of the filth which seems to have covered the floors of most turrets. In one turf-wall turret, 51a, a rough stone base

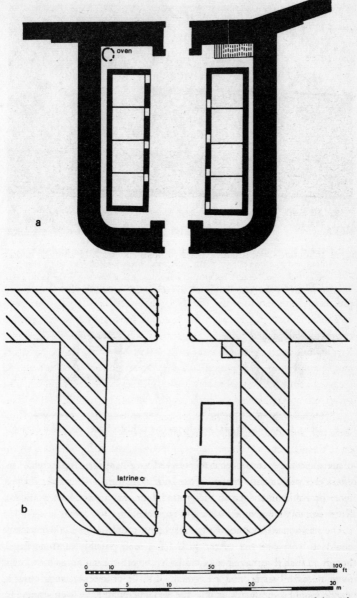

oven

a

latrine c

b

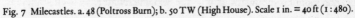

Fig. 7 Milecastles. a. 48 (Poltross Burn); b. 50 TW (High House). Scale 1 in. = 40 ft (1 : 480).

Plate 3 Model of a milecastle. The main features are: arched gateways with double doors front and rear, tower over north gate, small barrack-block (on right), shed (?), steps and oven. Modern reconstructions would add a tower over the south gate; it is possible that both towers had an extra storey to that shown.

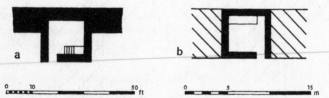

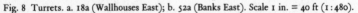

Fig. 8 Turrets. a. 18a (Wallhouses East); b. 52a (Banks East). Scale 1 in. = 40 ft (1 : 480).

in the south-west corner probably served as a base for a stair, while in others this presumably rested on the floor. The men in the turret if they slept there probably slept on the ground floor, and a stout bolt would be all the security they would normally require.

The height and roofing of the turret is a problem. The conventional view is to complete the turret with a flat roof, possibly of stone flags, though no such flags have been found. On the other hand slates have been found at some turrets, and a fragment of a tile at another, suggesting a peaked roof of some sort, but if so the remains found have been scanty. It

Plate 4 Turret 48a (Willowford East). A point of reduction in the width of the wall shows clearly on the extreme right.

is possible that the roofing material may have been thatch or wooden shingles and have left no trace today. The near-contemporary Trajan's Column shows towers with a hipped roof, a balcony providing an observation platform. A gabled roof has also been suggested. A hipped or gabled roof and a balcony seems preferable to the flat roof which would produce constant problems of weatherproofing in our climate, though few nails have been found at turrets. The designs on the Rudge Cup (Plate 6) and the Amiens Skillet, bronze vessels from the Roman period, generally dated to the second century A.D., have been taken as depictions of the Wall and its turrets, but this is far from clear. They may simply be stylized representations. A reasonable height for the turret may be presumed, to give a clear advantage in height over the wall top. Perhaps a minimum of 30 feet (9 m) to the viewing platform – twice the presumed height of the Wall – may be considered acceptable. This would have caused no difficulty to Roman engineering skill and would not have placed an undue strain on the foundations.

The turrets, besides providing regular observation posts, presumably

Plate 5 A reconstruction of a turret and stretch of wall at Vindolanda. This is one of several possible forms the turrets might have taken.

Plate 6 The Rudge Cup. Of mid-second-century date, this appears to portray the Wall as a running frieze, with the names of the forts above. Its diameter is 4 in. (100 mm) and its height 3 in. (75 mm).

also furnished shelter for the soldiers. All turrets would contain a hearth on the ground floor. It is probable that soldiers slept in turrets though in the nature of the archaeological evidence it cannot be proven; certainly excavation has demonstrated that turrets contained the normal detritus of life including quernstones, gaming counters and domestic artefacts. It would have been necessary to light the interiors by windows. These were probably simple affairs, perhaps holes closed by shutters, though window glass has been found at certain sites.

THE PURPOSE OF HADRIAN'S WALL

The milecastles and turrets provided the only accommodation for the soldiers on the Wall, for the original scheme included no forts on the line of the Wall. It must therefore be presumed that the forts already in existence behind the Wall on the Stanegate and on the south banks of the Tyne and Solway were to be kept in use. In some cases there were changes in the type of unit stationed in these forts, and it is possible that Burgh-by-Sands South was built at this time, specifically to provide a unit close to the Wall line, plugging the gap between Carlisle and Kirkbride. Behind the Wall in the east there is nothing north of the river Tyne between Corbridge and the new bridge at Newcastle, and south of the river only the fort at Washing Well is known.

This plan for Hadrian's Wall provided for the separation of the barbarians from the Romans, spoken of by Hadrian's biographer, by creating a continuous barrier. Surveillance over the ground north of the Wall would be exercised from the turrets and milecastle towers, so that attempts at unauthorized crossing of the barrier by raiding parties and the like could be foreseen and prevented. More serious trouble would be dealt with by signalling, or sending a runner, back to summon aid from the forts on the line of the Stanegate up to two miles (3 km) to the south. There was no point in signalling along the Wall since no milecastles had sufficient troops to deal with a major attack. The turrets therefore were watch-towers rather than signal-towers. David Woolliscroft has put forward an elaborate scheme for signalling from turrets and milecastles back to sites on the Stanegate, but only for the central sector, as too little is known of any putative Stanegate extensions east and west. Further evidence is needed.

The purpose of the barrier was to control movement, not to prevent it, as the liberal provision of gateways demonstrates. Civilians, whether merchants, local farmers moving their cattle and sheep or simply local people visiting relatives on the other side of the Wall, would be allowed through the gateways, though only presumably when they had satisfied the guards of their peaceable intentions and on payment of customs dues. The regulations known for the Rhine frontier, already referred to, lay down that the frontier can only be crossed, unarmed, under guard and upon payment of a fee. Although determined individuals or small parties might manage to clamber over the wall, movement on horseback, or in carts, or the driving of beasts, would only be possible through a controlled gateway.

So many gates were provided that travellers had to walk no more than half a mile (0.8 km) along the Wall to the nearest crossing-point. But the gates were also provided to allow troops to move easily through the Wall to deal with an attack from the north as well as conduct the more humdrum day-to-day patrolling. Not least the lavish provision of gates must have facilitated the maintenance of the wall and ditch. Lavish is the word, for there is a clear overprovision of gates and there is something artificial about their regular, even over-regular, spacing which led to milecastles and turrets being built in ludicrous positions on a steep hillside or with an almost precipitous drop immediately outside the north gate. This smacks of over-systematic planning, probably by Hadrian himself, with little attention to local topography.

There is, however, one major problem in any interpretation of the function of the milecastles. This is the fact that, except in the case of milecastle 50 on the turf wall, no causeways have been found in front of the north gates. So little excavation of the ditch has taken place that it is not possible to know if causeways once existed but were later removed, if timber bridges were constructed, or if no causeways ever existed. Some indication that the former may be the case came from discoveries at milecastle 54. Here a road was found apparently leading out of the north gate of the original turf and timber milecastle, and in the ditch opposite the end of the road was found a line of stone bottoming interpreted as the base of a stone culvert through a causeway. Clearly further work is necessary on this question, but it is interesting that the mile-fortlets on the Antonine Wall produce exactly the same problem, as few of them have causeways across the ditch in front of their north gates. Certainly the lack of causeways, and therefore access points across the ditch, clashes strongly with the provision of so many gates through the Wall. The latter suggests that this was to be an open frontier, the former a closed barrier.

Each milecastle contained one or two barrack-blocks to accommodate the men who guarded the gateways, controlled the traffic and manned the north tower. It is difficult to be sure how many men might have been stationed at each milecastle. Only seven milecastles have been completely excavated. Five contained a small two-roomed barrack-block and the two others two larger four-roomed buildings. The two-roomed unit is roughly equal in size to a normal *contubernium* or double-room (the old tent unit) for eight men in a full-sized barrack-block in a fort. Some milecastles may therefore have been garrisoned by only eight men, but others by four times that number, thirty-two men. Each turret and milecastle tower would have required a minimum of six men to maintain a constant watch so the soldiers manning the turrets on each side of a milecastle with sleeping accommodation for only eight could not on present evidence have slept at the milecastle. In fact the turret offered only slightly less space per man, if six be taken as the complement, than the milecastle barrack. Certainly the hearths associated with cooking-pots and animal bones in the turrets demonstrate that they cooked there. Even so eight men would hardly be sufficient to carry out all the necessary duties at a milecastle, including the guarding of the gate. There may have been as many as twelve if the men coming off duty simply took the sleeping places of the men relieving them.

It is usually presumed that troops also patrolled the wall top; indeed this has been seen as the major activity of the soldiers and the primary means of observation. In fact there is no evidence for this type of patrolling on the Wall; it is not only unattested but appears impossible on other frontiers where there was no provision of an elevated sentry walk – such frontiers were either timber palisades or narrow stone walls. Certain structural evidence may be cited as suggesting that the wall top was patrolled, but it is not unambiguous. The stair at milecastle 48 may have been only to allow access to the tower, not for patrols along the wall top. The blocking of turret recesses when they were abandoned may have been to allow the continuation of a wall-walk, but equally may have been to aid the structural stability of the Wall at these points. A bank of stone proposed as a ramp found uniquely at Peel Gap at one turret site, itself uniquely an addition to the Wall, need not be so interpreted. The original foot-bridge at Chesters is aligned on the Wall and may indicate a continuation of a wall-walk across the river, but it may have been that this was the most convenient place to locate the bridge while steps on each side of the river could have provided access only to the foot-bridge. The most that can be said safely is that the 10-foot-wide Wall was wide enough to allow a walk to have been provided along the top, that it is possible that the top was flat and therefore could have been patrolled, and that a parapet may have been supplied to protect such patrols. The Rudge Cup and the Amiens Skillet do not positively indicate that the Wall had a parapet. Some stones found at Cawfields have been interpreted as being from a crenellated parapet. Crenellation however is only appropriate for a defended wall top, and it may be doubted if it was provided for the Wall. On the turf wall the parapet was presumably of timber and, owing to the vast quantities of timber required, probably consisted of rough unseasoned posts and interwoven wattles. However, such a parapet did not need to be crenellated; it could have been a continuous low wall on both stone and turf sectors. Patrolling of the wall top could usefully supplement observation from the towers, particularly in mist or at night, and help to deal with observed unauthorized attempts to cross the Wall.

R. G. Collingwood pointed out long ago that the wall top did not serve as a fighting platform but as this idea constantly re-emerges his arguments bear repeating. The wall top, allowing for a parapet about 2 feet wide, would vary in width from 8 to 4 Roman feet. There was scarcely room to pass behind a man fighting from the wall top, and the only access points to bring up reinforcements or remove wounded men were milecastles and turrets, some 540 yards (494 m) apart. The Romans only fought from behind the shelter of walls as a last resort and developed no specialized weapons for fighting in this way until the changed conditions of the fourth century. There was no provision on the Wall for enfilading fire from projecting towers. Naturally there was no provision for artillery on the Wall, neither on the wall top itself nor at turrets. The Roman army was primarily intended to fight in the open and would if possible move out to engage the enemy long before the Wall was reached.

It has been suggested that equally narrow platforms and access points equally far apart have been found on city walls. The first point may be conceded, but there can be no comparison between city walls, perimeters guarded by a force placed inside, and the long ribbon of Hadrian's Wall. Men would have had to race from the forts some distance to the south to man the wall top before the barbarians could scale the Wall from the north. The cavalry would be useless for manning the wall top, of course, and would be wasted if dismounted for this duty. It should be pointed out that the presumed height of Hadrian's Wall is low in comparison with the known heights of Roman city walls. It has also been suggested that the turrets were 'fighting towers', but they are much more widely spaced than towers on city walls or camp perimeters. Finally, access points for troops need to be broad stairs or ramps, which are not attested on the Wall, not narrow stairs in turrets, while the 'fighting platform' in Roman forts appears to include the top of the earth bank behind the stone wall, absent on Hadrian's Wall.

The troops whose role it was to move out to meet the enemy in the open would come in the first instance from the forts immediately behind the Wall on the Stanegate; further support could be provided by the units stationed in the forts in the hinterland on the main roads which led to the Wall. The regular auxiliary units, infantry *cohortes* and cavalry *alae*, stationed at these forts might also have provided men for the milecastles and turrets. Lindsay Allason-Jones has noted that milecastles and turrets can be grouped together on the basis of the artefacts found there, which may point to soldiers being supplied from individual forts. If this is the case they would have needed regular reliefs and the sending-out of soldiers on such detached duties is regularly attested in Roman military documents, including some almost contemporary ones. A hundred years later men from the unit stationed at Dura on the Euphrates were sent out to serve in out-stations for three years and more.

On the other hand the men in the milecastles and turrets may have been members of a frontier militia specially raised for this purpose or drawn from the irregular units or *numeri* who may have occupied small forts on the Stanegate under Trajan, but which is otherwise unattested. Recent analysis of finds from the milecastles and turrets has emphasized their similarity to the material in the forts and therefore supports the theory that these troops were drawn from the units behind the Wall.

THE CUMBRIAN COAST

Milefortlets and towers on the Cumbrian coast carry the chain of observation posts for at least 26 miles (42 km) beyond the western end of Hadrian's Wall. The nature of these structures, so similar to those on the Wall, proclaims their function. Traces of fences and ditches too must, like the Wall, be connected to the establishment of supervised crossing-points, but as yet the details of these arrangements are obscure.

The milefortlets had ramparts of turf and were apparently about the same size as the milecastles with one exception, milefortlet 5, which measured 130 by 95 feet internally (about 40 by 29 m), about three times the norm. The barracks were probably of timber and in some fortlets hearths have been discovered; a timber tower usually appears to have been provided though not always over the gate. The towers, like the turrets on the Wall itself, were of stone. One tower, however, appears to have had a timber predecessor, and this may yet be demonstrated to be a regular feature. They were about 20 feet (6 m) square and were presumably similar in height to the turrets. In some, platforms with four or five steps leading to the top have been found; their purpose may have been the same as has been suggested for those in the turrets, namely to provide a base for a ladder leading up on to the first floor and the observation platform.

The frontier works continued beyond Maryport and may have run as far west as St Bees Head to control the movement of people across the Solway. What is in mind here is not seaborne assault, which could hardly be restricted to north of St Bees Head, but traffic across the estuary, probably of some antiquity. Suggestions that the line of fortlets and towers continued to Ravenglass and beyond are based on inadequate evidence; the notion is difficult to accept, as Ravenglass faces Man and Ireland, not the Scottish side of the Solway.

There is no substantial barrier here; the sea is a sufficiently clear boundary, simplifying observation. There are traces, still insufficiently understood, of a ditch or ditches and a fence or fences, through which the milefortlets provided gateways. They also provide accommodation, though very little is known of this, and, with the towers, continue the look-out system. It should be emphasized that these fences and the ditches associated with them are very slight, in comparison with the stone and turf walls and their ditches, and with the foot-square oak posts of the palisade in Germany. There is also a road associated with them.

These linear features were recorded for the first time in 1975. They have been traced from Bowness as far as Silloth to the south-west of Moricambe Bay. They are most complex, and the summary just given can only be the most provisional of interpretations. For the first mile or so beyond Bowness a pair of ditches, 150 feet (45.7 m) apart, has been located. The forward ditch measured 5 feet (1.5 m) across and 2 feet 8 inches (0.8 m) deep; it had been recut twice. The rear ditch measured 6 feet 6 inches (1.9 m) across by 2 feet (0.6 m) deep. A mile on, by tower 2b, only one ditch was found. It was 3 feet 6 inches (1.1 m) wide and 1 foot 4 inches (0.4 m) deep and had been recut on three occasions. Aerial photographs suggest the existence of this one ditch for at least a mile to milefortlet 4. Between milefortlet 4 and tower 4a a fence stood in front of the forward ditch. This ditch, 7 feet 6 inches (2.2 m) wide and 2 feet (0.6 m) deep, had been recut on two occasions. Located 100 feet (30 m) behind lay once more the rear ditch, 3 feet 6 inches (1.1 m) wide and 2 feet (0.6 m) deep, and recut twice. At tower 4b there was found a single ditch and behind it a fence, the fence apparently of two phases, and also a road. Both phases of the fence are thought to have preceded the construction of the stone tower, the first being associated with a timber tower, though the only evidence for this is a mass of clay, interpreted as the ground floor of the tower. At Silloth two phases of wattle fence and the road were located; the road has been traced on to at least the fort at Beckfoot.

The ditches and fences display a lack of uniformity. There was clearly a desire to keep them in operation, all the changes apparently occurring within a relatively short period. The recuttings of the ditch may have been due to the soft sand and gravel subsoil, but it is not clear why the fence required replacement. The most remarkable aspect of these remains is their slightness. This is true not only for the fence, but also for the ditches, which are frequently slighter than the minimum requirement stated in one Roman military manual of 5 feet wide and 3 feet deep.

THE EASTERN FLANK

Finds not associated as yet with clear structural evidence suggest that a fort was built at South Shields on the south side of the Tyne estuary, either now or shortly after, to keep an eye on the mouth of the river. There is some evidence too, that the whole of the south bank of the Tyne from Newcastle to South Shields was supervised by one or more small posts, possibly fortlets, but nothing to suggest that the system extended down the east coast, where the geographical situation, and perhaps the political too, was very different from that on the west.

THE OUTPOST FORTS

The three outpost forts north of the Wall at Bewcastle, Netherby and Birrens also apparently formed part of the first scheme for the Wall. Their purpose was not to give advance warning of an impending attack on the Wall – that could be done by scouts – but more likely to guard territory, presumably Brigantian, isolated from the rest of the province by the construction of the Wall. The discovery of a dedication to the goddess Brigantia, the personification of the tribe, at Birrens may suggest that this fort lay within, or on the very boundary of, the tribal territory. It is possible, however, that the dedicator had learnt to worship Brigantia at the legionary fortress of York, and his dedication to her while on a posting, probably temporary, to Birrens, is not evidence for the extent of her territory. If this territory was not Brigantian the forts are difficult to account for unless Rome was directly interested in this area. These forts had presumably become necessary because the Wall would hinder assistance from units to the south. It seems possible that they were built, or at least planned, at this time, for a special road through the Wall was provided at milecastle 50 TW, presumably to Bewcastle. If the outpost forts were a later addition the road would have passed through the Wall at the neighbouring fort of Birdoswald.

THE NEW FORTS ON THE WALL

Before this simple plan for a wall from Newcastle upon Tyne to Bowness-on-Solway, a regular series of milecastles and turrets from Newcastle to at least Maryport, and perhaps to St Bees Head, and three outpost forts had been completed, a major modification was made. This was the abandonment of the forts immediately behind the Wall and the construction of new forts on the Wall line. At the same time, or shortly after, it was also decided to construct an earthwork, known since the time of the Venerable Bede as the Vallum, behind the Wall all the way from Newcastle to Bowness.

When work was suspended the stone wall seems to have been completed for the most part from Newcastle westwards for 18 Roman miles to the Portgate, where Dere Street passed through the Wall, and work was proceeding between Portgate and the North Tyne and from the Irthing eastwards to turret 36b on the site of Housesteads. The turf wall had certainly been constructed in the Birdoswald area and, though evidence for the situation elsewhere is lacking, it may have been almost complete. Work was broken off so abruptly that sections of wall were left standing to a variety of heights and the decision came so soon that two of the new forts were virtually completed under the governorship of A. Platorius Nepos, who began the original plan (see Fig. 9).

The new forts varied in size from 3.35 to 9.32 acres (1.3 to 3.7 hectares) and were all large enough to hold whole auxiliary units, with the exception of Drumburgh, which was only 2 acres (0.8 hectares). The forts on the stone wall seem to have been constructed in stone, though undoubtedly many of the internal buildings would have been of timber on stone sill walls, and those on the turf wall of turf and timber.

The Wall forts, wherever local topography allowed, were positioned astride the Wall. This enabled three of the four main twin-portal gates to open north of the Wall. It seems clear that the main purpose of this change was to allow unrestricted access for major forces to the north. Hitherto the troops had to march a mile or two up to the Wall and then pass through a relatively narrow milecastle gateway before they could come to grips with the enemy; the Wall got in the way of effective army manoeuvres. Each fort astride the Wall now had the equivalent of six milecastle gateways through the Wall. There is no suggestion, of course, that this was to enable

Plate 7 The foundations of turret 36b: the turret was demolished when the fort at Housesteads was built over its site. The walls to right and left are of later fort buildings.

the men in the new forts to fight on top of the Wall. There is no evidence for the provision of access to the wall top from the forts, wide stairs or the like. If fighting from the wall top was the purpose there is no explanation of the most obvious feature of the new arrangements, the projection of forts beyond the Wall. There would also be no point in cavalry being stationed in the forts, both full cavalry regiments and units which were partly made up of cavalry, as riding on top of the Wall would be neither safe nor advantageous, even if possible. The decision to build these forts was not undertaken lightly for it led to the infilling of stretches of ditch, the dismantling of already constructed wall, turrets and milecastles, the abandonment of a number of forts in northern England and Wales and the construction of twelve or thirteen new forts on the Wall. This meant that the whole building timetable for the Wall had to be reorganized and more seasons allocated to it, for the new forts not only increased the amount of building in stone but required far more in the way of sophisticated building techniques. It also reduced the usefulness of the milecastles and turrets

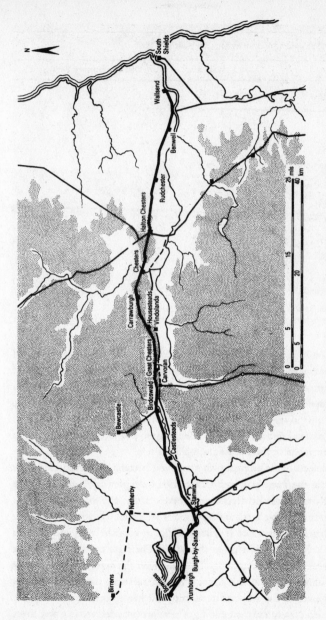

Fig. 9 Hadrian's Wall as completed at the end of Hadrian's reign. The open squares indicate forts possibly occupied at this time.

Table 2   The spacing of primary forts on Hadrian's Wall

Fort	Wall mile	Distance between forts
(South Shields)	–	
		c. 5½
Wallsend	0	
		6⅓
Benwell	6⅓	
		7
Rudchester	13⅓	
		8
Halton Chesters	21⅓	
		6
Chesters	27⅓	
		9⅓
Housesteads	36⅔	
		6⅓
Great Chesters	43	
		6⅓
Birdoswald	49⅓	
		7⅓
Castlesteads	56⅔	
		9
Stanwix	65⅔	
		6
Burgh-by-Sands	71⅔	
		8⅓
Bowness-on-Solway	80	

already built and those completed or built later. The army clearly viewed with concern the disadvantage under which it suffered in the original plan.

The provision of forts astride the Wall was an experiment to meet an unprecedented situation. When most of the forts had been completed it was discovered that they did not need to project from the line of the Wall itself. The final forts to be built, Great Chesters and Carrawburgh, were simply attached to the rear of the Wall.

The defects of the original plan must have become most apparent in the east where the stone wall had been carried from Newcastle almost to the North Tyne before the decision was taken to put the forts on the Wall. The fort at Washing Well, and any others which may have existed east of Corbridge, were separated by the river Tyne from the Wall and by both from effective action further to the north. The forts on the Wall in this sector were built early, although they involved the biggest destruction of already constructed wall and ditch. In the central sector the Stanegate forts, with no river in the way and a curtain wall hardly begun, continued to function effectively and the building of new forts was delayed for some time.

The forts were relatively evenly spaced along the Wall with no special regard for strong or weak points. They provided fighting troops in reasonable proximity to any point on the Wall, able to move out and deal with minor threats north of the Wall itself. In the face of a major threat these troops would use the road system to assemble for battle, abandoning the Wall. Some of their activities might be regarded as 'police work' rather than 'proper soldiering', but they remained fighting units of the Roman army. Police work always fell to soldiers before the appearance of police forces, and in some cases has done so since. Rome had virtually no police forces, though military units performed this function in Rome, Carthage and Lyons.

It would seem that the original plan was for twelve forts equally spaced at intervals of 7⅓ Roman miles. This was varied to allow for forts close to the river crossings on the line of the Wall at Chesters, Birdoswald and Stanwix. The spacing between Wallsend and Chesters is reasonably regular, the larger gap between Chesters and Housesteads (in its proper position) being plugged by a fort at Carrawburgh added after the construction of the Vallum. The space between Housesteads and the next river crossing, Birdoswald, was neatly halved by Great Chesters. Stanwix is almost at the position it should be if the forts were equally spaced. Castlesteads should have been situated halfway between Birdoswald and Stanwix but perhaps its position, a very odd one behind the Wall line, was dictated by a pre-existing fort. Finally, Burgh-by-Sands is not quite halfway between Stanwix and Bowness, because, like Bowness itself and the later fort of Drumburgh, it avoids a marshland site. It should be noted however that recent excavations have failed to find a Hadrianic fort here.

The forts on the Cumbrian coast followed a different pattern. New forts were built at Beckfoot, Maryport – possibly replacing an earlier fort – and Moresby, each pair some 12 miles (19 km), about a day's march, apart. Burrow Walls, it has been suggested, was not built till the fourth century.

It has been suggested that the forts which projected north of the Wall were cavalry forts, the infantry being content with only one twin-portal gate north of the Wall. However, it seems preferable to assume that all forts were intended to lie astride the Wall if possible. Examination of the size and ground plans of the forts, in conjunction with the slight epigraphic evidence, suggests that there were only three cavalry units on the Wall

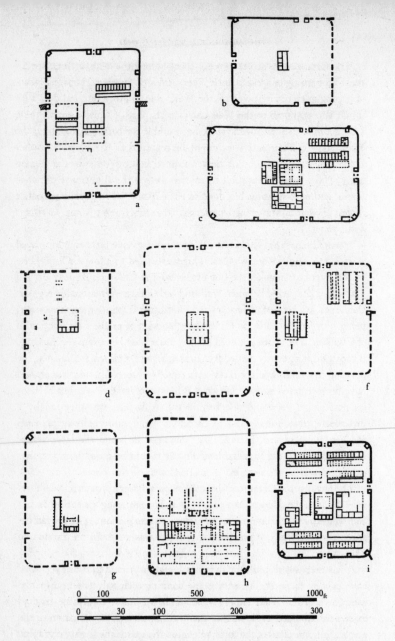

Fig. 10 Hadrian's Wall forts, Hadrianic plans (later buildings are omitted). From top left to bottom right: Birdoswald, Great Chesters, Housesteads, Carrawburgh, Chesters, Halton Chesters, Rudchester, Benwell, Wallsend. Scale 1 in. = 440 ft (1 : 5280).

Plate 8 Housesteads from the air looking east. Within the walls, complete with gates and towers, may be seen the central range of buildings – two granaries (to the left), headquarters with hospital to this side, and commanding officer's house – two barrack-blocks in the north-east corner (top left), the latrine in the south-east corner (top right) and civilian buildings outside the fort.

line (at Chesters, Stanwix and possibly at Benwell), three wholly infantry units (at Housesteads, Great Chesters and Birdoswald), while the other forts held mixed units of infantry and cavalry, *cohortes equitatae*. The three wholly infantry units were placed in the centre of the Wall furthest from the two main roads to the north, Dere Street passing through the Wall at the Portgate, and the road up Annandale crossing the Wall at Stanwix. The largest cavalry unit in the province, the *ala milliaria*, was placed at Stanwix on the main western route north; this fort also lay in the centre of the whole frontier complex including the Cumbrian coast, though this may be coincidental. The commanding officer of this unit was the most senior officer on the Wall, but this does not imply any command over his colleagues or that he was in any sense in charge of the Wall. The cavalry regiment at Chesters is in the best cavalry country available in the central sector, while the country around Benwell is also good for cavalry, if indeed the unit at the fort at this time was an *ala*.

Table 3   The suggested units in the Wall forts under Hadrian (see Appendix 2)

Fort	Acreage	Hectares	Unit
Wallsend	4	1.6	*cohors quingenaria equitata* (?)
Benwell	5.0	2.0	*ala quingenaria* (??)
Rudchester	4.5	1.8	*cohors quingenaria equitata*
Halton Chesters	4.3	1.7	*cohors quingenaria equitata*
Chesters	5.75	2.3	*ala Augusta ob virtutem appellata*
Carrawburgh	3.9	1.6	*cohors quingenaria equitata* (?)
Housesteads	5	2.0	*cohors milliaria peditata*
Great Chesters	3.36	1.35	*cohors VI Nerviorum quingenaria peditata* (?)
Carvoran	3.6	1.4	*cohors I Hamiorum quingenaria peditata*
Birdoswald	5.33	2.15	*cohors I Tungrorum milliaria peditata* (?)
Castlesteads	3.75 (?)	1.5	*cohors quingenaria peditata* (??)
Stanwix	9.32	3.7	*ala Petriana milliaria*
Burgh-by-Sands	4.9	2.0	*cohors quingenaria equitata* or *milliaria peditata* (?)
Drumburgh	2	0.8	(??)
Bowness-on-Solway	7	2.8	*cohors milliaria equitata* (?)
Beckfoot	2.55	1.0	*cohors quingenaria peditata*
Maryport	5.8	2.3	*cohors I Hispanorum milliaria equitata*
Moresby	3.6	1.4	*cohors quingenaria equitata* (?)

Total number of men on Hadrian's Wall:

Primary forts on Wall, excluding the Cumbrian coast: 7986 officers and men

All forts on Wall, excluding the Cumbrian coast: 9090 officers and men

In the eastern part of the Wall, from Wallsend to Carrawburgh, the only type of regiment employed, apart from the *ala* or *alae*, was the *cohors quingenaria equitata*, made up of infantry and cavalry. This was the most common type of auxiliary regiment, and was well adapted for frontier duties. In the centre, between Housesteads and Birdoswald, possibly even Castlesteads, all the units appear to be wholly infantry. The rest of the

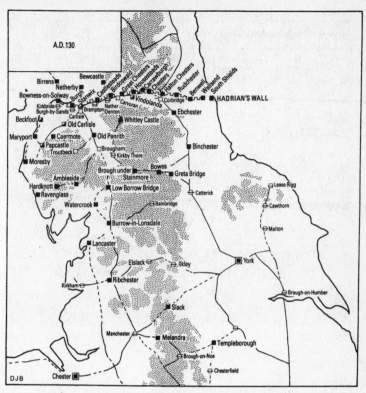

Fig. 11 Military dispositions in north England about 130. The open squares crossed through indicate forts considered to have been abandoned during the previous twenty years; open squares, forts possibly occupied at this time; and half-open squares, forts probably occupied.

western sector appears to have mixed units apart from the cavalry regiment at Stanwix, but the picture is less clear. There is a suggestion that the basic unit was a mixed one of infantry and cavalry, with pure infantry units being used in the centre, in the crags country, and the pure cavalry regiments placed strategically to take advantage of country suitable for their deployment.

These new forts were not replacements for existing ones immediately to the south, but in most cases additions. Several of the forts on the Stanegate, including Vindolanda, Carlisle and probably Corbridge, continued in

55

Plate 9 Aerial view of the central sector of Hadrian's Wall looking east, with the Wall following the crags on the left and the Vallum running behind the Wall on the right.

occupation. The 'fort decision' probably led to a reappraisal of the tactical position of many army units in the Wall area. Moreover, new units would have to be found for the additional forts. Presumably these would be withdrawn from stations in the Pennines and Wales, where several forts were abandoned about this time. There were now many more units based on the Tyne–Solway isthmus than at the beginning of Hadrian's reign.

THE VALLUM

The decision to construct the Vallum was contemporary with or immediately postdated the decision to move the forts up on to the Wall line. It cannot have been taken earlier as it would have reduced army movements

Plate 10 The Vallum crossing at Benwell looking north towards the fort. The ditch is shown dug to full depth, and to the north several periods of road are displayed as a series of steps.

to absurdity, while the relationship of the Wall and the Vallum in certain places suggests that they were almost contemporary. The Vallum consists of a flat-bottomed ditch 20 Roman feet wide and 10 deep with two mounds, 20 Roman feet wide, one on either side, set back 30 feet from the lip of the ditch (Plate 9). Thus a cleared area 120 Roman feet across was provided along the rear of the Wall which could not be crossed unwittingly or unobserved.

The Vallum was evidently a device to ensure the security of the Wall from the rear. The milecastles and turrets had been particularly vulnerable but now the population of the province, previously allowed to approach the Wall unhindered, were kept at a distance, only able to enter the Wall zone at forts, where causeways across the Vallum ditch were provided. These causeways of undug earth, together with gaps through the two mounds, seem to have been provided at every fort; they were guarded by massive gates, closed against the south (Plate 10).

The Vallum often passes so close to a fort that it has to deviate round it. This, together with the provision of undug causeways, demonstrates that the Vallum presupposes the existence of the forts. It has been argued that from the first there were also causeways across the Vallum at milecastles. This view is based upon excavations carried out before the Second World War at milecastles 50 TW and 51. The causeway at milecastle 50 TW seems a unique provision, combined with another feature unique at milecastles, a gap in the south mound, and with a causeway across the Wall ditch, which may not be unique, to permit the passage of a road, presumably to the outpost fort of Bewcastle, through the Wall. The blocking of the gap in the south mound, which followed almost immediately, would then be explained by the decision to direct the road to the new fort at Birdoswald. The interpretation of the excavations at milecastle 51 is far from clear. In more recent excavations at other milecastles no original causeways were found. Also on the evidence from milecastle 50 TW it has been argued that there was a patrol track along the south berm of the Vallum, between the ditch and the south mound. This could be purely a local feature; here the Vallum is very close to the milecastle, so close that the north mound of the Vallum is omitted to the east of the milecastle, all the spoil being placed on the south mound. Elsewhere metalling has been found on the north berm. This seems a more likely position for a patrol track, the fort causeways with their great guarded gateways providing the only access to it from the south, with the ditch as protection. Patrols and convoys on a south berm track would be separated by the Vallum ditch from troops on the Wall. Unbarred milecastle causeways make little sense alongside the gateways on the fort causeways, as the forts themselves needed no special protection. The gateways did not protect the forts but controlled access to the area between the Vallum ditch and the Wall, including the track along the north berm.

The track along the north berm would not only be used by army patrols, if these were considered necessary, but also perhaps by civilians. If they were allowed controlled passage through the Wall, it seems unlikely that they would be allowed through the forts themselves, especially if they were driving their flocks and herds. Instead, after crossing the Vallum at the fort causeway they would be directed along the track on the north berm to a milecastle where they could pass through the Wall itself. This presupposes the existence of causeways over the ditch, but milecastle gates without such causeways remain inexplicable. Supplies for the men in the milecastle would come by the same route; it is interesting that the road later provided along the Wall, the Military Way, frequently ran along the north mound of the Vallum. It is possible that the Vallum follows the line of a track which had been established during the building of the Wall. Excavations in 1987 revealed a metalled track immediately south of the Wall at Denton. Little investigation has been undertaken in this part of the Wall complex, that is between wall and Vallum, and it is possible that more evidence may come to light of a track or tracks in this position.

The Vallum reduced the number of cross-points through the Wall from an original seventy-nine or so to about fourteen, thereby greatly increasing the army's control over the movement of people. The Vallum also presupposes that resentment of the Wall and danger to it were coming from the south. Some incident may have made this obvious. The movement of the forts up on to the Wall line may suggest that free action by major forces north of the Wall had become a necessity. Such a large amount of work is unlikely to have been taken on simply from a desire to be more prepared for trouble. It is unfortunate that there is no more evidence as to where this possible trouble was coming from and how it was caused. Clearly, however, the task of Hadrian's Wall was proving more complicated than had been first visualized.

OTHER MODIFICATIONS

Work on the milecastles and turrets seems to have continued while the forts were being constructed, but a further modification was made to the Wall. The stone wall had been designed 10 Roman feet wide. It was incomplete when the decision to build the forts was taken. When nearly all the milecastles and turrets were completed but before work on the curtain had recommenced it was decided to narrow the wall. The new gauge is often stated to be 8 Roman feet thick, but narrower gauges are also attested. It seems as if working parties were allowed to complete the wall between 6 and 8 feet thick. This decision presumably speeded up the work, put well behind schedule by the building of the forts. Its value now lies in the clue it gives as to which work was done before the decision to build the forts, which after.

A number of minor modifications to the Wall remain to be noted. First, there is the extension of the Wall from Newcastle to Wallsend in narrow

Plate 11 The curtain at Planetrees. Here the wall is reduced in thickness from 10 Roman feet to 6 Roman feet. The foundations, incorporating a drain, had already been laid.

gauge, with a fort at Wallsend, but no Vallum to the rear. Presumably the river was considered to serve the purpose of the Vallum. Also, part of the turf wall was replaced in stone, probably towards the end of Hadrian's reign. A start was evidently made at the Irthing and the first 5 miles (8 km) west, up to about 54a, were completed. It may be, as has been suggested, that work was brought to a halt by the death of Hadrian in 138 and the decision to reoccupy Scotland. For part of these 5 miles (8 km) the Wall was rebuilt on a new alignment. From 49 to 51 the wall was realigned. A start had been made on replacing the original turf and timber fort at Birdoswald in stone. Now Hadrian's Wall was diverted from its earlier line to abut the north wall of the new fort leaving the two main side gates, previously north of the turf wall, behind the line of the new stone wall. This realignment may have been to provide more space behind the Wall at Birdoswald, for the fort sits uncomfortably close to the steep valley of the river Irthing; it was made possible by the realization that forts need not project to the north once they were placed on the line of the Wall – neither of the late forts of Great Chesters or Carrawburgh projects.

MORE FORTS ON THE WALL

Carrawburgh was a new fort added to the Wall to fill the extra-long gap between Chesters and Housesteads. This necessitated removing the mounds and filling in the Vallum ditch, which had already been constructed across the site. At the end of Hadrian's reign the fort of Carvoran was rebuilt in stone, on the site of an earlier fort, south of the Vallum. This was a useful addition, as Birdoswald was on the other side of the Irthing. It seems possible that Vindolanda was rebuilt late in Hadrian's reign too. The fort at Newcastle, however, does not appear to date to these years, not being built till later in the century.

The primary forts on the Wall had been placed at fairly regular 7-mile (11-km) intervals along the whole line of the Wall. By the end of Hadrian's reign that pattern had been altered by the building of Carrawburgh and the reoccupation or retention of Carvoran and perhaps Vindolanda. All three forts lay towards the centre of the Wall, between Wall miles 31 and 46. The total effect was to increase noticeably the number of units between the North Tyne and the Irthing, with Vindolanda and Carvoran brought back into use and Carrawburgh as an extra fort.

This concentration of troops faced northwards into an area very sparsely populated at this time, and not crossed by major routes so far as we know. There was no need to place more troops here to counter a major invasion. Such an area, however, might have required special treatment by the army. To the east and west lay settled agricultural communities. Any incursion of raiders would have been easily spotted either by Roman patrols or scouts or by the locals themselves and reported by their leaders to the army; certainly these people would have had a very real appreciation of the neighbouring power of Rome and the need not to offend it. The army, in fact, would have had to pay particular attention to those areas where there was no civilian population in order to learn what was happening; here its eyes and ears alone provided surveillance. These empty lands may well have been the preferred route for raiding parties, crossing the Wall and heading south into the hills.

THE EFFECT OF THE FORT AND VALLUM
DECISIONS ON THE FUNCTION OF THE WALL

The placing of the forts on the Wall has obscured the existence of two separate functions. The main purpose of the troops in those forts was to protect the province from attack, while the purpose of the barrier was to control the movement of people into and out of the province. The need to protect the province did not require the presence of the units on the Wall itself. What was perceived during the construction of the Wall were the great advantages to be gained by stationing the units on the Wall itself, and the disadvantages of having the units at a distance from the Wall and with no way through it except by the milecastles. The move forward of the forts enabled the regimental commanding officers to maintain closer supervision of the Wall and its operation, to patrol more effectively north of the Wall and to intervene more rapidly in any dangerous situation. This increased forward patrolling would have effectively rendered many, if not most, turrets superfluous. At the same time the construction of the Vallum and the consequent restriction of crossing points to those controlled by forts reduced the role of milecastles to one of Wall sector supervision and maintenance. The milecastles retained a role, as the occupation of several into the fourth century (and their appearance on the Antonine Wall) demonstrates, but the reduction in the width of so many milecastle gateways in the late second or early third centuries suggests that this role had changed from that envisaged when they were first built.

It has been suggested that the milecastles were now used as sallyports to surround a hostile force and trap it against the Wall. But the idea of penning an enemy against an obstacle is contrary to Roman military thought and practice; indeed it is officially proscribed in two surviving military manuals, since the enemy with nowhere to flee would fight all the harder, while the enemy could even foresee this possibility and turn the plan against the Romans. It was after all presumably in part the inadequacies of the milecastle gateways that had led to the siting of forts on the Wall. It is moreover unlikely that much action would take place immediately in front of the Wall; the army would try to deal with an attack before it got that far. More likely the milecastles continued to provide accommodation for the soldiers guarding the gates and manning the milecastle towers. These towers and the turrets presumably continued to act as watch-towers, though with reduced importance, but they now reported their observations to the forts on the Wall; certainly the system of milecastles and turrets was completed without apparent modification.

We do not know how responsibility for the Wall was divided. The most obvious method would be for each auxiliary commanding officer to take responsibility for the stretch of Wall on either side of his fort, for patrolling a sector of land to the north and for deciding when he required help from adjacent units or from further south. It is often suggested that there 'must have been' an officer in overall command of the Wall. No officer regularly commanding more than one auxiliary unit is attested for the Roman army anywhere in the first two-and-a-half centuries A.D., though *numeri* were occasionally subordinated to the auxiliary unit commander at the fort to which they were attached. The Roman army hierarchy cannot simply be assimilated to modern ones; note the absence of a regular commander for the legionary cohort. The prefect of the milliary *ala* at Stanwix outranked the other commanders on the Wall, but there is no evidence he exercised any special powers over them. The nearest senior officer possibly with authority over all the auxiliary units on the Wall was the legionary legate at York, but there is no evidence he exercised such authority.

The placing of forts on the Wall also raises again the problem of the manning of the milecastles and turrets. It would be most logical for each unit to man and control the milecastles in its vicinity. But did the cavalry attested at Chesters, for example, provide soldiers for the structures in its sector? This must remain one of the many unanswered questions about Hadrian's Wall.

HADRIAN, NEPOS AND BRITAIN

The general survey of the building of Hadrian's Wall is now complete but it is only half the story, for a combination of archaeological and documentary evidence allows its construction to be described in much greater detail. Before proceeding to examine this it is necessary to look at the evidence.

Some of the archaeological clues which help us to work out the sequence of the building of the Wall have been mentioned. They include the filling of ditches; dismantling of already-built wall, turrets and a milecastle in order to build forts; the Vallum's divergences round forts and its causeways of undug earth; and the fact that the stone wall was started in broad gauge and completed in a narrower gauge. This provides a sequence of building but gives no actual dates or timing.

The crucial evidence is supplied by the governor who was Hadrian's friend and chosen by him, it seems, to build his Wall, Aulus Platorius Nepos. He came to Britain not long before 17 July 122, for an auxiliary soldier discharged by the previous governor of Britain, Pompeius Falco, received a certificate of privileges, a diploma, with that date; on it Nepos is named as governor. The lapse of time between discharge and the certifying of the copy would be a matter of months, no more. Nepos came from the governorship of Lower Germany and it was from Germany that Hadrian came to Britain, again probably in 122. A third important movement from Lower Germany to Britain took place about this time, the transfer of the legion VI Victrix. As it worked on the Wall in the first full season of building the voyage may also have taken place in 122 or perhaps 123. It is certainly tempting to connect all three movements from Germany to Britain and place them in the same year.

Hadrian had come to Britain from Germany, where he appears to have initiated an artificial barrier, a timber palisade, apparently the first of its type in Roman history. There had been a frontier defensive system on the Taunus, Wetterau and Odenwald sections of the German frontier from the time of Domitian. This was most developed on the Taunus and Wetterau. Here the frontier system consisted of a path linking turf and timber forts. Also along the path were timber towers some 540 to 650 yards (494 to 590 m) apart. This is not so dissimilar from the contemporary Gask Frontier in Perthshire where the watch-towers, often rather closer together than in Germany, lay along the road leading north from a little south of Ardoch to Bertha. Under Trajan some new forts were built on the Taunus and Wetterau and fortlets were added to the frontier. The startling new development under Hadrian probably took place during the visit of the emperor to the area in 121–2. The reign of Hadrian saw the construction of such barriers not only in Upper Germany, Raetia and Britain but also perhaps in Africa, where the frontier complex known as the Fossatum Africae was possibly built at this time. Hadrian's Wall, however, is the best known, best preserved, and most explored of all the artificial barriers of Hadrian's reign or any other.

Plate 12 The diploma (grant of privileges) of 17 July 122 given to a man discharged by Pompeius Falco, the previous governor, the present governor being A. Platorius Nepos. The names of both governors and of the units discharging men can be picked out. Each of the two leaves measures 6½ in. by 5¾ in. (165 mm by 146 mm).

Most major modifications to the frontiers during Hadrian's reign seem to have followed, and presumably resulted from, the emperor's visit to the frontier region. Thus in 122 he came to Britain to solve the problem of the British frontier, perhaps even with the intention of building an artificial barrier. His friend Platorius Nepos was brought over from Lower Germany to share the task and the glory; he is the only governor to be named, after Hadrian, on inscriptions from the Wall. The summoning of the Sixth Legion from Vetera, the nearest occupied legionary base to Britain, may have been specifically for the Wall project, though Britain may in any case have been under-garrisoned if the Ninth had already left, as seems most probable. As already indicated (p. 26), the history of legion IX Hispana in its later years is uncertain. It has been suggested that it was based at Carlisle for a time before its final departure from Britain. This proposal is founded on the discovery of stamped tiles of the legion in and near to the city. On the other hand, recent excavations in Carlisle have provided no evidence for a legionary base.

C. E. Stevens, however, suggested that the Wall was actually begun before Hadrian set foot in Britain. He considered that Nepos' predecessor,

Pompeius Falco, had been instructed to put the Wall in hand. Hadrian, on arrival, saw the basic weakness of the plan, and modified it by insisting that the forts be placed astride the line of the Wall, not left to the south of it in their old positions on the Stanegate. Two things argue against this theory. First, our timetable of Wall building suggests that work did not start until 122, or even 123. Secondly, it seems unlikely that the emperor's presence was necessary to authorize the fort decision. The greater decision was surely that to build the Wall. There is much to be said for the convergence of emperor, governor and legion in 122 to take, or implement, that decision though it may be that the legion was only summoned when the Wall decision had been taken. Finally it makes better sense for the conception of Hadrian's Wall to follow that of the German palisade, each beginning under the eye of the emperor. Hadrian had never been to Britain and was unlikely to instigate so radical a plan without first-hand knowledge.

Nepos was still in Britain in 124, but his governorship is unlikely to have extended beyond 126. It seems probable that but for the fort decision the Wall could have been completed within the three-year term of a normal governorship. The name of Nepos appears on inscriptions from milecastles 37, 38 and 42 in the central sector of the Wall, on – by a reasonably probable restoration – a tiny fragment of a wooden inscription from milecastle 50 on the turf wall and on inscriptions at the forts on Benwell and Halton Chesters, thus demonstrating that the fort decision was made and implemented during Nepos' governorship.

THE NATURE OF THE EVIDENCE

To date more precisely this decision and others a new element must be introduced, an allocation of parts of the Wall system to working-gangs from different legions. This allocation can only be done because the evidence suggests that almost the whole of the Wall was built by the three legions of the army of Britain. These were II Augusta normally based at Caerleon in south Wales, XX Valeria Victrix from Chester and the new legion VI Victrix, which occupied the old home of IX Hispana, York. A certain amount of work was done by a detachment of the British fleet, who built the granary at Benwell, and probably also those at Halton Chesters and

Rudchester, and by one or more auxiliary units, who helped dig the Vallum, but they played only a small part.

Most of our evidence comes from the stone wall. Not only has there been much less excavation carried out on the turf wall, but only one fragment of a single original inscription has been found. Thus any allocation of structures in this sector has to be through extension of stone-wall types. Indeed information is so sparse along much of the turf wall that it has been possible to suggest that most of its construction was carried out by IX Hispana operating from a hitherto unlocated base at Carlisle (p. 64). This seems unlikely.

The legionaries did most of the work themselves, not simply supervised it. The legions contained craftsmen skilled in building, architect-engineers, surveyors, masons, carpenters, glaziers and so on, while the soldiers themselves were practised in the construction of forts and other military installations, both temporary and permanent. In one area only perhaps did help come from native levies, and that is in the carting of materials, though this is far from certain, for the Roman army also carried on its books carters and muleteers. The whole exercise was carried out by the army from the surveying of the line of the Wall through the cutting and dressing of the stone to the actual building operations.

Each legion built under the direction of its own officers to its own plans and consequently milecastles, turrets and even curtain built by each legion differed slightly. These differences can be best seen on the stone wall. Milecastles here vary in two particulars: in shape, according to whether their north–south axis is longer than their east–west axis (long axis) or shorter (short axis), and in the form of their gateways. Some gateways have one pair of responds for arches, some two. The combination of these features gives three types of milecastle. R. Hunneysett has pointed out that milecastles also vary in the position of their setting-out lines. Two legions seem to have used the internal face of the milecastle walls as their setting-out line, while the other legion used the outer face. Fortunately the two legions building long-axis milecastles used different setting-out lines so if other indications are lacking an alternative is available.

Turrets vary in the position of their doorways, either to east or west. Their walls vary in width from 3 to 4 feet (0.9 to 1.2 m), but tend to group around these two extremes, the thinner wall generally having an off-set at the third course. Two variations in the curtain have been recognized. In certain areas an off-set is introduced in the wall after the first course (standard A), elsewhere after the third or fourth course (standard B).

In the past it has been suggested that it is possible to allocate the different types of milecastles, of turrets and curtain to legions II, VI and XX. This was based upon the discovery of four inscriptions of legion II at three milecastles (37, 38 and 42), one of legion XX at a single milecastle (47) and another of legion VI at a turret (33b) together with the fact that the 15 Roman miles of stone wall from turret 7b to milecastle 22 divide into three 5-mile blocks of distinct milecastle, turret and curtain types, thus allowing the different types to be allotted to the three legions (see Table 4). However, the epigraphic evidence has all been found in that part of the Wall where work was disrupted by the decision to build forts on the Wall. The evidence for the disruption can still be seen at milecastle 37 where the north gate had not reached the height of the impost caps at the time of dislocation, and milecastle 42 where the north wall was narrowed immediately beyond the side walls, which unusually are not bonded in with the north wall. As the inscriptions were erected over the gates, it is possible that in both cases one legion started building the milecastle and another completed the work, and the same may be the case with the other structures which did not survive so well. It is thus not possible to be certain that, for example, legion II started building milecastles 37, 38 and 42. In fact, it is most unlikely that it did; it is much more likely that the milecastles were commenced by another legion to be completed by legion II. As it is not possible to be certain which legions built which structures, the letters A, B and C are here assigned to the three legions.

There is also some evidence for different milecastles and turrets on the turf wall. Both long-axis and short-axis milecastles are found. Two types of turrets are also known. The variant with an east door has walls 2½ feet (0.76 m) thick, while the other type has a west door and walls 3½ feet (1.06 m) thick. Both types of turret are found in conjunction with long-axis milecastles – no turret in association with a short-axis milecastle has yet been excavated.

R. L. Bellhouse has been able to adduce evidence for differences in the construction of milefortlets and towers on the Cumbrian coast. All the known milefortlets are of the same size, if the anomalous milefortlet 5 (Cardurnock) is left to one side, and although most seem of long-axis type,

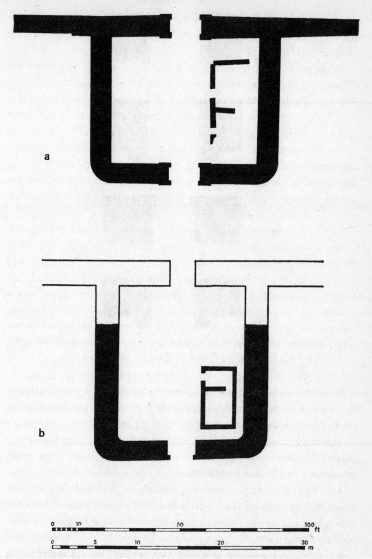

Fig. 12 Milecastles. a. 37 (Housesteads) built by legion A: completed by legion II; b. 9 (Chapel House) built by legion B. For the legion C type milecastle see Fig. 7a. Scale 1 in. = 40 ft (1:480).

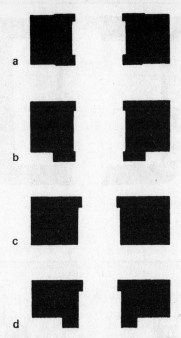

Fig. 13 Milecastle gates. a. legion A; b. legion C; c. legion B (Broad Wall); d. legion B (Narrow Wall). Scale 1 in. = 22 ft (1:264).

a short-axis milefortlet has been inferred. The towers vary in three ways: the footings for the walls (four types), the internal platform for the ladder (three positions), and the siting of the door (either left or right, equivalent to west and east in the turrets). These differences suggest three basic tower types but much more work needs to be done before either these or the milefortlets can be allocated to legions.

Two legions are attested building forts on the Wall and the Cumbrian coast, VI Victrix at Halton Chesters and XX Valeria Victrix at Moresby. Differences in shape and measurement between forts of roughly the same area have been noted. For example, three forts (Chesters, Birdoswald and Stanwix) share a common length of 580 feet (177 m). Housesteads, of similar size to Birdoswald, is markedly longer and thinner. This distinction can be recognized in smaller forts; Rudchester is almost the same size as Halton Chesters but is longer and thinner. It is tempting to define here

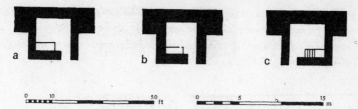

Fig. 14 Stone Wall turrets. a. legion B (7b); b. legion A (13a); c. legion C (19a). Scale 1 in. = 40 ft (1:480).

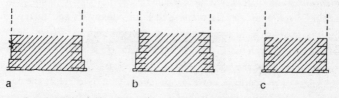

Fig. 15 Curtain: a. standard A (legions A and B); b. standard B (legion C); c. standard C (later Hadrianic work). Scale 1 in. = 13 ft (3.9 m) (1:168).

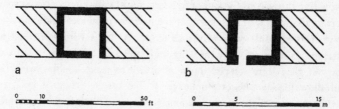

Fig. 16 Turf Wall turrets. a. legion B (?) (52a); b. legion C (?) (54a). Scale 1 in. = 40 ft (1:480).

two groups of forts, and this possibility is heightened by differences in the masonry of the gates, still visible at Housesteads and Chesters. Other forts do not fit readily into either group and may reflect the work of a third legion. The variety of types of units requiring forts and the existence of at least two if not three legions building these forts complicate the picture and prevent the certain allocation of forts to legionary builders.

It is possible to reconstruct the building programme on the stone wall, and to a lesser extent on the turf wall, by the allocation of the different types of milecastles, turrets and curtain to the three legions, and by the other evidence already cited. Before this is attempted, however, it is necessary to examine the order and method of construction of the length of wall assigned to each legion.

CONSTRUCTION ORDER AND METHODS

The primary task of each legion in its allotted length was to construct the milecastles and turrets, and there is some evidence that they were occupied as they were built. On the stone wall both milecastles and turrets were built with short wing walls ready to receive the curtain. Where the stone curtain was completed to the 10-foot Roman gauge these wing walls are not noticeable as they are bonded to the curtain. The reduction in the thickness of the curtain, however, produced an ugly effect at the edge of the wing wall where the wall abruptly narrowed by 2 Roman feet or more at a corner or 'point of reduction'. This point of reduction can be seen at both milecastles and turrets. Usually it takes the form of a vertical re-entrant extending through all the four or five feet of wall still standing but at some turrets the wing wall is so low that the narrow curtain wall rides up over it to meet the side walls of the structure. At these turrets at least no attempt was made to carry the wing walls up to the full height of the wall top but they were stepped down gradually to make bonding with the curtain wall easier (Plates 4 and 11).

The digging of the ditch apparently commenced while the structures were being erected; at Chesters, for example, the ditch was dug before work on the curtain was completed, but it is difficult to follow its progress in detail. One legion made a start on the curtain before it had built all its structures, while another appears to have completed all its milecastles and turrets and the wall foundation before it started on the curtain. Each legion divided the stretch of curtain allotted to it among its constituent cohorts and within each cohort among individual centuries. Each century, cohort and indeed legion marked both ends of its block of work by the erection of inscriptions. Sometimes all three appear on the same stone, sometimes separate stones are used. These stones are called 'centurial stones'. Since the Second World War many of them have been found *in situ*. Unfortunately few have been found at the eastern end of the Wall, that completed before

Table 4   The evidence for the allocation of work on Hadrian's Wall

Stone wall

Milecastles – 3 types
Turrets – 3 types
Curtain – 2 types

These types can be allocated as follows (the legions named on the inscriptions need not be the original builders):

| Legion | Evidence from inscriptions | Milecastles | Structural evidence from: | |
			Turrets	Curtain
A	Milecastles 37, 38, 42 Platorius Nepos Legion II	short axis 2 pairs responds	broad wall (4 feet) (1.2 m) east door	A 1 course below off-set
B		long axis 1 pair responds	narrow wall (3 feet) (0.9 m) east door	A
C	Milecastle 47 Legion XX	long axis 2 pairs responds	narrow wall (3 feet) (0.9 m) west door	B 3 courses below off-set

Turf wall

Milecastles – 2 types known
Turrets – 2 types known

| Legion | Evidence from inscriptions | Structural evidence from: | |
		Milecastles	Turrets
A		short axis	
B	Milecastle 50 TW Platorius Nepos Legion VI (?)	long axis	narrow wall (2½ feet) (0.76 m) east door
C		long axis (?)	broad wall (3½ feet) (1.06 m) west door

Plate 13 A building stone recording work by the century of Tertius in the sector 49—49a.
Inscriptions such as this are commonly termed centurial stones.

the fort decision, where there was no disruption in the work. Although
more have been found in the central sector they are too few to determine
just how much wall each century constructed, while there is the unknown
factor of disruption introduced by the decision to build the forts. It is not
even certain that the three legions were present in full strength. There is
some evidence that not all cohorts were complete. Few stones recording
the second, fourth, seventh and ninth legionary cohorts have been found.
These are the cohorts which, according to Vegetius' description, had the
less important place in the legion's line of battle. To argue from this that
these contained the highest number of recruits and would therefore have
remained at the legionary fortress to train is probably to strain the Vegetius
passage too far. These difficulties make it impossible to commence the
study of the building of the Wall by examining the centurial stones; it is
better to start with the allocation of the milecastles, turrets and curtain
to the three legions.

THE BUILDING OF THE WALL

This evidence makes it now possible to follow in detail the building of the Wall. Assuming Hadrian, Nepos and VI Victrix arrived in Britain in 122, the decision to construct the Wall was probably taken in that year. Elaborate preparations in the way of surveying, summoning of the three legions from their respective bases and organization of the working parties and transport would have been necessary. All this may have taken weeks if not months and the building operations may therefore not have commenced until the following year. The first year's work seems to have been the construction of 3 Roman miles of wall from milecastle 4 to about milecastle 7 with the bridge at Newcastle. The bridge would have considerably facilitated work at the east end, for the lowest bridge on the river previously was 15 Roman miles upstream at Corbridge. There may have been time in 122 to construct this short stretch of wall and the bridge. It seems better to assign it to this year rather than assume that the surveying and other preparations took a whole year.

Another reason for postulating a short stretch of actual building in 122 is that the next stretch, from about milecastle 7 to milecastle 22, divides up fairly neatly into three legionary blocks, that is, three stretches of similar length containing the same ratio of turrets, milecastles and curtain wall. Although proof is impossible it seems reasonable that these represent a season's work for each of the legionary 'gangs', however constituted. This also accords with the completion of these sections and more under Platorius Nepos and before the change in plan.

The second season was the first full season, and probably included work on the stone wall, the turf wall and on the Cumbrian coast. Firstly the stone wall. As already mentioned the stretch of Wall from about milecastle 7 to milecastle 22 falls neatly into three legionary blocks, each legion constructing about 5 Roman miles of Wall, with the attendant milecastles and turrets. So far as can be determined, most of this stretch of Wall was completed to the broad gauge. On the turf wall there is only one recognizable legionary block, the most easterly 5 miles. Here there are long-axis milecastles and turrets with narrow walls and east doors. The next turret to the west, 54a, has broad walls and a west door, suggesting work by a different legion. If each legion therefore built 5 Roman miles of Wall, as is most probable, the 31 miles of the turf wall would presumably have been divided into two three-legion blocks of 15 miles each, one three-legion block being constructed at the same time as the stretch from milecastle 7 to milecastle 22. The stone wall was built from east to west, but the turf wall may have been built from east to west, or from west to east. Progress on the Cumbrian coast is much harder to determine. With no wall to construct work should have proceeded much more quickly and it is possible that half was completed in this season.

The next year will probably have seen the completion of most, if not all, of the turf wall and the Cumbrian coast. On the stone wall the situation was very different. In this season there was a redistribution of the three working parties. One legion commenced building westwards from milecastle 22 at least as far as turret 27a, for that turret was started before Chesters fort, and had to be demolished to make way for it. They also presumably had to construct the bridge over the North Tyne at Chesters. Another legion was sent off to another major river crossing, that of the Irthing, and built eastwards from that point. Next door was the third legion, the last structure of its allocation being turret 36b, later to be demolished to make way for Housesteads fort. Interestingly each legion seems to have been given a little more work to do than in the previous season, 6 Roman miles of Wall or 5 miles and a bridge. This strengthens the supposition that 5 Roman miles had been the allocation for the previous season. For uncertain reasons in the Irthing sector two milecastles, 47 and 48, and possibly others which have not been investigated, were constructed to a larger size than those built in the previous seasons, thus providing more accommodation in the fortlet. This is part of a general trend, for many of the later stone milecastles built on the turf wall were larger than earlier stone milecastles.

During the second full season, 124 on our reckoning, there was dislocation of the work. Between milecastle 22 and turret 27a there are stretches of half-built or just-started broad wall, broad foundation with a narrower wall on top, a turret built to receive broad wall with broad curtain on the west side and narrow on the east, and so on. In the 12 miles eastwards from the Irthing the same phenomena recur: broad wall built, a few courses of broad wall laid, milecastles and turrets built to receive broad wall with narrow wall brought up to them. The bridges over the North Tyne and the Irthing appear to have been erected, but work was slower in the crags sector, presumably due to the difficulties of working here, where transport

Table 5 The building of the stone and turf walls

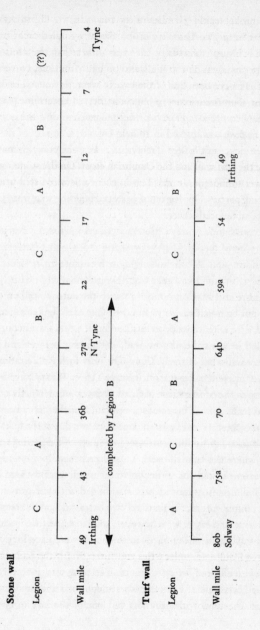

Stone wall

Legion	C		A		B		C		B		A		B		(??)
Wall mile	49 Irthing	43	36b	27a N Tyne	22	17	12	7	4 Tyne

Turf wall

Legion	A		C		B		A		C
Wall mile	80b Solway	75a	70	64b	59a	54	49 Irthing

completed by Legion B

of materials would have been slow and arduous. The impression is that all three working parties were called away by some dramatic change of plan.

That change can hardly have been other than the decision to build the twelve new forts on the Wall, and probably, in time, two on the Cumbrian coast. The construction of these forts certainly started under Nepos. How long it took the legions to build the forts is uncertain. It was presumably in order to speed up the building programme that the detachment of the British fleet was drafted in to help construct certain of the fort granaries. The presence of the fleet is recorded on an inscription discovered at Benwell and the efficiency of its engineers is attested by the strength of the granary foundations here. The similarity between this granary and those at Rudchester and Halton Chesters suggests that the same men were responsible for all three.

Benwell and Halton Chesters were completed, or nearly so, before the departure of Nepos, that is by about 126. Great Chesters was completed in 128 or later. Wallsend ought to be earlier than Great Chesters as it projects, though like Great Chesters it is bonded in with the narrow wall. Housesteads, which is bonded in with the narrow wall on the north-west, may not be much earlier than Great Chesters, and Chesters appears to be bonded in with the narrow wall on both sides. Carrawburgh may also be bonded in with the narrow wall; it does not project and was built after the construction of the Vallum. The only fort with a more precise date is Carvoran, which was rebuilt in stone 136–7. It may have been a Stanegate fort up to the construction of Great Chesters but virtually nothing is known about its history. It may be assumed that Rudchester came early, along with Halton Chesters and Benwell. Less is known about the forts in the west.

All forts, as has been stressed, were at first designed to lie astride the wall where the land allowed. This placed them in a unique position: easy movement in and out of the fort to the north was provided by three double gates while ready contact was maintained with the province to the south by a double gate at the rear and two extra side gates, themselves a unique provision in forts. It was, however, soon realized that if a fort was actually on the Wall line fewer gates to the north were necessary. The main west gate of Halton Chesters fort, one of the first to be built on the Wall, was therefore blocked before it was completed as was, it seems, the east portal of the north gate at Housesteads, though the situation is not so clear here. Great Chesters, a primary fort but one of the last to be constructed, is completely south of, albeit still attached to, the Wall, though it could have projected. At Carrawburgh, too, the fort, a later addition to the primary series, was attached to the rear face of the curtain. A few years later when the turf wall flanking Birdoswald was rebuilt, the Wall was realigned to come up to the north corners of the fort, not the south guard chambers of the side gates, demonstrating again that forts on the Wall line did not need three double gates to the north. This apparently led to the disuse and later blocking up of some gates. On the Antonine Wall all the forts were built behind the Wall, none projected.

Some gangs apparently were left to complete the Wall for the inscriptions from milecastle 37 (and 38 and 42) date to the governorship of Platorius Nepos. During this process and soon after the decision to add the forts it was decided to reduce the thickness of the curtain from 10 Roman feet to 8 feet or less. The remaining structures and the rest of the curtain were completed at this reduced gauge, accounting for the unusual, and rather ugly, spectacle of conjoining stretches of broad and narrow wall. These points of junction are especially strange in the stretch of wall eastwards from the river Irthing. Here up to five courses of broad wall, including in places the off-set course, had been laid. Instead of these dressed stones being reused in the narrow curtain they were left in position, the low broad wall forming a sort of step on the south side of the curtain. The new builders even sank new foundations for the narrow wall into the core of the existing broad wall, so deeply in places as to create a shallow gully between the south face of the narrow wall and the top courses of the old broad wall. The narrowing of the wall was undoubtedly to speed up work. But for the fort decision this stretch of wall from turret 27a to the Irthing could have been completed in 125; the building of the forts had added at least three seasons to the working period.

The burden of the Wall builders was further increased by the extension of the Wall 4 miles (6.4 km) down the Tyne from Newcastle to Wallsend. On spacing considerations the new fort at Wallsend was one of the primary forts but the 4-mile (6.4-km) length of wall, with which the fort was bonded in, was built to the narrow gauge, probably late in the works programme. This stretch of wall would have been nearly one year's work for one legion.

Plate 14 The later narrow wall built on top of the surviving bottom five courses of the broad wall at Willowford, looking west.

COMPLETION OF THE WALL

While the forts were built and the curtain finished off the Vallum was constructed. The decision to add the Vallum was probably taken at the same time as the decision to move the forts up on to the Wall, or possibly a little later, but its construction may have proceeded at a faster rate than the building of either the forts or the curtain. In the Limestone Corner area the Wall and Vallum are so close as to suggest that the latter was constructed first. However, in places further east Wall and Vallum come very close together, and appear to be laid out independently. Perhaps this, and the fact that the Vallum diverges around forts rather than is laid out to pass to the south of them, suggest that the Vallum did follow the line of a pre-existing track, conceived and perhaps in use before the decision to add the forts. More significant perhaps is the fact that at Limestone Corner the Vallum ditch was dug for over a mile through solid rock while the Wall ditch was left unfinished. Again this makes better sense if the Vallum ditch was completed before, rather than after, the decision to abandon the completion of the Wall ditch. Help for the legionaries in this operation was forthcoming in this case from the *auxilia*, for an inscription from the south mound of the Vallum between turret 7b and milecastle 8 attests work by the *cohors I Dacorum*.

It is difficult to say when Hadrian's Wall was completed. Great Chesters and the adjoining stretch of curtain were not built until 128–38. The fort of Moresby on the Cumbrian coast, built by XX Valeria Victrix, falls into the same period. The building of all the forts on the Cumbrian coast may have been left until the completion of all, or most, of the Wall itself. Since a road was apparently provided in the first scheme from milecastle 50 TW north to Bewcastle it would appear that the outpost forts were planned from the first. It is not possible to place them accurately within the building programme but they were probably completed by 130. The last dated work on the Wall comes from the very end of Hadrian's reign. In 136/7 the fort of Carvoran, just south of the Wall 3 miles (4.8 km) west of Great Chesters, was being rebuilt in stone. Either it had continued in use as a survivor from the Stanegate system or it had been abandoned only to be reoccupied towards the end of the reign. Also near the end of Hadrian's reign the rebuilding of the turf wall in stone commenced and the legions played a part in this work. The milecastles were built by VI Victrix and XX Valeria Victrix and they are all larger than the earlier stone-wall milecastles, a modification probably resulting from earlier experience. Another change was the introduction of regular drains through the Wall. Hitherto these had only been placed at some points; now they were provided at regular intervals of 20 feet (6 m) or so. One minor modification, started some years before when the stone curtain in the vicinity of milecastle 45 was being completed, was the eradication of the off-set. From now on all the curtain was built without an off-set; this particular stretch to the narrow gauge, 8 Roman feet thick.

There is other evidence to suggest that the building progress was not smooth. At Birdoswald, for example, there was a break during the construction of the fort sufficiently long for scrub to grow on the site before the builders returned.

Hadrian's Wall was being continually modified and improved throughout the life of its designer. Much of the Wall bears the imprint of that designer: the rigidity in the spacing of milecastles and turrets, the regular spacing of forts, the provision of three twin-portal gates north of the Wall for the forts, and the Vallum, another experiment not tried elsewhere. All these clearly show that the Wall was conceived by someone with little time to study the problem of the northern frontier in detail. Nevertheless Hadrian did create an enduring monument to his name and foresight.

THE WALL AS AN ENGINEERING ACHIEVEMENT

How great an achievement was Hadrian's Wall? A hundred and fifty years ago Collingwood Bruce supplied figures, not entirely correct ones, to an engineer of his day, Robert Rawlinson, who was used to working with navvies without the benefit of bulldozers on large engineering projects. Rawlinson produced estimates of 1,702,115 cubic yards of masonry, in his day costing £1,021,269. Each cubic yard entailed the movement of a ton of material – stone, lime and water – and this would have to be done by ox-drawn wagons.

Rawlinson reckoned each cubic yard required from quarrying to setting as at the least the energy of one man per day, so a force of 10,000 men would have taken 170 days to build the curtain alone, reckoned as 68 miles long, 16 feet high and 8 feet wide. The forts, milecastles and turrets were not taken into account by Rawlinson, nor were the forts on the Cumbrian coast, and the three outpost forts, whose existence was not then known. The nineteenth-century excavator could move 20 cubic yards of earth a day; Rawlinson only allowed his second-century counterpart 8 cubic yards, and made no estimate of the increased labour occasioned by cutting through rocks, though compensating for this by taking no account of the lack of ditch on the crags. Seventy days was allowed for the digging of the ditch, and for the Vallum 46 days. His force of 10,000 would therefore have constructed the curtain and dug the ditch in 240 days. Rawlinson considered that work would be possible only 200 days of the year, so the operation would have been completed in a year and a half, two years allowing some leeway.

Although the stone wall was 45 miles long, not 68, and 10 feet wide, not 8, Rawlinson's estimate of a working force of 10,000 may not have been far wrong, so if the minor structures are brought into the calculations an estimate of almost three years for the first scheme may not be far out. This is remarkably close to the time which the archaeological and epigraphical material suggests. The construction of fourteen or fifteen forts must have greatly lengthened the building programme, and obtaining materials – more dressed stone and turf together with vast quantities of timber, nails and the like – must have further held up work. Interestingly the Vallum was only a relatively minor addition to the workload: Rawlinson allowed 46 days for its construction.

Hunter Davies obtained in 1974 from Laings a figure of £55 million for building the wall in reinforced concrete then. This was for a much narrower wall; a wall to Roman width would cost £80 million. No quotation was obtained for dressed stone, as a stone-faced wall's cost would be too astronomical to contemplate at contemporary prices – in 1850 a cubic yard of facing stone cost 12 shillings, in 1974 £10.

Rawlinson's figures give some idea of the human labour involved, and the possibilities, Hunter Davies's of the size of the undertaking, though neither set of figures can be pressed too far. Bruce's specifications for Rawlinson were incorrect; Hunter Davies gives no details of his specifications. The undertaking was certainly vast, with special difficulties in providing the required quantity of water on the crags. On the other hand it must be remembered that it was not expensive for Rome. The army supplied the labour, with perhaps carting and other unskilled services imposed on the provincials. The quarries belonged to the state, or to anyone with the skill to work them. Nevertheless the Wall as an engineering feat would have been notable in any age.

Table 6   The building of Hadrian's Wall

ORIGINAL SCHEME

Milecastles (and milefortlets), turrets (and towers), curtain (stone and turf), ditch.

Stone wall c. milecastle 4–River Irthing (Willowford Bridge)

(i)   c. milecastle 4–c. milecastle 7 (with bridge at Newcastle)

(iia)	c. milecastle 7–milecastle 12	3 legionary blocks built together
(iib)	turret 12a–milecastle 17	
(iic)	turret 17a–milecastle 22	

(iiia)	milecastle 22–turret 27a+	3 legionary blocks built together under Platorius Nepos (122–c. 126)
(iiib)	turret 36b–milecastle 43(?)	
(iiic)	turret 43a(?)–Irthing	

The second 3-legion block had not been completed before the second scheme was started.

Turf wall River Irthing (Willowford Bridge)–turret 80a(?)

Milecastle 49–turret 53b or milecastle 54 constitute one legionary block of 15 or 16 structures, 5 Roman miles, and it is possible that all the 96 or 97 structures on the turf wall were divided into 6 blocks of 16 structures, that is two 3-legion blocks. It is not possible to say whether the turf wall was built east to west or west to east, but the eastern end was completed under Platorius Nepos.

Provisional Scheme

(ia)	River Irthing–milecastle 54	3 legionary blocks built together under Platorius Nepos (122–c. 126)
(ib)	turret 54a–turret 59a	
(ic)	turret 59b–turret 64b	

(iia)	milecastle 65–milecastle 70	3 legionary blocks built together
(iib)	turret 70a–turret 75a	
(iic)	turret 75b–turret 80b	

Cumbrian coast turret 80b(?)–milefortlet 40(?)

This system of milefortlets and towers is probably part of the original scheme. Differences have been noted in the structures but it is not possible to make out any pattern yet.

Forts

(i)   The auxiliary units were to be left in the forts behind the Wall on the Stanegate.

(ii) The outpost forts probably fall into the original scheme, for a road was provided now from milecastle 50 TW north to Bewcastle. However, they may not have been built till later: Bewcastle was possibly built between 124 and 130, Netherby and probably Birrens before 128.

SECOND SCHEME

Forts were built on the line of the Wall and the Vallum added to the south of the Wall.

Forts

(i) Primary forts: Wallsend, Benwell, Rudchester, Halton Chesters (built by VI), Chesters, Housesteads, Great Chesters, Birdoswald, Castlesteads, Stanwix, Burgh-by-Sands, Bowness-on-Solway. Started under Platorius Nepos (122–c. 126).
  These forts were probably all intended to project north of the Wall wherever possible. Not completed until 128–38.

(ii) The forts on the Cumbrian coast may also be primary forts: Beckfoot, Maryport, Moresby (built by XX 128–38).

Vallum

The decision to construct the Vallum was contemporary with or postdated the decision to build the forts, though the actual construction of the Vallum may have preceded some or all of the forts. It diverges round Benwell, Halton Chesters, Birdoswald and Castlesteads, crosses the site of Carrawburgh, excludes Carvoran and ends at Newcastle not Wallsend.

Stone wall

Completion of milecastle 22 to Willowford Bridge over the Irthing not finished before 128–38. After most of the milecastle gates and the turrets had been built in this sector the gauge of the stone wall was reduced from 10 Roman feet (broad) to 8 Roman feet or less (narrow), and the remaining structures and curtain completed. (Turret 44b is the only narrow wall structure known.)

FURTHER MODIFICATIONS

The Wall was extended eastwards for 4 miles (6.4 km) to Wallsend in narrow gauge.

Before all the primary forts were completed it was decided that it was not necessary for the forts to project north of the Wall. Great Chesters was therefore built behind the Wall (128–38).

Carrawburgh added behind the Wall.

Carvoran rebuilt in stone 136–7.

The turf wall from the Irthing to just west of milecastle 54 was rebuilt in stone under Hadrian. The Wall around Birdoswald was realigned so that the fort no longer projected. The rest of the turf wall was probably completed in stone about 160.

Table 7 A draft chronology for the building of Hadrian's Wall

Date	Stone wall	Turf wall	Cumbrian coast	Forts	Vallum	Bridges
122	milecastle 4—milecastle 7					Newcastle
123	milecastle 7—milecastle 22	milecastle 49—turret 64b (?)	turret 80b milefortlet 20 (?)	outpost forts planned (and commenced?)		
124	milecastle 22—turret 27a turret 36b—Irthing	milecastle 65—turret 80a (?)	milefortlet 20—milefortlet 40 (?)			Willowford Chesters
Dislocation by fort decision						
	remaining structures turret 27b—Irthing	continuing (?)	continuing (?)	primary forts commenced	commenced	
125	continuing			continuing	continuing	
126	reduction in gauge of curtain (?) continuing work on Wall milecastle 22—Irthing			continuing	continuing	

Governorship of Platorius Nepos ended (?)

127 continuing   extension to Wallsend

128–38 completion of curtain

           continuing   continuing (?)

           continuing

           completion of primary forts (Great Chesters behind Wall)

           Carrawburgh added behind wall

           Cumbrian coast forts completed

rebuilding in stone commenced   outpost forts completed (by c. 130?)

136–7   Carvoran rebuilt in stone

3

THE ANTONINE WALL

THE MOVE NORTH

Hadrian's Wall was scarcely completed – in fact it was probably undergoing renovation in the turf wall sector – when it was abandoned shortly after the death of its designer in 138. The new emperor, Hadrian's adopted son Antoninus Pius, immediately decided on a new forward policy in Britain. He sent a new governor, Lollius Urbicus, with orders to reoccupy southern Scotland and construct a new Wall across the Forth–Clyde isthmus.

The occasion for this change of policy is not certain, but a Greek travel writer, Pausanias, writing about 176, mentions in his *Description of Greece* a disturbance in Britain which may be relevant. He comments that Antoninus never voluntarily involved the Romans in warfare but on two occasions he did make war. The first was against the Moors, the second was in Britain. He states that the emperor deprived the Brigantes of most of their territory because they had taken up arms and invaded the Genounian 'district', whose people were subject to the Romans. There are two problems here: the Brigantes lived within the province and so could hardly be deprived of territory, while the location of the Genounian 'district' is not known. However, the name of the Brigantes was sometimes used instead of Britons, in the same way as English is wrongly used for British today, and so might be taken to mean in a general way the tribes beyond the frontier. Whatever the explanation the event was probably connected with the reoccupation of southern Scotland since no other war in Britain is recorded under this pacific emperor, and this is the only war for which he took a salutation as victor (*imperator*). J. G. F. Hind has drawn attention to the occurrence of Brigantii and Genauni in Raetia (modern southern Germany), and suggested that Pausanias in describing something that occurred relating to the Brigantes in Britain included in error a tribe that were neighbours to the Brigantii in Raetia. He suggests as an alternative but less probable explanation that Pausanias was describing otherwise unrecorded troubles in Raetia under Pius. A. L. F. Rivet and C. Smith in their study of place-names draw attention to the fact that 'in Britain' seems to be a later insertion into the manuscript of Pausanias, and consider there may have been a conflation of incidents in Britain and Raetia. That is not impossible, but it still seems incredible that Pausanias should have referred to some other troubles otherwise unknown and pass over the campaigns of Lollius Urbicus in silence.

The advance in Britain was clearly important to Pius for as has been noted it was the only time that he took the title *imperator* – victorious general – after his succession, in spite of achieving later military victories and even pushing the frontier forward in Germany, though here, it seems, without fighting. But why did he do it, if not provoked in any way?

Moving the frontier of the province 100 miles (160 km) further north may imply that Hadrian's Wall was not a success. On the other hand its replacement by another Wall suggests that this failure was not absolute. Was it perhaps out of touch with the main centres of resistance to the Romans, hence the move forward? Hadrian's Wall would then be a tactical success but a strategic failure.

More than a logical reappraisal may have been made. It has been argued that military men chafing under the restrictions imposed by Hadrian won this advance as a concession from Pius. Equally, however, Hadrian may have ignored obvious weaknesses in his brain-child. There is a further consideration. Pius' succession to Hadrian was not secure. He lacked military prestige, and he or his advisers may well have felt that a victory would strengthen his position, just as Claudius had in 43, and Britain may once more have seemed eminently suitable for a triumph. Certainly the abandonment and dismantling of the Wall, Hadrian's most impressive monument to his defensive policy, would have appealed to the generals who were frustrated opponents of Hadrian's ideas. However, the advance in Britain is so out of character with the rest of Pius' reign that it should have some connection with Pius' own problems. A relatively short war and a spectacular advance, piloted by the emperor from his palace, as Fronto represented it, would have political advantages in Rome far outweighing any long-term disadvantages for frontier control in Britain. The construction of new barriers, in Britain and in Germany, demonstrates that the new emperor fully accepted the principle of linear frontiers: the advances only resulted in the drawing of new lines.

The decision to move north must have been taken within months of Pius' accession in July 138, for preparations in Britain commenced in 139. In this and the following year inscriptions were erected at Corbridge, where Dere Street crosses the Tyne, recording the construction of buildings by legion II Augusta under the supervision of the governor Lollius Urbicus. A new fort was required here on the road north for the new campaign and occupation.

The duration of the campaign is not known but it clearly took place between the reoccupation of Corbridge in 139 and 140, and the acclamation of Antoninus Pius as *imperator* in 142 and the issue of commemorative coins in 142 or early 143. The campaigning must have ranged through Lowland Scotland and into Strathmore, but few marching camps belonging to this period have been recognized. The construction of the new Wall commenced in the governorship of Lollius Urbicus, but may have been completed under his successor.

THE ABANDONMENT OF HADRIAN'S WALL

Hadrian's Wall was presumably not abandoned until the Antonine Wall was completed. It does not seem to have been deliberately destroyed, but simply rendered open to traffic, both military and civilian. The milecastle gateways were opened, possibly the gates removed completely, for there is evidence at some sites of damage to the gate pivots, and the Vallum slighted. In certain areas the north and south mounds were backfilled into the ditch to form causeways at regular intervals of 135 feet (41 m). It seems best to assign the slighting to this period; analysis of vegetation remains below a crossing on Cockmount Hill suggests that the ditch was

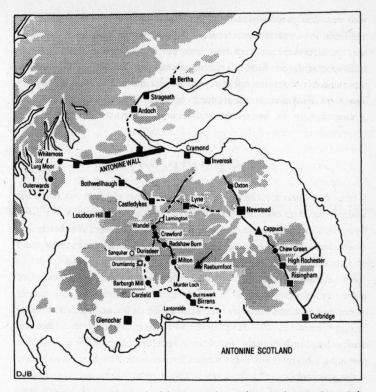

Fig. 17 Military dispositions north of the Tyne–Solway isthmus in the Antonine period, about 142–58. Forts are marked by large and small squares, small forts by triangles and fortlets by circles. Open squares and circles indicate sites possibly occupied at this time.

only open for a short time. But if the Wall itself was abandoned the Wall forts may not have been. Inscriptions at two forts, Chesters and Benwell, have been taken to indicate that the auxiliary garrisons were replaced at this time by legionaries. Their interpretation is, however, uncertain. Diplomas of A.D. 146 found at Chesters and at Vindolanda may imply the presence of normal auxiliary garrisons at these two sites. It has recently been argued on the basis of coins and pottery that Birdoswald continued in occupation throughout the Antonine period. A difference in the treatment of the forts and the Wall is possible because their functions were completely different. The purpose of the Wall was to control the movement of people; the forts had a military function independent of the Wall. When the Wall was abandoned the forts retained their military functions, and some might still be garrisoned. Corbridge, Vindolanda and Carlisle appear to have remained in occupation, all lying on the Stanegate. The abandonment of Hadrian's Wall thus would appear to have revived the importance of the Stanegate, a crucial line of communication between east and west.

THE SCOTTISH LOWLANDS

The units to garrison the new forts constructed in the Scottish Lowlands and on the Antonine Wall were withdrawn from Hadrian's Wall and from forts in the Pennines, such as Slack, Brough-on-Noe, Binchester and Ebchester — the last two stations were replaced by a new establishment at Lanchester about halfway between them. Other units also appear to have been withdrawn from Wales at this time. These new forts, often placed on or near the sites of earlier Agricolan foundations, lay mainly along the two trunk roads leading north to the Antonine Wall, Dere Street taking the eastern route while to the west the road passed up Annandale, with a loop up Nithsdale, and down Clydesdale. One of these new forts was at High Rochester, the Roman Bremenium. The first-century fort there was replaced by a new establishment constructed, as an inscription demonstrates, under Lollius Urbicus and many, or all, of these forts may have been built, or at least started, in the same governorship. The purpose of these forts and fortlets was to police and control the inhabitants of Lowland Scotland and the Borders, as well as providing bases for the army which would meet major invasions in the field. The most troublesome tribes appear to have been the Selgovae and the Damnonii. However, troublesomeness tends to be assumed on the basis of the number of forts and fortlets in a tribal territory, so the argument is apt to be circular.

It has been suggested that a method employed to bring peace to the northern frontier at this time was to draft the newly conquered barbarians into the army and transport them and their families to the Upper German frontier. This suggestion was based on the first appearance there in 145–6 of at least ten *numeri* of *Brittones*, many bearing subsidiary titles taken from the river by which they were stationed. This is unusual and has been

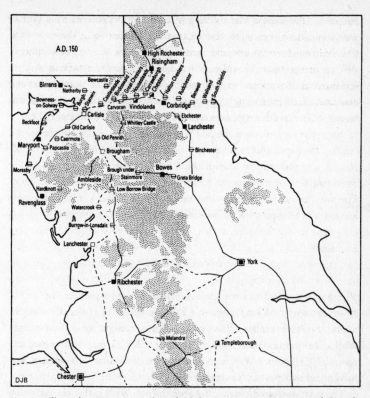

Fig. 18 Military dispositions in north England about 150. Open squares crossed through indicate forts considered to have been abandoned during the previous ten years; open squares, forts possibly occupied at this time; and half-open squares, forts probably occupied.

taken to imply that the *numeri Brittonum* were not ordinary military units but communities of men with their wives and children. The tribesmen conquered by Lollius Urbicus would have no legal rights and therefore could have been so drafted – the same happened in reverse some thirty years later when 5500 conquered Sarmatians were sent to Britain. However, excavations by Dietwulf Baatz at Hesselbach on the Odenwald sector of the Upper German *limes*, the station of the *numerus Brittonum Triputiensium*, have cast doubt on this. He points out that the type of garrison of the fortlet in the 140s was already in residence by 130 and probably earlier.

Indeed on the basis of the building history of the site alone this type of unit could have been at the fortlet from its foundation at the end of the first century. It seems unlikely therefore that there was any new influx of Britons in the 140s. This theory has also come under attack in Britain. Extensive field work and excavation by George Jobey in Northumberland and Dumfriesshire and by the Royal Commission on the Ancient Monuments of Scotland have demonstrated the existence of a substantial population in the area between the two Walls at this time. Indeed in the second century the population may have been increasing. Certainly it is improbable that it was reduced by transplanting entire tribes of barbarians to the continent. On the contrary the barbarians stayed at home and throve under the *pax Romana*, extending their existing farms and constructing new homesteads to cope with the increase in population.

THE ANTONINE WALL

The Antonine Wall had one great advantage over its predecessor: it was 37 miles (nearly 60 km) long, only half the length of Hadrian's Wall. In many ways it was similar to Hadrian's Wall. An examination of the Antonine Wall and a comparison with its predecessor will illustrate the function and purpose of Hadrian's Wall both in the reign of Hadrian and when it was reoccupied on the abandonment of the Antonine Wall.

The most obvious difference between the two Walls is that the Antonine Wall was of turf. The turf rampart was built on a heavy stone base usually 15 Roman feet wide. It almost certainly stood 10 feet (3 m) high and may have been higher. If there was a walk along the top this may have been protected by a timber breastwork. The Antonine turf rampart was only two-thirds the width of its predecessor on Hadrian's turf wall, thus saving materials and time, while the greater stability of a stone base would have allowed the Antonine Wall to be the same, or almost the same, height. The stone base may also have resulted from other experience. Hadrian's Wall, as has already been noted, suffered from a drainage problem; when the turf wall was rebuilt in stone the number of drains through the curtain was increased to allow water ponding up beside the wall to drain through it. It is not known if, or how regularly, drains were provided on the turf wall; certainly drainage through it would have been difficult. A stone base

Plate 15 The Antonine Wall ditch at Watling Lodge survives with almost its original profile, measuring about 40 feet (12.2 m) across and 12 feet (3.66 m) deep.

made the turf superstructure more stable and at the same time made the provision of culverts easier.

One important question which remains is why turf should have been used for the Antonine Wall at a time when the turf wall of the abandoned Hadrian's Wall was being rebuilt in stone, unless the long-drawn-out building of Hadrian's Wall created a desire for a quicker result. In fact on an empire-wide basis the use of stone was unusual, the other frontier barriers of this period being turf, earth or timber. However, the original intention may have been to build the Antonine Wall in stone. The fort of Balmuildy, one of the first on the new Wall to be constructed, was provided with stone walls and stone wing walls just like the milecastles on Hadrian's Wall. Stone wing walls would not bond with a turf rampart – which incidentally had not yet been built – and interpreted strictly should mean that the Wall would be of stone. In that case only while work was actually proceeding were plans changed and the Wall built in turf.

If the wall itself was slighter than its predecessor the ditch to the north was not, though again there are hints of modifications during building. In the eastern half of its length, that part usually considered to have been dug first, the ditch was normally 40 feet (12 m) wide and about 13 feet (4 m) deep, except in front of the forts, and was separated from the rampart by a berm 20 feet (6 m) wide. In places the distance between the rampart and the ditch was much wider; on Croy Hill, owing to the configuration of the ground, it reached 100 feet (30.5 m) while at Kinneil, near the east end of the Wall, for no apparent reason, the width of the ditch was only 18 feet (5.5 m) and the berm 24 feet (7.3 m). In its western half the ditch nowhere exhibits the uniformity of the eastern half. Its width varies from 19 to 36 feet (5.8 m to 11 m) while its depth can be as little as 6 or 8 feet (1.8 to 2.4 m). The berm is more usually nearer 30 feet (9 m) than 20 feet (6 m). A constant distance of 40 feet (12 m), however, generally appears to have been maintained between the front of the rampart and the centre of the ditch, presumably reflecting the lines originally laid out by the Wall surveyors. The reason for the variations in the width of the ditch and the berm is not understood, though the immediate impression is of reduced efficiency; the legionaries may have been getting tired of their task.

It has been suggested that the greater width of the berm on the Antonine Wall was to allow the army more room to corral the enemy between the rampart and the ditch. However, we have already seen how unlikely it was that either Wall was used in that way. More probably the wider space was for structural reasons, the greater width being safer. The material from the ditch was thrown out on to the north side to form a mound, usually termed the upcast mound or the outer mound. This earth would, of course, be of no use in the construction of the rampart.

Another feature ran along the whole length of the Wall, a road, known today as the Military Way. This road, about 18 feet (5.5 m) wide, was placed a little to the rear of the rampart. No pre-existing road ran across the Forth–Clyde isthmus and this new road seems to have been constructed even before some of the structures on the Wall. Presumably this was in order not only to improve lateral communications but also to assist with the transport of building materials.

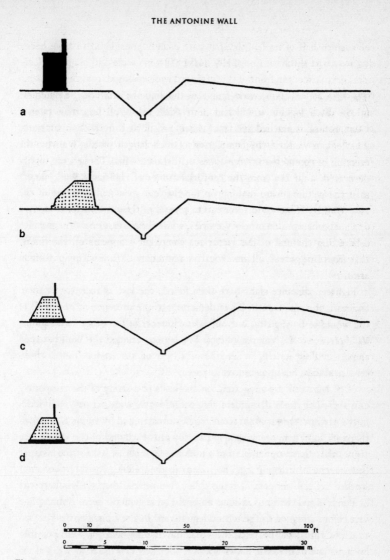

Fig. 19 Sections across the two Walls. a. Hadrian's stone wall; b. Hadrian's turf wall; c. the Antonine Wall, eastern sector; d. the Antonine Wall, western sector. Scale 1 in. = 40 ft (1 : 480).

THE BUILDERS

The rampart was constructed, and presumably the ditch dug, by soldiers of the three legions which had built Hadrian's Wall less than twenty years before; some soldiers may have taken part in both operations. The legions marked the completion of each length of the Wall by the erection of commemorative plaques or distance slabs. These were highly decorated, a far cry from the centurial stones of Hadrian's Wall, almost as if the soldiers were making up for the less spectacular nature of the new Wall by these vivid records. On several of the stones appear captive or slain barbarians, on others Victories, while the *suovetaurilia* – the sacrifice celebrating the end of the victorious campaign – appears on the finest, that from Bridgeness; all are evocative reminders of the success of Roman arms.

Eighteen distance slabs have been found, the last as recently as 1969, and part of a nineteenth. They demonstrate the presence on the Wall of the whole of II Augusta, but only detachments of the other two legions, VI Victrix and XX Valeria Victrix. The legions divided the Wall between them, building mostly in lengths of 3, 3⅔ or 4⅔ Roman miles, these sectors always being measured in paces.

G. S. Maxwell has suggested, on the basis of a study of the temporary camps used by the Wall builders, that these lengths were in turn subdivided. In the eastern stretch of 4⅔ Roman miles constructed by legion II Augusta there are four temporary camps, two towards each end of the length. He argues that these are bases from which the legionaries issued to construct this stretch by working from both ends to the middle. Possibly two gangs worked on the rampart and the other two on the ditch. Elsewhere the evidence is less clear but in some areas the arrangements seem similar. The four camps assigned to the second legion vary in size from 4 to 8 acres (1.6 to 3.2 hectares) and between them may have held as many as four, possibly even six cohorts. Further west a camp of either VI Victrix or XX Valeria Victrix was as large as 11 acres (4.4 hectares), though most were in the 5- to 6-acre (2- to 2.5-hectare) range. Since all three legions appear to have constructed a similar length of Wall it is probable that some four to six cohorts, or 2000 to 3000 men, of both legions VI and XX were present on the Wall. The remaining cohorts of II Augusta were presumably allotted other tasks, and indeed the legion is attested constructing the fort at Balmuildy under Lollius Urbicus.

Although no temporary camps are known at the west end more than half the distance slabs come from the last 4 miles (6.4 km). These demonstrate that the Wall here was divided into six short lengths, each less than a mile long, and each measured in feet not paces. Sir George Macdonald argued in his study of the distance slabs that this stretch was constructed last, building having started at the Forth. Nothing has been found to disprove this theory, though it does not completely explain the anomalies on the Wall.

Junctions in the stone base and differences in the treatment of the turf superstructure and in the width of the base and the ditch have been recorded. These may indicate the activities of different legions, but equally may reflect the work of separate gangs operating within legionary allocations.

FORTS AND FORTLETS

A variety of structures have been identified on the Antonine Wall – forts, fortlets, small enclosures and 'expansions'. The relationship of these structures to the Wall varies. Some forts were built before the rampart, others later. Two fortlets preceded the rampart, but most were contemporary. The single small enclosure examined was structurally later than the rampart, though not by long. The one 'expansion' thoroughly excavated was built at the same time as the rampart. Some of these differences have long been recognized. At first it was suggested that they reflected the time-lag between the construction of the rampart and the forts – the rampart was built from east to west and the eastern forts are either contemporary with or later than the rampart, while the western forts usually precede it. In 1975 J. P. Gillam put forward a more convincing explanation. He suggested that originally the Antonine Wall was planned to have only six forts, placed about 8 miles (12.8 km) apart, with fortlets at intervals of 1 mile (1.6 km) between them, but that during building operations the number of forts was significantly increased, so that when completed the distance between forts was reduced to about 2 miles (3.2 km). Since 1975 this theory has been tested by the spade. While it has not been

Table 8   The spacing of the 'primary' forts on the Antonine Wall

	Internal acreage	Hectares	Distance between forts in miles (km)
Carriden	c. 4	1.6	
			7¾ miles (12.4 km)
Mumrills	6.5	2.6	
			9 miles (14.5 km)
Castlecary	3.5	1.4	
			6 miles (9.6 km)
Bar Hill (?)	3.2	1.3	
			9 miles (14.5 km)
Balmuildy	4	1.6	
			9 miles (14.5 km)
Old Kilpatrick	4.2	1.7	

proved beyond all shadow of doubt the circumstantial evidence, the location of another five fortlets in particular, now is so strong as to suggest that it is most likely to be correct. It is therefore accepted here.

The original plan for the Antonine Wall called for the construction of six forts along the Wall with fortlets at intervals of 1 mile (1.6 km) between them. Most of the forts choose themselves, for they all precede the construction of the rampart. The forts, Mumrills, Castlecary, Balmuildy and Old Kilpatrick, are large and widely separated from each other. Mumrills and Castlecary are 9 miles (14.4 km) apart, Castlecary and Balmuildy 15 miles (24 km), Balmuildy and Old Kilpatrick 9 miles (14.5 km). The central 15-mile (24-km) stretch may have been broken by a fort: although Auchendavy, 8 miles (12.8 km) from Castlecary and 7 miles (11.2 km) from Balmuildy, may be a candidate, Bar Hill, more asymmetrically placed but on a high eminence with a fine view to the west and north, and detached from the Wall, is another possibility. Its position behind the rampart may suggest its construction beforehand; if the Wall was already there the fort would surely have been simply attached to it. At the east end of the Wall the large fort at Carriden nearly 8 miles (12.8 km) from Mumrills probably belongs to the same series.

Five of these six forts were large enough to hold complete auxiliary regiments, though in the case of Castlecary both of the two units known to have been posted there at different times in the second century –

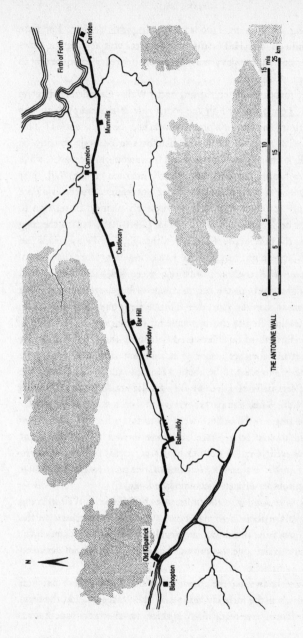

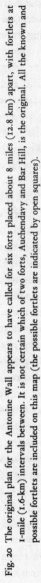

THE ANTONINE WALL

Fig. 20 The original plan for the Antonine Wall appears to have called for six forts placed about 8 miles (12.8 km) apart, with fortlets at 1-mile (1.6-km) intervals between. It is not certain which of two forts, Auchendavy and Bar Hill, is the original. All the known and possible fortlets are included on this map (the possible fortlets are indicated by open squares).

thousand-strong cohorts – were too large for this particular fort. The sixth fort is more difficult. Bar Hill held quingenary cohorts at different times during its life, but Auchendavy may have had difficulty in squeezing in even a regiment of this size.

The primary forts actually on the line of the Wall – Carriden lay beyond the east end – were all placed on the south side of the rampart, though still attached to it (Bar Hill, if a primary fort, may be an exception). This is in keeping with the position of the last forts to be built actually on Hadrian's Wall, such as Great Chesters and Carrawburgh. However, while on the southern barrier the forts were clearly imposed on the Wall, their internal arrangements being planned without any reference to the existence of the Wall, the Antonine Wall forts were clearly planned in relation to the Wall. Thus on Hadrian's Wall the front gate usually lay on the long axis, which was the normal procedure, even though, as at Housesteads and Great Chesters, this might result in the fort facing east rather than north. On the Antonine Wall the forts, with one exception, faced north, even though this might result in the central range of buildings running along the long axis rather than the short one. This closer integration of forts and Wall marks a further step in the development of frontiers.

All the nine fortlets so far discovered belong to the original plan, for they were constructed either before or at the same time as the rampart. They were clearly intended to be about a Roman mile apart, though the actual distance varied. The fortlets are very similar in size to the milecastles on Hadrian's Wall. Their ramparts were of turf on a stone base, usually protected by a single ditch. There were gates to both north and south. Timber buildings have been located in some fortlets. The building at Duntocher measured 36 by 18 feet (11 by 5.5 m) and is so close in size to its counterpart in the Hadrian's Wall milecastles as to suggest a similar estimate of the number of men accommodated, eight.

The fortlets were similar to the milecastles on Hadrian's Wall in being placed at intervals of about 1 Roman mile, but as there were forts on the Antonine Wall from the beginning they could not be an unbroken chain. It is also not certain that one was provided at every mile site not occupied by a fort.

No turrets are known on the Antonine Wall. Turrets were built on Hadrian's Wall when the forts lay behind on the Stanegate, and the forts on the Wall itself may have made many of these watch-towers superfluous.

Plate 16 Aerial view of the Antonine Wall at Rough Castle looking east. The fort lies to
the right of the rampart and ditch, with the fortified annexe immediately beyond.

However, a new feature was provided, the 'expansions'. When these were
first recognized they were called expansions because visually they appear
to be southward extensions of the rampart. Only six are known and they
always appear in pairs, two on the west brow of Croy Hill and two on
either side of the fort of Rough Castle. The one at Bonnyside East, a few
yards west of Rough Castle, on excavation was found to consist of a turf
platform on a stone base 18 feet (5.5 m) square, butted up against the rear
of the Antonine Wall. The two bases were constructed separately, but the
turfwork of 'expansion' and rampart overlapped, suggesting contemporan-
eity of construction. The 'expansion' was presumed to rise to the same
height as the wall top.

Around the base was found a considerable amount of burnt wood and
burnt turf presumed to have come from fires on the platform. The spacing
and position of the 'expansions' have been thought to suggest that they

were concerned with long-distance signalling. The discovery of two pottery vessels beside this particular 'expansion' led to the suggestion that a small detachment of men might have camped there from time to time.

There are problems with this interpretation of the function of the 'expansions'. It is by no means clear how such 'beacon-stances' could have worked. They could only have sent the simplest of messages and for anything more a man would have to be dispatched. Furthermore, there would have been many occasions when they would have been inoperable owing to climatic conditions. The burning is not evidence in itself of fires on top of the 'expansions'. It seems best to leave these structures as having undetermined functions.

The discovery of the last type of structure on the Antonine Wall to be discussed was announced as recently as 1978. The examination of aerial photographs led to the identification of three small enclosures, attached to the rear of the Wall, in the vicinity of Wilderness Plantation. The only excavated example consisted of a single ditch surrounding a slight turf rampart and enclosing an area about 18 feet (5.5 m) square. No structure was found inside it, and no entrance was located. It was constructed after the rampart, but the time-lag was probably not great. No convincing explanation has yet been put forward for the function of these small enclosures.

It seems probable that the Military Way also falls into the first plan. There is some evidence for this suggestion. At Rough Castle a quarry pit, dug to provide material for the adjacent road, was overlain by an 'expansion', the turfwork of which bonded in with that of the rampart.

The first plan for the Antonine Wall was close in many respects to Hadrian's Wall as completed. The running barrier was modified, being in turf not stone, a Vallum was not provided, though a road was, but the main features were similar. Forts, generally for whole units, were established at regular intervals of 8 to 9 miles (12.8 to 14.4 km) with fortlets every mile in between. No turrets are known on the Antonine Wall, but instead smaller structures appear, 'expansions' and small enclosures.

THE REVISED SCHEME

The differing relationships of the forts and fortlets to the Wall demonstrate unmistakably that new proposals were tabled and implemented before work on the original plan was completed. These called for the construction of at least ten new forts on the Wall. The decision seems to have been taken when the construction of the rampart had reached the area between Bearsden and Duntocher. Two fortlets in the western 4 miles (6.4 km) of the Wall, Cleddans and Duntocher, had been constructed before the rampart. Indeed the latter had been replaced by a fort, to which it became a sort of annexe, before the rampart builders arrived. Four miles (6.4 km) from the western end of the Wall lies Castlehill, where the unit of measurement for the Wall changed from paces to feet. This may be the point reached when it was decided to add to the number of forts on the Wall; even if this was not the exact spot, the change resulted from the fort decision. It is possible that most of the rampart-builders were redeployed to build the forts leaving only small detachments to complete the rampart. However, the building of the new fort at Duntocher before the rampart-builders reached the site may imply that all the gangs were taken away to build the forts and some time elapsed before the rampart was completed; such a lapse of time would best explain the change in the unit of measurement from paces to feet.

All the new forts were added to the rear of the rampart, the fort ramparts usually resting against the Antonine Wall rampart; Bar Hill may be an exception if it was not a primary fort. The secondary forts were all smaller than the first series – again Bar Hill may be an exception. None exceeds 3 acres (1.2 hectares) in internal area and nearly all were capable of holding only a detachment and not a whole unit. This marks a significant departure from the pattern of Hadrian's Wall, which itself was based upon halving the earlier spacing of about 14 miles (22.5 km), a day's marching distance.

The new forts throughout the western two-thirds of the Wall were on average about 2 miles (3.2 km) apart. The spacing is much more irregular in the eastern third. There have been several attempts to locate forts at hypothetical positions, all fruitless. It seems possible that here forts were not built on a regular 2-mile (3.2-km) spacing, perhaps because the outpost forts to the north helped to provide cover for the Wall.

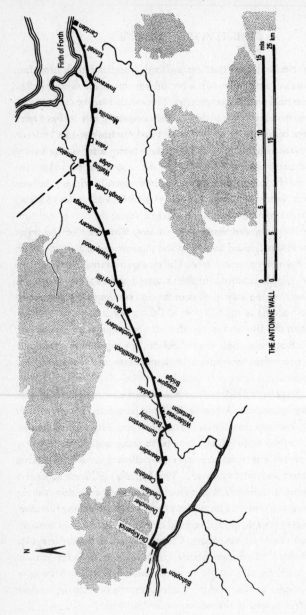

Fig. 21 The Antonine Wall as completed, with all the known forts and fortlets marked. The small squares on either side of Wilderness Plantation fortlet mark the sites of the small enclosures. The open square indicates a fort possibly occupied.

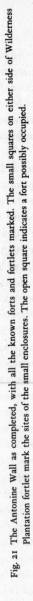

THE FORTS IN DETAIL

The forts on the Antonine Wall range in size from tiny Duntocher with an internal area of half an acre (0.2 hectare) to Mumrills, 6½ acres (2.6 hectares) internally and larger than most forts on Hadrian's Wall. The forts had from two to four ditches and although most had turf ramparts, between 12 and 20 feet (3.6 to 6.0 m) wide, two – Balmuildy and Castlecary – had stone walls. All other forts and fortlets constructed in Scotland at this time had turf ramparts. In general this is in keeping with Hadrian's Wall where the forts on the turf wall appear originally to have had turf ramparts, with the exception of Birdoswald which lay east of the Red Rock Fault.

The internal buildings also varied little in their materials of construction from their counterparts on Hadrian's Wall. The principal buildings were normally of stone, the barracks, stables and storehouses of timber. Although most barrack-blocks on Hadrian's Wall appear to have been built of stone, the surviving walls may have been sill walls supporting a timber superstructure.

In their internal arrangements, however, the Antonine Wall forts display none of the uniformity of the Hadrian's Wall forts. At Croy Hill, for example, a granary was placed in the *praetentura*, while a large part of the *praetentura* at Cadder apparently was left empty. The bath-house was usually placed within the fort; later changes resulted in some bath-houses being placed in the annexes. In keeping with the later practice on Hadrian's Wall none of the forts lay astride the rampart but all lay to the south, though in all but two cases (Carriden and Bar Hill) still attached to the Wall. We have also seen that with one exception the Antonine Wall forts face north, be it across or along the long axis. The overall impression is of much more flexibility in siting, planning and designing the forts on the Antonine Wall than was evident on Hadrian's Wall twenty years before. The construction of the Antonine Wall seems to reflect another step towards the dispersal of troops along a line for frontier police duties, as opposed to the concentration that would have been desirable for military operations.

The legionaries played a part in constructing the forts as well as the wall. Croy Hill, Bar Hill, Auchendavy, Cadder, Balmuildy, Bearsden, and

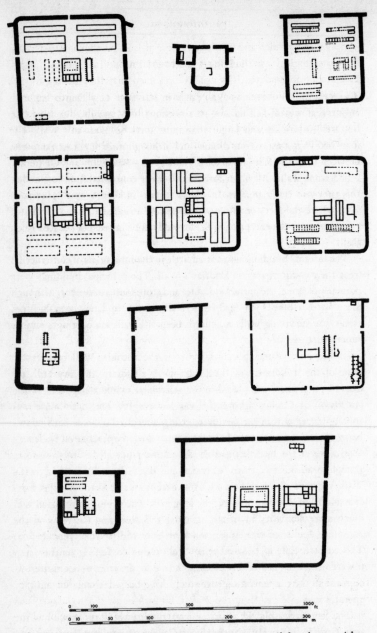

Fig. 22 The Antonine Wall forts, early Antonine plans. From top left to bottom right: Old Kilpatrick, Duntocher, Bearsden; Balmuildy, Cadder, Bar Hill; Croy Hill, Westerwood, Castlecary; Rough Castle, Mumrills. Scale 1 in. = 440 ft (1 : 5280).

possibly also Carriden and Castlecary, were at least partly constructed by legionaries, for legionary building stones have been found at them. Although these stones are undated it is usually presumed that they belong to the first period of building. They attest the activities of all three legions. However, several forts have also produced auxiliary building inscriptions. The headquarters building and possibly more of Rough Castle was built by *cohors VI Nerviorum* while at Castlecary *cohors I Tungrorum* was at work and at Bar Hill *cohors I Baetasiorum*. These three units were building under Antoninus Pius; the inscriptions may date to the original building of the Wall early in his reign or to a later rebuilding. Since none of the inscriptions specifically refers to restoration as opposed to building it may be best to assign them to the earlier period. The weight of the evidence suggests that most of the work fell on the shoulders of the legionaries with the auxiliaries acting in a secondary capacity, possibly concentrating on the buildings inside the forts.

The division of the Antonine Wall forts into two series may explain their great variation in size and lack of standardization. A certain degree of standardization can be recognized in the forts of Hadrian's Wall: for example, 580 feet appears in the dimensions of three forts, Chesters, Birdoswald and Stanwix. On the Scottish Wall there is no sign of standardization, mainly due, no doubt, to their construction by three legions and perhaps also a number of auxiliary units, but also because the forts were built in two stages. Thus Balmuildy and Cadder, two adjacent forts, were built by the same legion, II Augusta (so it appears), and for the same size of unit, or at least with a similar complement of buildings, but at different stages. They bear no resemblance to each other in size, dimensions or barrack-blocks.

One experiment on Hadrian's Wall, the Vallum, was not repeated. Instead, the forts were provided with a new feature, annexes, which appear to be an afterthought. These lay to one side of their fort and were often almost as large as or even larger than the forts themselves. Annexes are found outside many forts from the first century onwards. They are absent on Hadrian's Wall presumably because they were rendered unnecessary by the Vallum, which served among other things as an elongated annexe running the entire length of the Wall. The bath-house when outside the fort was usually within the annexe. Timber buildings have been found in some annexes, Mumrills, Cadder and Bearsden for example, but neither the purpose nor date of these buildings is known. It is highly unlikely that civilians were allowed to build houses and shops in the annexes. These enclosures had a military function, as had the Vallum, and would accommodate equipment and stores which could not be housed in the forts. Civilians were not allowed in the area between the Wall and the Vallum, the 'Hadrianic annexe', and there is no reason to suppose that the Antonine annexes were treated differently. Excavation, admittedly not very extensive, at Mumrills, Rough Castle, Castlecary, Bar Hill, Bearsden, Duntocher and Old Kilpatrick has produced no evidence of civilian buildings in the annexes though the excavators of the annexe at Camelon, just north of Watling Lodge fortlet, did suggest that buildings there were used by civilians.

THE UNITS ON THE WALL

Information about the units occupying these forts derives both from inscriptions and from the plans and layouts of the forts and their buildings. The largest fort was Mumrills, where was stationed the *ala I Tungrorum*, the only cavalry unit attested on the Antonine Wall. Inscriptions at Castlecary, 8 miles (12.8 km) to the west, record the *cohors I Tungrorum milliaria peditata*, which as we have seen helped to construct the fort, and the *cohors I Vardullorum milliaria equitata*. Both are large infantry units, the latter also containing cavalry, and the only units of this size to be attested by name on the Wall. The only sizeable areas of Iron Age settlements known for 20 miles (32 km) north of the Wall lie at the east end of the Campsie Fells just north of Castlecary, and this may account for the presence of the milliary units there. The position of Mumrills close to the road which led north through the Wall at Watling Lodge may have governed the nature of the unit based there. Inscriptions record the presence of several quingenary (500-strong) cohorts on the Antonine Wall, at Rough Castle, Bar Hill and at Castlehill. The size and number of barrack-blocks at Old Kilpatrick at the west end of the Wall suggest a *cohors milliaria peditata*, which quingenary cohorts may have been stationed at Cadder and Balmuildy. At another fort, Bearsden, possible cavalry barracks have been excavated. Many sites along the Wall have produced inscriptions recording legionary detachments – for example, Westerwood, Croy Hill and Auchen-

Table 9 The units suggested for the Antonine Wall forts

	Internal acreage	Hectares	Unit
Carriden	c. 4	1.6	
Inveravon (?)	small		
Mumrills	6.5	2.6	ala I Tungorum cohors II Thracum
Falkirk	small (?)		
Rough Castle	1	0.4	part of cohors VI Nerviorum quingenaria peditata
Castlecary	3.5	1.4	part of cohors I Tungrorum milliaria peditata part of cohors I Vardullorum milliaria equitata vexillation of legions II and VI
Westerwood	2	0.8	vexillation of legion VI (?)
Croy Hill	1.5	0.6	vexillation of legion VI (??)
Bar Hill	3.2	1.3	cohors I Baetasiorum quingenaria peditata cohors I Hamiorum quingenaria
Auchendavy	2.7	1.1	vexillation of legion II (?)
Kirkintilloch	(?)		
Cadder	2.8	1.1	cohors quingenaria peditata
Balmuildy	4	1.6	cohors quingenaria peditata
Bearsden	2.4	0.9	the fort probably included cavalry
Castlehill	2.6	1.0	cohors IV Gallorum quingenaria equitata
Duntocher	0.5	0.2	part of a unit
Old Kilpatrick	4.2	1.7	cohors milliaria peditata cohors I Baetasiorum quingenaria peditata

The primary forts are marked in bold; it is not clear whether Bar Hill or Auchendavy was the primary fort in this sector, though the former is more likely.

davy. Although the inscriptions are not dated they may belong to the first period of the occupation of the Wall. Some forts, such as Westerwood and Croy Hill, are in any case too small for a complete auxiliary unit, as are others, Rough Castle and Castlecary, where such units are specifically attested. Clearly part of these units must have been permanently out-stationed, possibly at the smaller forts along the Wall. Two forts extens-ively excavated, tiny Duntocher and the more normally sized Bearsden, do not appear to have contained headquarters buildings, suggesting that they were the home of detachments rather than complete units.

It is difficult to distinguish any general policy governing the garrisons of these forts. Different types and sizes of auxiliary units are mixed together with legionary detachments apparently at random. It is, however, notable that very little cavalry is attested on the Wall. Only one *ala* is known to have served on the Wall, one *cohors milliaria equitata*, and two *cohortes quingenariae equitatae*, one probably succeeding the *ala* at Mumrills later in the second century. In comparison one *cohors milliaria peditata* is attested and three smaller peditate cohorts, while legionary detachments, presumably composed completely of infantrymen, served at a further three forts. Finally the layout and barracks of a further three forts suggest that they too were occupied by infantry cohorts, one of milliary size. Only one-seventh of the troops on the Antonine Wall may therefore have been cavalry compared to a quarter on Hadrian's Wall. This emphasis on infantry may suggest a different strategy of frontier control, though alternatively it may have been in response to local terrain and conditions. The valleys of the Kelvin and the Carron in the Roman period would have been very boggy and unsuited to cavalry.

The total number of troops stationed in the Antonine Wall forts was only slightly less than that on Hadrian's Wall, which was twice as long. Put another way, there were nearly twice as many soldiers per Wall mile stationed in the Antonine Wall forts as in those of Hadrian's Wall. The strengthening of the frontier line under Antoninus Pius reflects not just the local situation but also the general nature of the Antonine reoccupation of Scotland. The Scottish Lowlands were now controlled by more forts and fortlets than either before or later and more than was usual in other similar areas, for example north England or Wales. The impression is that the Roman army moved north in great strength. The fact that some of these sites, both forts and fortlets, were abandoned within a few years suggests that the army may have overestimated the problem in the 140s and placed a greater occupation force in the Scottish Lowlands than was really necessary.

The second point is that the weight of the Wall garrison lay towards the west. Six of the eight western forts of known size were large enough to hold complete auxiliary units compared to only three out of the seven in the east. Certainly the eastern sector of the Wall was shielded by the outpost forts, but the comparison with Hadrian's Wall is striking. The first plan for forts on the Antonine Wall shows no particular emphasis on any sector. As on Hadrian's Wall, the addition of more forts was to affect the balance. Now the main body of troops lay in the west-central sector, facing the open and largely unpopulated Campsie Fells and Kilpatrick Hills. As on Hadrian's Wall it may have been the need to keep special watch on these hills that led to the establishment of more troops in the sector of the Wall facing them.

THE OUTPOST FORTS

North of the Antonine Wall, towards its eastern end, lay a number of forts. The first, Camelon, was only about half a mile (0.8 km) beyond the Wall, overlooking the crossing of the river Carron. Another fort probably lay beside the crossing of the Forth in the vicinity of Stirling while two others were Ardoch and Strageath, beside the river Earn. It is probable that Bertha on the Tay was reoccupied at this time, though that is not certain. These forts were linked to the Wall by a road. They presumably did not act as advance warning stations but protected and controlled friendly tribespeople in Fife and around the head of the Forth, the area which later became part of the kingdom of the Manau Gododdin. The style of their houses suggests strong connections between the tribes in Fife and those south of the Forth at this time.

THE FLANKS OF THE WALL

The south shore of the Forth was also protected by forts during the Antonine period, though no complex system such as the Cumbrian coast scheme is known. Eleven miles (17.7 km) beyond the eastern end of the Wall lay the fort of Cramond at the mouth of the little river Almond. Nine miles (14.4 km) further east was Inveresk, the base, apparently, of a complete *ala quingenaria*. An extensive civil settlement grew up outside this fort in the mid second century. The west flank of the Wall was protected by a fort at Whitemoss, Bishopton, and two fortlets at Lurg Moor and Outerwards.

THE BUILDING PROGRAMME

An attempt can now be made to reconstruct the building programme of the Antonine Wall. The easternmost length, built by legion II, is 4⅔ Roman miles long. This is very close to the lengths of 5 Roman miles which frequently recur on Hadrian's Wall, and taking account of natural geographical divisions the nearest convenient distance to 5 miles. Since further west the distance slabs record remarkable uniformity of lengths allocated to the legions, it is a reasonable assumption that legions VI and XX also built about 4⅔ Roman miles of the Wall. Each legion seems to have been divided into gangs with their own temporary camps. Nine of these camps have been found between Bridgeness and Castlecary. While the three legions were at work in this area other soldiers had started building the primary forts. Old Kilpatrick, Balmuildy and probably Castlecary were all built before the rampart, while the excavators of Mumrills suggested that work was actually proceeding on the fort when the rampart builders arrived. II Augusta certainly built Balmuildy, and possibly the others as well.

It may have been intended to divide the whole Wall into three lengths of about 13 Roman miles each, each in turn subdivided between the three legions. But if that was the intention it was not followed in the next length to be constructed. This stretch, which probably had Seabegs as its eastern boundary, is apparently only 10½ Roman miles long. The reason for this is uncertain, though Sir George Macdonald linked it with the difficulty of digging the ditch over Croy Hill and, we may add, Bar Hill. The next stretch, 11 Roman miles long, brought the Wall builders to Castlehill, 4 Roman miles from the Clyde. Here there is the puzzling change from paces to feet as the unit of measurement, probably connected with the addition of some thirteen new forts. All the primary forts may have been completed by now but the extra work was a considerable undertaking. Some soldiers may have been left to complete the Wall, but the change in the unit of measurement implies a break in the building programme and this is reinforced by the sequence at Duntocher, where the new fort was built before rampart builders arrived on the site.

The original intention may have been to build the Antonine Wall in three years, with each legion allotted a complete year's work at a time, 4⅔ Roman miles or thereabouts in the first season. The acclamation of Antoninus Pius as *imperator* took place in 142, and it is usually considered that construction started then. The decision to add more forts, and annexes, will have lengthened the building programme. Vivien Swan has argued that the work may have been slowed even further by the dispatch of British troops to participate in the war fought in Mauretania (modern Morocco) in the late 140s. This suggestion was prompted by the appearance of pottery with North African affinities in the later levels of some forts on the Antonine Wall: returning soldiers are the most likely vehicle for the introduction of exotic cooking methods. The construction of some forts by auxiliaries is paralleled by auxiliaries building on other frontiers and at Carvoran at the end of Hadrian's reign. In addition to the Wall the army had to build the outpost forts and the new forts in the Scottish Lowlands. Only one of these forts, High Rochester, has produced an inscription, which demonstrates that the *cohors I Lingonum equitata* was responsible for the erection of at least one building in the fort, though an inscription recording work by XX Valeria Victrix has also been assigned to this period. The auxiliary units may have built their own stations, leaving the construction of the Wall to the legionaries.

THE PURPOSE OF THE ANTONINE WALL

The Antonine Wall was designed, built and garrisoned in the light of experience gained on Hadrian's Wall, and then modified to suit the special problems of building – and occupying – a wall on the Forth–Clyde isthmus. The tactical purpose of the two Walls was the same: to control the movement of people into and out of the province at a convenient point (not necessarily the political or administrative boundary of the province). In the event of an attack on the Antonine Wall the army would move out to deal with the enemy in the open, just as they would on Hadrian's Wall. The Antonine Wall was presumably modified to create a frontier complex able to deal effectively both with the day-to-day difficulties of frontier control and the more serious dangers of a major attack. If the emperor and his advisers considered that the movement north and the provision of a new Wall would settle the disturbed conditions on the northern frontier they were mistaken. Sixty years were to elapse before peace came to the north.

4

THE TWO WALLS

The intention, presumably, was that the construction of the Antonine Wall should lead to permanent occupation of southern Scotland. The military installations show no signs of being temporary: the extensive use of turf and timber was normal in constructing new forts. During the occupation the frontier was repaired, forts and their buildings were modified, while the tentacles of supply stretched south, deep into the province and beyond. Civilians followed the soldiers north, and in one case at least a civil settlement gained self-governing rights, while a new pottery industry was established as is attested at several forts. Recent excavations have even suggested the existence of an amphitheatre at Inveresk.

There is no literary evidence for the period during which the Antonine Wall was occupied. A coin issue of 155 portrayed Britannia, the personification of the province, seated disconsolately with her head bowed. This has been taken to imply a disturbance, possibly an invasion or revolt, put down shortly before. Her attitude may simply be ringing the changes from earlier coin issues of Hadrian and Antoninus Pius depicting the personification of the province, though her demeanour does suggest an unhappy event in Britain. This coin issue appears, from its distribution and workmanship, to have been minted in Britain.

The history of the sixty years from 155 to the reign of Caracalla in the early third century is most confused. Certain events are known from literary evidence, and there is a sprinkling of building records and other inscriptions, though their relevance is not always clear. Additional evidence is provided by the structural history of the forts and the frontiers, as well as the coins and pottery found there. There is no consensus among scholars as to how a meaningful history of the Roman north in this period can be constructed. All that can be done is first to detail the evidence relating to events, real or imaginary, secondly to describe the structural evidence and the varying conclusions of ceramic and numismatic experts, and finally to put forward the interpretation that seems best to reconcile all the evidence.

The written evidence for the later second century tends to consist of scattered references in the literary sources to trouble in Britain and building inscriptions and dedications under various governors, among whom Iulius Verus under Antoninus Pius, Calpurnius Agricola under Marcus Aurelius and Ulpius Marcellus under Marcus and Commodus and later Commodus alone stand out for the number of references to them. Finally comes Clodius Albinus, governor of Commodus and rival emperor to Septimius Severus. There is no clear literary reference to the governorship of Verus, but a passage from Pausanias and the coin issue of 155 have been taken to hint at trouble under him, as have a number of inscriptions dating from his governorship. There is no need to rehearse again the case against the relevance of Pausanias (see pp. 88–9 above), and a dedication to Mars the Avenger from Corbridge has been re-read as a straightforward building-record. Three other inscriptions which have been taken to indicate problems under this governorship deserve longer treatment.

An inscription found in the river Tyne at Newcastle refers to a detachment or detachments coming from or destined for the armies of the two Germanies. It is a circular argument to say the soldiers must be coming to Britain, because we know of no trouble in the Germanies but do know of trouble in Britain, as the evidence for trouble in Britain depends heavily on this particular inscription. The Tyne is a curious place for soldiers going to or from the three legions, though a convenient port if the legions were all in the field in the north, and it is experienced soldiers, not raw recruits, that are referred to. Certainly on epigraphic grounds the interpretation of the inscription as referring to detachments going to the two Germanies has much to recommend it.

An inscription at Birrens records building at the fort in 158. The archaeological evidence may be dealt with at this point. Excavation has shown that Birrens was certainly rebuilt in 158 after destruction. The cause and nature of the destruction, though, are not known. The fort may have been sacked by an enemy, but the damage might have been done accidentally or even by the Romans themselves. With timber forts, when a change in the unit stationed there was contemplated, it was often simplest to demolish the existing fort, in order to build a new fort of different dimensions and accommodation. It is known that the unit at Birrens changed at this time. Re-excavation does not appear to have given a decisive answer. There is an inscription from Brough-on-Noe in Derbyshire, restored with probability as being under the governorship of Iulius Verus. The fort was certainly rebuilt at this time but unlike Birrens it had been abandoned for thirty or more years. The rebuilding of the fort may therefore have been occasioned not by unsettled conditions in the area but as part of a redeployment of forces in north Britain.

Finally under this governorship two inscriptions were found in the eighteenth century but subsequently lost referring to rebuilding on Hadrian's Wall, one dated to A.D. 158, apparently of the curtain rather than of its structures. The significance of this, and the general evidence for activity under this governorship, will be considered when the archaeological evidence has also been taken into account.

There may have been trouble, not perhaps connected with the Brigantes, in the 150s but in the past it may have been dated too late. If the coin issue of 155 is relevant it should celebrate a victory even earlier, before the governorship of Iulius Verus. His activities may be consonant with a strategic withdrawal to Hadrian's Wall, unaccompanied by fighting. The inscriptions from Hadrian's Wall showing rebuilding of the curtain in 158 may suggest this, for repair work to the curtain of the Wall ought to imply reoccupation of the whole Wall. If so it is not impossible that the rebuilding at Birrens was connected with a change in function from a hinterland fort of the Antonine Wall to an outpost fort of Hadrian's Wall, while Brough-on-Noe may have been reoccupied by a unit returning from Scotland. If the inscription from Newcastle could refer to detachments being sent from Britain to Germany, the implication is that Britain could spare troops.

LITERARY AND EPIGRAPHIC EVIDENCE FOR THE LATER SECOND CENTURY

At the beginning of the reign of the next emperor, Marcus Aurelius, who succeeded his adoptive father, Antoninus Pius, in 161, his biographer states 'war was threatening in Britain', and Marcus sent against the Britons Calpurnius Agricola. The description is reminiscent of the scene facing Hadrian in Britain at his accession forty years before: 'Britain could not be kept under Roman control'. This raises an interesting question of biographical criticism. At the opening of the reigns of four successive emperors, Hadrian, Antoninus Pius, Marcus Aurelius and Commodus, there is reference in their biographies or in the contemporary histories to a difficult situation in Britain. Although these may have been accurate – indeed in some instances there is corroborative evidence – it is also possible, if not probable, that this emphasis on the disturbed conditions which his hero inherited and forcefully dealt with is part of the stock-in-trade of the imperial biographer. Hadrian responded by visiting Britain and building a wall, Pius by sending Lollius Urbicus to reconquer the Scottish Lowlands and build a new Wall, and now Marcus by sending to Britain Calpurnius Agricola. Nevertheless the writer cannot have created an event which did not happen; there must have been a germ of truth in his account. Certainly Britain was a difficult province to govern, for the best generals of the day were sent here in the second century. Iulius Severus was governor of the province when called upon to deal with the Jewish revolt in 132, Lollius Urbicus had a distinguished military record, as did Iulius Verus himself; both served in the Jewish revolt, Urbicus on Hadrian's staff, and Verus as a tribune under Severus, his father. Statius Priscus, governor in 161 or 162, was recalled in less than a year to cross the Empire to take command in Cappadocia against the Parthians, while in the reign of Commodus, Helvius Pertinax, governor in succession of four major provinces and a future emperor, was to be sent to Britain. For most of these men the governorship of Britain was the climax of their careers; they had previously served a long apprenticeship in both civil and military posts usually including a junior governship of one or two of the Danubian provinces and also the senior governorship of Lower Germany. Little is known of the earlier career of Calpurnius Agricola, but he did go on to govern the three united Dacian provinces.

Calpurnius Agricola was evidently concerned with Hadrian's Wall, in particular perhaps the Stanegate, for building inscriptions of his governor-ship have been recovered from the forts at Carvoran and Vindolanda, and also from Corbridge; he was also active in the Pennines, for building at this time is recorded at Ribchester and possibly also Ilkley. A few years later, in 166–9, building is attested on Hadrian's Wall, this time at Stanwix and Great Chesters.

Unsettled conditions apparently continued in Britain for the rest of the reign of Marcus Aurelius. The emperor's biographer records, apparently in the early 170s, that war was again about to break out in Britain. When in 175 peace was concluded on the Danube and the Sarmatians provided 8000 cavalry for the Roman army, 5500 were sent to Britain. They may have been required to support a hard-pressed provincial army, or Britain may simply have been an isolated place to which to send troops of uncertain loyalty.

If the nature of these disturbances is uncertain, those which afflicted the province in the early 180s are somewhat less obscure. Cassius Dio in his *History of Rome* records that

the greatest of the wars of Commodus' reign was fought in Britain. The tribes in the island crossed the wall that separated them from the Roman forts, doing much damage and killing a general and the troops he had with him; Commodus in alarm sent against them Ulpius Marcellus, who ruthlessly put down the barbarians.

This passage clearly indicates the nature of the troubles in Britain at this time, an invasion of the province, involving the death possibly of the governor himself, or one of the legionary commanders, and the destruction of his army. However, unfortunately the location of 'the wall' is not given, and it is necessary to turn to archaeological evidence to try to determine this.

Nor is the date entirely clear. An inscription from Benwell records Marcellus as governor under two joint emperors. This has led in the past to the suggestion that there were two governors of the same name, one serving later, under Severus and Caracalla. A military diploma has come to light, however, recording Ulpius Marcellus as governor in Britain on 23 March 178 under the joint emperors Marcus and Commodus. Commodus could hardly have 'sent' Marcellus at the beginning of his sole reign in 180 if he was already in Britain. Perhaps Marcellus had completed his term in

Britain and was sent back. This would be specially appropriate if the general killed had been the governor and needed urgent replacing. Alternatively Dio's phrasing is loose and Marcellus was still governor in 180.

Cassius Dio, or rather his epitomist, instead of narrating useful information relates Ulpius Marcellus' reputation as a martinet, with supporting anecdotes. It is perhaps no coincidence that the army of Britain was in a mutinous state in 185. Their resentment of an attempt by Commodus' favourite and praetorian prefect Perennis to replace their senatorial commanders by equestrians helped to lead to the downfall of Perennis, and they were still mutinous when Pertinax arrived to take charge of them in 185. Although he had some success, after almost losing his life he finally asked to be relieved of his command because of the resentment towards him nourished by the troops.

The next tribulation which befell Britain was a result of the murder of Commodus on 31 December 192. In the ensuing power struggle the governor of Britain, Clodius Albinus, was bound to become involved, as governor of one of the three major military provinces. In the final act of that struggle Albinus led his troops across the Channel to face Septimius Severus, governor of Upper Pannonia (modern Hungary), who had made good use of his central position and the proximity of his province to Rome. In February 197 Albinus was defeated at a hard-fought battle at Lugudunum (Lyons) in southern France.

The following years cannot have been happy for Britain. Families in the military areas lost husbands, sons and fathers in the fighting while many of the province's leading families must have suffered as a result of their support for Albinus. Meanwhile the tribes north of the frontier were restless. Cassius Dio refers to the conditions which faced Virius Lupus, Severus' first governor:

since the Caledonians did not keep their promises and made ready to assist the Maeatae, and since at that time Severus was devoting himself to the Parthian war, Lupus was forced to purchase peace from the Maeatae for a great sum, receiving back a few prisoners.

It has been considered that in 196 Albinus withdrew the units on the Wall for his fight with Severus, allowing the northern tribes to attack and destroy the Wall. There is, however, no mention of this in the contemporary literature. Ten years later Herodian does record that 'the barbarians had risen and were overrunning the country, carrying off booty and causing great destruction . . .' But neither Herodian nor Cassius Dio mentions a single geographical place-name in their discussion, though the latter does state that 'the Maeatae live close to the wall which divides the island into two, and the Caledonians beyond them'. Unfortunately again which Wall is not made clear, for this would have been known by the people living at the time and reading the account. Because these references in the sixty or seventy years following the construction of the Antonine Wall are so brief the events of these years are obscure and likely to remain so. While new inscriptions may from time to time be discovered, new literary evidence is unlikely to be found. Meanwhile archaeologists and historians will have to rely on more imperfect tools for tracing the history of the second half of the second century, namely coins and pottery.

NUMISMATIC EVIDENCE FOR THE LATER SECOND CENTURY

The coins found on northern sites give clear and unquestioned dates, but dates of minting, not of loss. The latest stratified coin from the Antonine Wall is of Antoninus Pius, was minted 154–5 and comes from the debris found in the outer west ditch at Mumrills. Unstratified coins of a rather later date are known. A coin of 164–9 has been found within the fort at Old Kilpatrick and another of 173–4 has been found near Mumrills, while from Kirkintilloch comes a coin of Commodus recorded by a nineteenth-century antiquarian and from Bar Hill a coin tentatively assigned to the same emperor. Since these coins are unstratified they may not be relevant to the date of the abandonment of the Antonine Wall. The may have been dropped by a passing Roman patrol or by local natives at a much later date. Coins of Marcus and his son Commodus are absent from other Roman forts in Scotland, apart from Cramond on the Forth, which was reoccupied under Severus, and Newstead, always a special case, as it was occupied for some years after the abandonment of the Antonine Wall. However, an important coin-hoard has been found at Rumbling Bridge in Kinross-shire. Although a few miles north of the Antonine Wall, Rumbling Bridge lies within the area protected by the outpost forts. The hoard of 179 coins contains eight of Commodus, the latest a fairly fresh specimen minted in

186–7, but the reasons for its deposition and whether a Roman or a native buried it are unknown. The owner of the hoard could have obtained his coins from the Antonine Wall forts or from the outpost forts, though Newstead, held almost certainly until 180 and possibly beyond, 60 miles (100 km) to the south, may have been the source. The hoard was within that part of Britain shielded by the outpost forts in the Antonine period and over which the army may have maintained surveillance and some sort of physical presence from the abandonment of these permanent bases to the fourth century. Quite possibly the coins have no historical importance at all and formed a hoard built up by a civilian, army veteran or even deserter and buried fortuitously at this time. Certainly the hoard does not prove that the Antonine system continued down to 186–7 nor do the unstratified coins from the Wall itself. The numismatic evidence does attest the occupation of the Antonine Wall down to 154–5, and the unstratified coins of later date hint at some continuing Roman presence in the Antonine Wall area.

The coin from 155 referred to above (p. 117) is a rather different use of coin evidence, as its value depends on its depiction of Britannia being significant, not on where it is found, though its confinement to Britain may be significant.

ARCHAEOLOGICAL EVIDENCE FOR THE LATER SECOND CENTURY

Excavation at many sites in the north of Britain has provided a considerable body of material relating to the history of individual stations and the frontier generally. This evidence consists of the structural sequence of buildings within the forts, and the objects found at the sites. The coins at least provide a clear *terminus post quem*, though few stratified coins have been found in north Britain. The pottery, which is more abundant, is not self-dating and has to depend on its relationship to contexts dated by inscriptions and literary sources. Where these are lacking in the second half of the second century the pottery is difficult to date. However, typology of the vessels and comparison of pottery from different sites, some securely dated, together with the detailed examination of the potters' stamps on samian ware and *mortaria* (mixing-bowls), do allow some conclusions concerning the occupation of individual sites in relationship to each other. Nevertheless nearly all this evidence is open to more than one interpretation and in reconstructing the history of the northern frontier at this time this awkward fact must be borne in mind.

Excavation has demonstrated complexity in the occupation of forts and fortlets in southern Scotland during the Antonine period. Some sites exhibit only one phase of occupation; others major rebuilding; while some have what appears to be a third phase. N. Hodgson has recently suggested that instead of there being two main periods of occupation most of the major changes could be a consequence of the decision to increase the number of forts on the Antonine Wall during its construction. This would account for the evidence for rebuilding and/or unit changes at the primary forts, outpost forts such as Strageath, and hinterland forts like Crawford. At Birrens and Newstead the second phase probably related to the changes following the abandonment of the Antonine Wall rather than during its occupation.

The pottery found in north Britain suggests that the Antonine Wall and the other Scottish forts, except Newstead, Birrens and probably Cappuck, were abandoned by the middle years of the decade beginning in 160. This conclusion rests on separate studies of the imported samian ware and the British-made *mortaria* and other pottery. Analysis of the samian ware demonstrates that pottery stamps and decorated vessels of the period 160–200 are not represented on the Antonine Wall and in the outpost and hinterland forts, though they are found at several civilian sites in Scotland. Stamped *mortaria* of the same period are also absent from military sites, while the finds of other coarse pottery would also suggest an abandonment of the Antonine Wall shortly after 160. While the evidence of all three types of pottery is in agreement none of this evidence carries its own date. Dating is provided by a relatively small number of deposits and sites, and therefore lacks total certainty.

Excavation attests that the Antonine Wall ended in the destruction of the forts, and some of those on Hadrian's Wall suffered the same fate at the end of the second period in the second century. But excavation rarely allows the cause of the destruction to be determined. It could have been the result of the demolition of the fort by the Romans before abandonment of the site, or due to a successful attack by the enemy; it could also have been accidental. Sir George Macdonald long ago suggested that the distance

Table 10 Events of the second century

Date	Emperor	Literary	Evidence Epigraphic	Numismatic	Archaeological
119	Hadrian			Britannia issue	
122		Hadrian visits Britain and builds Wall	Diploma: Nepos becomes governor July 122: building inscriptions		Wall building commences
139–42	Antoninus Pius	Pius conquers barbarians and builds Wall	Urbicus governor: building inscriptions	Coin issue 142	Wall building commences
155				Britannia issue	
158			Hadrian's Wall and Birrens building inscriptions		Scotland (apart from Newstead) abandoned: Hadrian's Wall and hinterland forts reoccupied?
161	Marcus	British war threatens: Calpurnius Agricola sent	Building inscriptions on Hadrian's Wall and in hinterland		
170–72		British war threatens			
175		5500 Sarmatian cavalry sent to Britain			

Year	Emperor / Governor	Events	Inscriptions	Coins / Destruction
178				Destruction at Corbridge, Halton, Rudchester
	Ulpius Marcellus governor			
180	Commodus	The barbarians cross a Wall: Ulpius Marcellus sent against them		
184				Coin issue for British victory
197	Severus	Defeat of Albinus at Lyons: Maeatae and Caledones restless	Building inscriptions in hinterland	
205–7			Building inscriptions on Hadrian's Wall and outposts	
208		Barbarians overrun province, emperor and sons arrive		
210		British victory		Coin issue for British victory
211		Caledones and Maeatae revolt: death of Severus		
213			'Loyalty' inscriptions: building inscriptions on Hadrian's Wall and hinterland continue into 260s	

slabs had been removed from the Wall and carefully buried to prevent their desecration by the natives. Recent excavations at Bearsden have suggested that the army demolished and burnt the timber buildings before evacuating the site. At other sites the situation is not so clear. Doubtless the action of the withdrawing units varied from site to site.

The evidence from Newstead clearly indicates the difficulties in interpreting the evidence. During the course of the excavations carried out at the site before the First World War many pits were emptied. The Antonine pits were found to contain debris cleaned out of the fort, including damaged armour, tools, personal ornaments, and even human skulls; this has been interpreted as evidence for the sacking of the fort. But by an alternative interpretation it is rubbish, unwanted odds and ends, and armour awaiting repair, all abandoned when the fort was evacuated and demolished by its garrison, which may not have been able to carry away all its equipment and accumulated possessions. The metalwork will have been buried not just to leave the site tidy but also to hide it from hostile tribesmen. For the same reason no doubt all the nails left when the fortress of Inchtuthil was evacuated seventy years before were buried deeply. The human skulls may also have had a less spectacular if no less gruesome explanation. On Trajan's Column can be seen Roman auxiliaries in action brandishing the heads of slaughtered Dacians, and even gripping these heads in their teeth as they fought. In another scene two such heads are fixed on stakes outside a Roman camp. The heads found in the pits at Newstead may therefore have been of British or Caledonian tribesmen killed in earlier wars and displayed as trophies in the fort. It has been suggested that these were ritual pits, but there is no conclusive evidence that this was so. Clearly the material from Newstead cannot be taken as unequivocal support for the sacking of the fort at this time.

THE ABANDONMENT OF THE ANTONINE WALL

The dating of the abandonment of the Antonine Wall has been complicated in the past by the need to fit in two periods of occupation, and a feeling that Pius would not have abandoned it, so in earlier editions of this book c. 158–c. 163 was suggested for the second period on the Antonine Wall. The return to Hadrian's Wall has tended to be associated with the activity of Calpurnius Agricola, recorded in the literary sources as sent because of war threatening in Britain and on inscriptions as undertaking building work on and south of Hadrian's Wall. The lost inscriptions recording building work apparently on the curtain of Hadrian's Wall have, however, long suggested an earlier return to Hadrian's Wall, and the elimination of the second period on the Antonine Wall largely removes any difficulty in accepting it. The rebuilding at Birrens, dated epigraphically to the same year, could then relate to a change of unit consequent upon its role changing from that of a hinterland fort of the Antonine Wall to an outpost fort of Hadrian's Wall. The work at Brough-on-Noe under Iulius Verus might relate to its reoccupation by troops returning from Scotland. If legionary troops were being sent to Germany under Verus of course that might increase the pressure to reduce commitments in Britain by the withdrawal to Hadrian's Wall. The rebuilding and repair under Calpurnius Agricola might then be seen as the continuation of a process begun a few years earlier, after Agricola had dealt with the threat of war he had been sent to counter. This may suggest that the withdrawal from Scotland was undertaken over several years, perhaps interrupted by campaigning, and this might account for the coin of 164–9 from Old Kilpatrick. The general date of 158–164 for withdrawal is supported by the pottery.

Although units were no longer permanently stationed in central and south-western Scotland the army did not lose all interest in this area. The continuing occupation – in strength – of Newstead on the north side of the Cheviots points to a considerable interest in the tribes of this frontier region, and there is a hint that Newstead was not the most northerly base. Late Antonine samian ware has been found at Castlecary on the Antonine Wall as well as at Newstead and Birrens. Although the quantity of late Antonine samian at Castlecary is very small it does receive support from an altar discovered at the site. The dedication to Mercury, found just outside the fort, records the erection of a shrine and statue by soldiers of VI Victrix who were citizens of Italy and Noricum (Austria). The most straightforward way that soldiers from that part of the Empire could have entered VI Victrix is by transfer from II Italica, the one legion of Noricum, raised in Italy in 165. (Only new legions recruited Italians – most Italian recruits entered the Rome units such as the praetorian guard or the urban cohorts.) That would date the inscription within the period 165 to 190, probably later rather than earlier as the number of Noricans is large enough to warrant special mention. Moreover it is unlikely that soldiers could have been spared from the Danube until after 180; indeed it is possible that the soldiers were sent to Britain to make up losses suffered in the invasion of the early 180s when not only was a Roman general killed but also his army. However, this is speculation; the troops may have arrived some years earlier. Nevertheless the altar does attest a continuing Roman interest as far north as the Forth–Clyde line after the mid 160s. This altar, if correctly dated, is the only inscription from the Antonine Wall certainly later than the reign of Pius.

The continuing Roman preoccupation with the land – and the tribes, the Caledonians and the Maeatae – north of the Forth in the late second and early third centuries could imply that the Antonine Wall was held until the end of the century. Speaking of the Severan campaigns of 209–11 Cassius Dio says that 'the Maeatae live close to the wall which divides the island into two, and the Caledonians beyond them'. The Maeatae lived just north of the Forth – their name is commemorated in the place-names of Dumyat and Myot Hill in the Central Region – and so the Wall which they lived beside was the Antonine. This, together with the inscription from Castlecary, is the best evidence for the continuing occupation of the Antonine Wall in the later second century. But it is not unequivocal proof of a late date for the abandonment of the Wall. It directly contradicts pottery evidence, which is unanimous in suggesting a date in the mid 160s, and the lack of epigraphic and numismatic evidence later than the 180s. Castlecary may have been held for some time as an advance base. It was an important fort in the first and second centuries, lying on the watershed of the Carron and Kelvin valleys, possibly beside a natural route north.

Why was the Antonine Wall abandoned? The reason does not seem connected with the local situation. The army experienced no difficulty in controlling northern England and southern Scotland and the withdrawal cannot be connected with a need to strengthen control over the Pennines. The hostile attitude of the Caledonians alone would not have forced the Romans to withdraw – it is inconceivable that Rome at the height of her power would be forced into a 'strategic withdrawal'. The reason for the abandonment of the Scottish Lowlands must be closely connected with the reason for its occupation twenty years before. If the move into Scotland in 140 was mainly a scheme to gain Antoninus Pius easy military prestige then the withdrawal a few years before Pius' death could follow recognition in Rome that it no longer justified holding on to Scotland. Pius had no continuing concern with Britain, which he failed to visit as he failed generally to visit the provinces. Also choices may have had to be made. Pressures were building up elsewhere under Pius, to break out into war under Marcus, but Britain had her share of problems also. It is significant that one of the first acts of Marcus' reign was to transfer Statius Priscus, the newly arrived governor of Britain, to the Parthian war that had just broken out, as the best man available, and then to dispatch Calpurnius Agricola to deal with the threat of war in Britain. Troops were being called for, from Britain as well as from other provinces. The withdrawal from the unnecessary commitment in Scotland would help Britain's problems and the rest of the Empire. Given a free hand, the Roman army could have conquered the whole of Britain. Under Agricola it failed because a legion was required more urgently elsewhere; it would fail under Severus because the emperor died and his sons had other priorities. The move forward to the Antonine Wall had perhaps never been more than a clumsy compromise, given total conquest was the optimum solution; it was abandoned as the two attempts at total conquest were because Britain was never an absolute priority for Rome.

THE REOCCUPATION OF HADRIAN'S WALL

The overall nature of the reoccupation of the frontier complex in the mid 160s is fairly clear. Hadrian's Wall itself was put back into working order much as before. The forts were repaired and reoccupied, usually by a unit of similar size and type to the one which had left twenty years previously. The milecastle gates were replaced, the barracks repaired and the turrets rebuilt. The rebuilding was quite extensive, and either now or later included the replacement of the original clay core by mortar. This is presumably why the curtain itself was repaired in places in 158. Work on the curtain in the west probably included the completion of the rebuilding of the turf wall in stone. The Vallum was cleaned out and the silt dumped on the south berm forming an extra mound (the 'marginal mound'). One addition to the frontier complex, a road, seems to have been made at this time, perhaps resulting from experience gained on the Antonine Wall. The discovery of side roads linking turrets abandoned some years later with this road, the Military Way, suggests that the road (clearly not part of the Hadrianic plan, for in places it overrides or runs along the top of the north mound of the Vallum) was built at this time. The bridge at Chesters was probably rebuilt at this time to take a road rather than a mere walk, though that at Willowford may not have been rebuilt until the early third century.

If the Wall was reoccupied as before, and even improved, other parts of the frontier complex were not. Very few of the towers on the Cumbrian coast seem to have been repaired and reoccupied at this time, though recent work suggests that a number of milefortlets were recommissioned now and occupied until about 180. The three definitely Hadrianic forts continued in use – Burrow Walls if built under Hadrian certainly did not continue in occupation till the 160s. The large-scale abandonment of the Cumbrian coast system was realistic for that system had resulted from over-anxiety with the problems of security in the west on the part of Hadrian and his generals.

The units withdrawn from the Antonine Wall and its associated forts had to be found new homes, and many sites in the Pennines were reoccupied at this time. Inscriptions demonstrate rebuilding, and therefore presumably reoccupation, in 158 at Brough-on-Noe, in the 160s at Ribchester and Ilkley, and in the 170s at Lanchester, while a recent survey of the ceramic evidence has suggested that the forts at Ambleside, Bainbridge, Binchester, Chester-le-Street, Ebchester, Lancaster, Manchester, Old Penrith and Templeborough were all reoccupied at this time. The renewed activity at these forts, spread over the whole of the north of England from Derbyshire to the Wall, does not imply any local disturbance but simply the need to find bases for the returning units.

The return to Hadrian's Wall in the years following 158 did not break all contact with the area to the north, as seems almost to have happened under Hadrian. In the west Birrens and Netherby certainly continued to be held, and therefore presumably Bewcastle also. In the east, as we have seen, the hand of the army stretched even further north. Newstead was rebuilt about 160 and continued in occupation for another twenty years or so. The forts on Dere Street linking it with the Wall presumably were also held (Risingham alone had produced clear evidence for a garrison in these years). Patrols may have maintained surveillance over an area almost coterminous with the abandoned territories, if the evidence from Castlecary is accepted. This system of outpost forts, and the patrolling which must

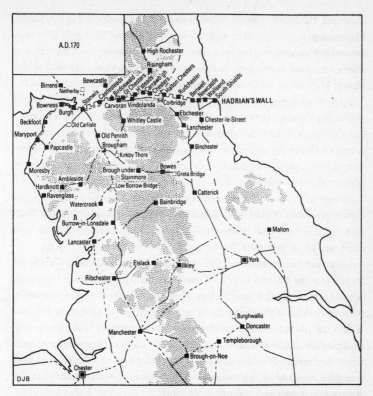

Fig. 23 Military dispositions in north England about 170. The open square crossed through indicates a fort considered to have been abandoned during the previous ten years; the open squares, forts possibly occupied at this time; and the half-open square, a fort probably occupied.

have accompanied it, heralds the later 'third-century' organization which lasted unchanged almost to the end of the Roman period in Britain.

THE INVASION OF THE EARLY 180s

Britain was unsettled throughout the 170s but in the early 180s trouble erupted spectacularly. A Roman general was killed and his army massacred when the barbarians crossed the Wall. Which Wall was crossed is not recorded and some scholars have suggested that the peculiar wording of the passage – 'the wall that separated them from the Roman forts' – may imply that the unoccupied, but not forgotten, Antonine Wall was crossed. However, there does appear to have been damage to Hadrian's Wall at this time. The fort at Halton Chesters seems to have been destroyed, its neighbour Rudchester, and also the station of Corbridge two miles to the south. But none of the other forts where excavation has taken place recently can be shown to have suffered damage at this time. Some milecastles and turrets exhibit signs of repair perhaps following destruction by enemy action, or as part of a general overhaul of the frontier complex, possibly over a period of years.

There is an altar at Kirksteads between Stanwix and Burgh-by-Sands by a legate of VI Victrix recording successful operations beyond the Wall. It may have been dedicated at this time, but it could equally well have been set up at any time in the second half of the second century. An attempt has been made to identify this legate with a man who was consul in 158. As the office of consul followed that of legionary legate, generally after a few years, this would strengthen the case for the reoccupation of Hadrian's Wall in the mid 150s. The identification is uncertain, but it is a genuine possibility. If it were proven we might have to conclude that Hadrian's Wall was reoccupied earlier in the 150s than presently envisaged, with the Antonine Wall evacuated, but perhaps several forts retained in southern Scotland. It is a comment on the nature of our evidence that this possibility cannot be laughed out of court.

Ulpius Marcellus, 'sent' by Commodus, retrieved the situation, and his victory was celebrated in 184. Marcellus also seems to have made changes in the military dispositions. The pottery evidence suggests that the forts at Birrens and Newstead were abandoned at this time. Risingham on Dere Street may also have been given up, for an inscription erected over the south gate of this fort twenty-five years later records the rebuilding of this gate and the adjoining length of wall, which had fallen down through old age. It is difficult to envisage an occupied fort with its gates and walls in ruins, so the fort may have lain abandoned for the last years of the second century. However, a similarly worded inscription dated to 221 comes from Chesters, where the unit had been stationed continuously for at least fifteen years, so the continued occupation of Risingham cannot be ruled out. Unfortunately nothing is known of High Rochester, the next fort along

Dere Street, at this time. The abandonment of Newstead and possibly also of Risingham, points to a lessening of the Roman grip on Dere Street after the disaster of the early 180s. Marcellus may have made treaties with the Caledonians and the Maeatae; a passage in Cassius Dio's *History of Rome* implies such a treaty, which might have been made either at that time by Marcellus or ten years later by Clodius Albinus, or indeed at any time between the early 180s and 197.

THE MODIFICATIONS TO HADRIAN'S WALL IN THE 180s

The hand of Ulpius Marcellus can also be recognized on the Wall itself. At several forts the regiment appears to have been changed. For example, two inscriptions from Chesters, which should probably be dated to this time, record building at the fort by the *ala II Asturum*. There seems to have been an infantry unit at the fort in the 160s and 170s, so the change to an *ala* was presumably made by Marcellus. The *ala II Asturum* was destined to have a long connection with Chesters, for it remained for over 200 years into the early years of the fifth century. The *cohors I Aelia Dacorum*, recorded at Birdoswald in 205–7, and the *ala I Asturum* at Benwell in 208, may both have been moved to these forts by Marcellus. The presence of a cavalry commander at Benwell, some time in 178–80, however, may imply that the *ala I Asturum* had been moved to the fort before the invasion of the early 180s. Indeed some unit changes may have occurred in the late 150s or early 160s.

The modifications did not just affect the forts, but extended to the smaller structures as well. It seems that many of the turrets along the line of the Wall were abandoned. The establishment of military units on the Wall in the second Hadrianic scheme must have made many of these observation posts redundant, although none seem to have been relinquished. All the ones investigated seem to have been put back into working order on the return to Hadrian's Wall in the 160s, unlike their counterparts on the Cumbrian coast, but reoccupation may have been only half-hearted. So little pottery of this period was found in turret 33b, for example, that the excavators felt the reoccupation was only very brief or spasmodic. Some turrets exhibit traces of blocking in their doorways. After an initial brief reoccupation in the late 150s or early 160s the turrets may have gone out of use and the doors been built up. Later in the century more drastic alterations were carried out at these turrets and at others. The structure was demolished, sometimes removing almost all trace of it, and the curtain wall built across the recess on the north side of the turret. Pottery dropped during this operation helps to date it to the later years of the second century or the early years of the third. The recess may have been built up in order to eliminate a point of structural weakness in the Wall. To suggest that it was done to maintain a wall walk, as some have done, raises problems, as the elimination of the turret would lengthen considerably the distance between places of shelter and accommodation, and destroy an access point to the wall top. It seems easier to interpret the abandonment of the turret as the dropping of whatever system of observation and patrolling was linked to it, either because it had proved unnecessary or because it was being done by patrols from the forts. In some areas turrets were abandoned wholesale: in the central crags sector of the Wall no turret between 33b and 41b inclusive is known to have been retained, though a few miles further west turret 44b in a splendid signalling and observing position did continue in use. Elsewhere the pattern is more irregular; in the Irthing–Birdoswald area, for example, some turrets were abandoned, others retained, with no discernible pattern. One turret, 51b, was abandoned, but the recess was not built up; it saw reuse in the fourth century. Some of the milecastles and turrets which did continue in use may have been abandoned during the third century; certainly few survived into the fourth.

The milecastles did not go untouched at this time. Every milecastle where investigation has revealed sufficient surviving evidence had one of its two gates narrowed so that it was only passable by pedestrian traffic. Usually the north gate was treated in this manner, but sometimes the south, while the north gates of milecastle 22 between Halton Chesters and the Portgate, and of milecastle 35 on the crags, were blocked completely. The latter gate may never have been an opening, as there is a precipice immediately outside it. However, only one milecastle, 27, seems to have been abandoned at this time, though the interiors of few milecastles have been examined and published. These alterations, like the changes to the turrets, follow realistic assessment of the situation on the Wall. There was an overprovision of milecastles – and gates – at the beginning so these changes were probably no more than an adaptation of the structures to meet the real situation.

Plate 17 Turret 33b (Coesike). The blocking in the doorway dates to the second century. Later the turret was demolished down to the lowest four courses and the recess on the north side built up. Beyond this blocking can just be seen the original inner north wall of the turret.

THE MID 180s AND AFTER

Ulpius Marcellus, sent by Commodus to retrieve the situation in Britain, may have restored the frontier defences but he was not able to solve all the province's troubles. This disturbed state of affairs in Britain makes the history of the next twenty years correspondingly obscure. It is not until 213 or so that the mists shrouding the events of these years clear and the organization of the frontier defences can be better understood. Marcellus' victory over the barbarians was celebrated in 184 but in the following year the British army, now probably under a new governor, mutinied and their complaints led directly to the downfall of the senior army officer, the praetorian prefect, Perennis. Helvius Pertinax was appointed governor of Britain and tried to restore discipline, but with limited success. A legion mutinied again and in the disturbances Pertinax was almost killed. He retired prematurely from his command at his own request. The lack of building inscriptions dated to the reign of Commodus is not confined to Britain but is general to the Empire. Perhaps the damnation of his memory after his murder resulted in the smashing of the inscriptions bearing his name. This makes unsafe any conclusions based on their absence in Britain. Be that as it may, the last years of his reign were not conducive to good and stable provincial government, while his assassination on the last day of 192 led to a civil war which lasted four years.

While the governor of Britain, Clodius Albinus, was preparing for his challenge to the new emperor, Septimius Severus, he cannot have been too concerned with the northern frontier. He was playing for higher stakes: if he won the Empire he would have enough troops to settle any frontier trouble, and if he lost it would no longer be his concern. However, he may have made or renewed treaties made some years before by Ulpius Marcellus with the northern tribes, the Caledonians and Maeatae, to help safeguard the frontier. Immediately after Albinus' defeat in February 197, while some or all of the units normally based in the Wall forts may have been absent on the continent, these tribes may have invaded the province and caused extensive damage on Hadrian's Wall. While there is no definite evidence of this the Maeatae were clearly causing trouble, for Cassius Dio states that Severus' new governor Virius Lupus was forced to purchase peace from the Maeatae for a great sum, receiving back some prisoners, when the Caledonians did not keep their promises but made ready to assist the Maeatae. It is not recorded precisely what the Maeatae were doing but it clearly involved hostilities with the Romans. Possibly the Maeatae had attacked one of the pro-Roman tribes of the Scottish Lowlands, they may even have crossed the Wall, but it is perhaps unlikely that they destroyed the frontier complex and the forts of north Britain wholesale at this time. Severus, across the Channel in Gaul, made no move to come to Britain but instead turned east to fight the Parthians. This war was of his own choosing and it seems probable that he would have come to Britain if he was needed. Nevertheless the statement by Dio is unmistakable evidence for unsettled conditions on the northern frontier, which seem to have continued for some time. Nearly ten years later, again according to Dio, Severus was angry at the thought that, although he was winning wars in Britain through others, he had shown himself no match for a robber in Italy. The victories of these years may be commemorated in the dedications to Victory at Benwell on the Wall and at Greetland in Yorkshire, though the former may have been erected in 207 on the anniversary of the Parthian victory won in 198, and the latter, since it is dedicated to the goddess Victoria Brigantia, for the putting-down of a more local disturbance or Severus' own victories.

While fighting these wars Severus' governors still found time to rebuild at many forts. Ilkley, Bainbridge, Bowes, Brough under Stainmore and Greta Bridge in the Pennines all underwent repair; inscriptions on Hadrian's Wall at Chesters, Housesteads and Birdoswald are testimony to the work of army maintenance staff while Risingham and High Rochester north of the Wall have yielded building stones dated to these years. More building activity is recorded on these inscriptions than at any time since the construction of the two Walls, and it has long been taken as evidence that the forts of the north of England had recently suffered destruction. However, the long period of building continued until about 240 and over the forty years affected a score of sites from Yorkshire to High Rochester. Work over such a long period cannot have been occasioned by enemy action but rather by two other considerations: the need to undertake necessary repairs to forts occupied for some years, and a desire to improve facilities at these now-permanent stations. Hence the building inscriptions at two sites, South Shields and Chester-le-Street, record the bringing of water into the fort, while at Netherby a cavalry exercise hall was built. Chesters, Vindolanda, Great Chesters, Lanchester and some years later Lancaster all received major repairs after they had been occupied for some years.

SEVERUS IN BRITAIN

Although the Romans were winning victories in the middle years of the first decade of the third century, in 208 the tide again turned against them. Herodian states that the governor wrote to Severus 'that the barbarians had risen and were overrunning the country, carrying off booty and causing great destruction, and that for effective defence either more troops or the presence of the emperor was necessary'. Severus responded by coming to Britain himself with more troops. The emperor brought his two sons, Caracalla and Geta, with him. Both Herodian and Cassius Dio are in agreement that Severus wished to get his sons away from the flesh-pots of Rome where they were being corrupted by the 'luxuries and pleasures of the capital'. Indeed A. R. Birley has gone so far as to suggest that their father engineered the request from the governor of Britain as an excuse to give them a taste of military life and discipline. However, Cassius Dio states that Severus intended to conquer the rest of the island and emphasizes this by his remark that the emperor almost reached the end of the island. The costly and far-reaching preparations made by Severus for the campaign suggest this was his intention even before he arrived in Britain, which would be consonant with his general policy of expansion to solve frontier difficulties. Severus' love of warfare is also cited by Herodian as a reason for the campaign, while Dio remarks that the emperor considered that the army was becoming slack through inactivity and required exercise.

Preparations were put in hand for the forthcoming campaign. At Corbridge on the traditional invasion route into Scotland they included the rebuilding of a granary. The fort at South Shields at the mouth of the Tyne was extended and thirteen new granaries built there in addition to the two already standing within the fort. This energetic work suggests preparations not just to serve for the duration of a single campaign but afterwards to supply a new system of permanent forts in Scotland. A supply base at South Shields demonstrates that the campaign was to be supplied by sea, and now or within a short time the fort at Cramond on the Forth was reconditioned, presumably as a link in the supply line. As far as land communications were concerned Risingham and High Rochester on Dere Street had already been occupied – if indeed they had ever been abandoned – and Newstead may also have been reoccupied for a time.

The imperial family with an army consisting of part, possibly most, of the praetorian guard and legionary vexillations arrived in Britain in 208. The exceptionally large marching camps which are generally dated to these campaigns seem to reflect the size of this considerable army. The camps of the largest series extend to a massive 165 acres (66 hectares); the camps assigned to the second campaign over 130 acres (52 hectares); the smallest camps are 63 acres in area (25.5 hectares). The 63-acre (25.5-hectare) camps form two lines through Strathmore and may mark the progress of two divisions of the army, subsequently amalgamated in the 130-acre (52-hectare) camps, which have been demonstrated by excavation to be later constructions. The rate of discovery of new marching camps in Scotland and changing views about their date cast doubt on any theories which determine the extent of the Severan campaigns on the basis of study of the location of the camps.

While Geta was left to gain experience in administration in south Britain, Severus and Caracalla moved north. The Caledonians and Maeatae sued for peace, but Severus would have none of it and sending their envoys

Plate 18 Aerial view of the fort at South Shields looking south-west. Within the central, modern enclosure the headquarters building and parts of nine granaries can be seen.

home prepared for war. The campaign was probably mounted in 208 and during its course the Roman army reached, according to Dio, almost the end of the island. The barbarians answered Rome's might with guerrilla tactics and Severus lost many men before they capitulated and, in the words of Dio, ceded 'not a small part of their territory'. Severus and his sons assumed the title Britannicus, while Geta was made co-emperor with his father and brother. The epithet Britannica was added to the titles of legion VI Victrix. Construction of the new legionary base at Carpow on the Tay may have started at this time. Less than 30 acres (12 hectares) in size, it was too small to hold a complete legion, and may have been designed for legionary detachments, possibly from II Augusta and VI Victrix, the two units which built the fortress. The establishment of a base here emphasizes that Severus intended to reoccupy southern Scotland at the minimum.

After the conclusion of peace Severus and Caracalla returned to York, the nearest legionary base. Some months later they heard there that the

Maeatae had revolted. While they were preparing for a new campaign news came that the Caledonians had joined the revolt. Severus was too ill to join his army – he had been carried on the previous campaign in a litter – so Caracalla was left in command. But he was more concerned with securing army support than prosecuting the campaign, according to contemporary writers, and the death of his father at York on 4 February 211 brought a speedy end to the fighting. Caracalla signed a new treaty with the barbarians, withdrawing from their territory and abandoning some forts. He then joined his mother and brother and returned to Rome, the centre of power.

An inscription recording building activity at Carpow in 212 or perhaps a little later suggests that Caracalla's abandonment of his father's conquests may not have been as abrupt as his contemporaries imply. A series of inscriptions erected in the forts of north Britain in 213 emphasizing the army's loyalty to Caracalla may have been necessary after his murder of his younger brother Geta, whose interests, according to Herodian, had been protected by the army in Britain. The disgrace and possible execution of a governor of Britain in 213 emphasize the unsettled state of the army. It has also been suggested that the troops from the two Germanies attested at Piercebridge under Caracalla or his successor may have been brought over to stiffen the loyalty of the British units, but this is unlikely four years after 213.

The occupation of Carpow did not long survive the departure of Caracalla. The fortress was demolished and abandoned after a short life. With Carpow presumably also went Cramond on the Forth and whatever presence may have been established at Newstead on Dere Street. The supply base at South Shields, however, survived, perhaps to service the needs of Hadrian's Wall.

THE SCOTTISH LOWLANDS IN THE THIRD CENTURY

The frontier defences after the final abandonment of the Scottish forts were very different from those when the Wall was built nearly a hundred years before. Although the Wall itself no doubt retained its bureaucratic function of frontier control the weight of the military units defending the province was moved north to the outpost forts. Four such forts appear to have been occupied now – High Rochester and Risingham in the east, Bewcastle and

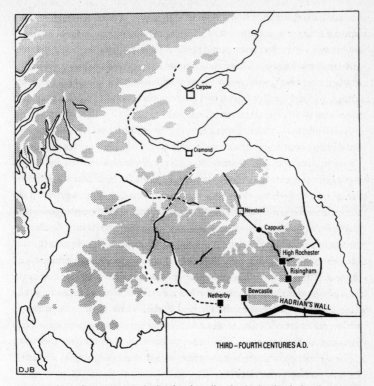

Fig. 24 Military dispositions north of Hadrian's Wall in the third and early fourth centuries. Severan sites are marked as open squares.

Netherby in the west. Thus the farthest-flung outposts in the east, Cappuck and Newstead, were abandoned, though third-century inscriptions found at Jedburgh near Cappuck demonstrate a military presence there at this time, while in the west Birrens, one of the original Hadrianic outpost forts, had been given up. In the east Risingham and High Rochester were bases for perhaps the most versatile auxiliary units in the Roman army, the thousand-strong mixed infantry and cavalry units, the *cohortes milliariae equitatae*. There were only five such units in Britain and it has been suggested that four of them were in the outpost forts, Bewcastle and Netherby matching Risingham and High Rochester. The evidence for Bewcastle is far from convincing, however (see p. 263). Risingham and High Rochester had additional support in the form of *exploratores*, scouts, while the former was the base for a detachment of spearmen from Raetia (modern southern Germany). Netherby, interestingly, was called Castra Exploratorum (Camp or Fort of the Scouts). These troops must have patrolled the Cheviots and southern Scotland; the parent forts could not have accommodated the scouts, and indeed Risingham and High Rochester could hardly have held the whole of the cohorts based there.

The Ravenna Cosmography, a list of places in the Roman world compiled at Ravenna in the seventh century, records various *loca* in north Britain. These include the *locus Maponi*, *locus Manavi*, *locus Dannoni*, the *Segloes* and the *Tava*. The first was clearly connected with the god Maponus, whose shrine may have been at or near the town of Lochmaben; nearby Clochmabenstane on the northern shore of the Solway also preserves the name. Manavi may refer to the tribe whose full name was the Manau Gododdin, Gododdin deriving from the Votadini of Ptolemy, who apparently had their capital at Traprain Law in East Lothian. In the seventh century A.D. the seat of the tribe, or kingdom as it then was, had moved to Edinburgh. Possibly in the third century the Manau were a sept or division of the tribe living at the head of the Firth of Forth, where their name survives in the place-names Clackmannan and Slamannan. The Dannoni are clearly the same as the Dannonii, who seem to have been centred on the lower Clyde valley, and the Segloes the tribe named as the Selgovae by Ptolemy. Tava is probably the river Tay.

The difficulty is in knowing whether *loca* is being used in one of its senses, that of meeting-places. In the late second century meeting-places were established north of the Danube in territory recently evacuated by Rome, but still subject to its control. The arrangements included the fixing of where these tribes should assemble and when, and that such assembly should only be in the presence of a Roman centurion. It is possible that the north British *loca* were similar meeting-places set up by the army following the abandonment of the Antonine Wall. Ammianus Marcellinus writing in the late fourth century about the events of 360 (see p. 235 below) refers to the Scots (i.e. Irish) and Picts laying waste *loca* near the frontier. Again we cannot be certain that the word is being used in a technical sense, but it does go some way towards strengthening the translation of *loca* as meeting-places. It is interesting that the *loca* appear to have extended as far north as the Tay, the northern limit of the province in Antonine times. If this interpretation of *loca* is correct it would appear that although the army withdrew south in the 160s it still intended to maintain surveillance over the former provincial territory. Whether or not the word *loca* in the Ravenna Cosmography can be translated as 'meeting-places' it is likely that the army did establish something similar in the wake of its abandonment of the Antonine Wall.

HADRIAN'S WALL IN THE THIRD CENTURY

The establishment of a broad zone of defence in advance of the Wall was accompanied by changes on the Wall itself. The building-up of the recesses in many turrets rendered obsolete as observation posts by the presence of military units on the Wall can probably be dated to these years. The Vallum also appears to have gone out of use at this time. In the peaceful conditions of the third century it seems to have been simply forgotten about; civilians were allowed to build houses and shops between the Vallum and the forts, even filling in the ditch and levelling the mounds where it suited their purpose. This process may even have started before the end of the second century, at least at Benwell, where the pottery recovered from the filling of the Vallum ditch would support such a date.

WALL REGIMENTS IN THE THIRD CENTURY

Although many turrets were abandoned, milecastles had their gates narrowed and the Vallum was built over, the forts continued in use and the total number of men based on them was increased. Four cavalry regiments are now attested on the Wall as opposed to two or three in the Hadrianic period. Most units contained an element of cavalry, indeed only three or four forts are known not to have contained at least some cavalry. At many sites the normal auxiliary unit was strengthened by the addition of irregular units or *numeri*. The *cohors I Tungrorum milliaria* stationed at Housesteads, for example, was supplemented (rather than replaced, as has been suggested) by the *cuneus Frisiorum*, a cavalry unit, and the *numerus Hnaudifridi*, Notfried's regiment. Often the fort could not hold the troops technically stationed there and many soldiers must have served away from base, unless there was accommodation in the civil settlement outside the fort or more room created within it. At several forts the earthen rampart backing was removed in places and buildings erected there, suggesting pressure on space within the forts. With these extra units the total number of troops based on the Wall forts was nearly 12,000, about 3000 more than in the Hadrianic period. The increase in the number of men based in the Wall forts gave not only greater protection to the province but also strong additional support to the outpost forts, themselves the bases of considerably augmented forces (with the exception of Bewcastle, perhaps). The strengthening of the cavalry element on the Wall not only gave more mobility in the case of an impending invasion, but also allowed these troops to participate to greater effect in the patrolling of the area to the north of the Wall.

This system of frontier control, which was to last well into the fourth century, is often attributed to the emperor Caracalla but there is some evidence that it was established before the death of his father Severus in 211. The auxiliary units stationed in one of the outpost forts, Risingham, and two of the Wall forts, Chesters and Birdoswald, in the third century were in residence in 205–7 when they were rebuilding or repairing the forts, while by 213 the auxiliary regiment in Risingham had been joined by the irregular troops, the *Raeti gaesati* and the *exploratores*. There are building inscriptions of this date at High Rochester and Housesteads but unfortunately both are fragmentary and the name of the units missing. The altar to Victory erected at Benwell in the governorship of Alfenus Senecio, 205 to 207, mentions the *ala I Asturum*, the third- and fourth-century unit in the fort. At few forts can the unit based there be shown to have changed between the early third century and the drawing up of the *Notitia Dignitatum*, probably in the early fifth century. Thus it is possible that along most of the Wall the unit which was to be stationed there for the next two hundred years was already in residence by the middle of Severus' reign, before his campaigns against the Maeatae and Caledonians. There is the possibility, mentioned above (p. 135), that the unit at Chesters, the *ala II Asturum*, was already there in the late 170s. If that was the case other forts might have received their third-century units at this time. Probably the other major modifications to the Wall, which were to last through the rest of its history – the abandonment of the turret system and the narrowing of the milecastle gateways – were made at this time. Perhaps these years saw a thorough rethinking of the purpose and

Table 11   The units on Hadrian's Wall and in the outpost forts in the third century

Fort	Unit
South Shields	*cohors V Gallorum quingenaria equitata*
Wallsend	*cohors IV Lingonum quingenaria equitata*
Newcastle	*cohors I Ulpia Traiana Cugernorum quingenaria peditata*
Benwell	*ala I Asturum*
Rudchester	*cohors (Frisiavonum?) quingenaria peditata*
Halton Chesters	*ala I Pannoniorum Sabiniana*
Chesters	*ala II Asturum*
Carrawburgh	*cohors I Batavorum quingenaria equitata*
Housesteads	*cohors I Tungrorum milliaria peditata, cuneus Frisiorum, numerus Hnaudifridi*
Vindolanda	*cohors IV Gallorum quingenaria equitata*
Great Chesters	*cohors II Asturum quingenaria equitata, vexillatio Raetorum gaesatorum*
Carvoran	*cohors II Delmatarum quingenaria equitata*
Birdoswald	*cohors I Aelia Dacorum milliaria peditata, venatores Bannienses*
Castlesteads	*cohors II Tungrorum milliaria equitata*
Stanwix	*ala Petriana milliaria*
Burgh-by-Sands	*cohors I Germanorum milliaria equitata, cuneus Frisiorum* (later *numerus Maurorum Aurelianorum*)
Drumburgh	(?)
Bowness-on-Solway	*cohors milliaria*
Beckfoot	*cohors quingenaria* (?)
Maryport	*cohors milliaria* (?)
Moresby	*cohors II Thracum quingenaria equitata*
Netherby	*cohors I Aelia Hispanorum milliaria equitata, exploratores*
Bewcastle	*cohors milliaria*
Risingham	*cohors I Vangionum milliaria equitata, numerus exploratorum, vexillatio Raetorum gaesatorum*
High Rochester	*cohors I Vardullorum milliaria equitata, numerus exploratorum*

function of the Wall, though not perhaps a complete overhaul of its installations, which came some years later under Virius Lupus, Valerius Pudens and Alfenus Senecio, Severus' governors.

It is more than possible then that the units on the Wall were in position before Severus' campaign and perhaps since the 180s or slightly earlier. There was a milliary cohort at Risingham before Severus came to Britain and the other milliary cohort or cohorts may have taken up position. Is there any evidence to suggest that the system of basing scouts on the outpost forts commenced before the campaigns? If so all the elements in the 'Caracallan' organization were in place before 208. There had always been individual *exploratores*, which simply means scouts, in the Roman army, for patrolling was always important. Units of *exploratores* develop first in the second century, as the frontiers settle down. What is special about the 'Caracallan' system is that *exploratores* known by the fort name, for example the *exploratores Habitancenses*, are attached to the outpost forts. At Netherby the evidence is its name, Castra Exploratorum. But the name itself comes from the Antonine Itinerary, a collection of routes prepared for special journeys by Caracalla and others, and the route in which Castra Exploratorum appears begins at Blatobulgium (Birrens), which was apparently abandoned by about 184. If it took some time for this name to become established the *exploratores* must have been stationed at Netherby for some time before the death of Severus, perhaps as early as the 160s.

Seen in this context the campaigns of Severus mark a complete break with his governors' policy of overhauling the system based on Hadrian's Wall; this had been pursued since perhaps the 180s when the last changes in the garrisoning of the Wall took place, on lines that had been laid down in all probability in the 160s when the outpost forts on the east were held for the first time. After the campaigns of Severus, Caracalla simply reverted to this system.

THE DEVELOPMENT OF THE FRONTIER FROM HADRIAN TO CARACALLA

The system of frontier control and defence which had been established by the early third century did not materialize out of thin air; it was the result of many years, rather decades, of experiment on the northern frontier.

Hadrian's Wall in the 120s had been added to an existing network of forts and roads which covered the north of England. These forts controlled the local population and the units based in them could be brought together to form a field army in the event of an enemy invasion. The movement of people into and out of the province was supervised by a number of forts, small forts and watch-towers stretching across the Tyne–Solway gap, at that time the most northerly dispositions of the army. It was presumably the failure of this system of frontier control which led to the construction of the only effective substitute in the absence of a natural barrier, a Wall: a barrier indeed, but not designed to thwart an attack in strength, for Hadrian's Wall was not a medieval town or castle wall. Its position was a matter of historical and geographical accident. It was not in the best situation geographically, which was later occupied by the Antonine Wall, nor politically, for the northern limit of the British tribes (who on the whole may have been friendly and not too troublesome) – as opposed to the fiercely anti-Roman 'Caledonian' or Pictish tribes – also followed the Forth–Clyde line.

Hadrian's Wall was a barrier, not a fighting platform, and no military units were placed on it at first. This was quickly remedied and thereafter army units were always stationed on the Wall, be it Hadrian's or the Antonine. They would operate in front of the Wall against minor threats. To meet major threats they would move into the field to deal with the enemy in the classic Roman manner, leaving their forts empty, and no units 'guarding the Wall'.

The Wall was to control movement into and out of the province, and allow the peaceful economic exploitation of the northern part of the province, but it was not the provincial boundary. Three outpost forts north of the Wall protected that part of the province isolated by the Wall. These forts were not advance warning posts or forward patrolling bases, for there was no reason to provide these on the west and not on the east.

The Antonine Wall broadly follows this pattern. The forts were more closely integrated with the Wall, and there was in the second plan provision for units or part-units to be stationed at shorter intervals, 2 Roman miles rather than 7. Troops were thus available more rapidly to deal with small problems. The function of the regiments nevertheless was probably much the same as on Hadrian's Wall. There were proportionally more troops on the Antonine Wall than on Hadrian's, almost twice as many per Wall mile, though the cavalry content of the forces was reduced considerably. This is in keeping with the occupation force in the Scottish Lowlands, which was much stronger then than earlier or later. Outpost forts again protected Rome's interests beyond the Wall, though this time they lay to the east not the west; they extend so far north that the Wall clearly falls within the province.

The establishment of units actually on the Wall line in Hadrian's reign must have reduced the importance of watch-towers and milecastles though the latter at least are retained on the Antonine Wall. When Hadrian's Wall was reoccupied about 160 the milecastles and turrets seem initially to have been recommissioned though the Cumbrian coast system was to a large measure abandoned. During the following years some of the Wall turrets may have been abandoned, but in the main everything was as before. This was not true of the forts in advance of the Wall. There is no evidence that the western outpost forts were abandoned at this time but there were new stations on the east. When the rest of Scotland was given up the fort of Newstead and the stations along Dere Street linking it to Hadrian's Wall were retained. These allowed the army to exercise much closer control over events north of the Cheviots, a difficult task for troops based sixty miles (100 km) to the south.

This system formed the basis of the third-century organization. Risingham and High Rochester on Dere Street were now held and a base or station further north near Cappuck, while the most westerly fort, Birrens, was abandoned. Essentially, however, these sites did not protect local friendly tribesmen, but rather formed the bases of auxiliary units and scouts who patrolled the land to the north.

While the army was groping for a military solution to frontier defence, and arriving at one which effectively ignored both Walls, Hadrian's Wall itself was being reappraised. This led to the large-scale abandonment of turrets and the narrowing of milecastle gateways. This reappraisal was long overdue, for the original system of turrets and milecastles was rendered meaningless by the addition of forts to the Wall and had only survived through inertia. Attention was now focused on the forts, and in some cases the number of troops based in them was increased, though not to the number per Wall mile on the Antonine Wall.

The system of frontier control and defence which was to survive for close on two hundred years was thus born out of many years of experiment and change under energetic governors of a province containing the largest

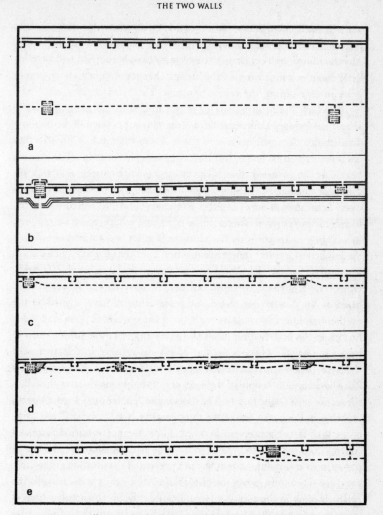

Fig. 25 Diagram to illustrate the development of the mural frontier: a. Hadrian's Wall as planned; b. Hadrian's Wall as completed; c. Antonine Wall as planned; d. Antonine Wall as completed; e. Hadrian's Wall in the third century (milecastle causeways are assumed though unproven).

army in the Empire. It saw the invasions – and counter-invasions – of the reign of Severus and the reoccupation of Scotland considered and abandoned. Any modifications after these years seem to have been slight and have left little mark in comparison to the abrupt changes of policy every twenty years or less during the second century. The third century received a legacy which it saw no reason to reject. Indeed it was more difficult to alter than before. Under the Severi the single province of Britain was divided into two, perhaps in two stages. From this time on the governor of Lower Britain no longer had three legions at his disposal. The division left the senior governor, that of Upper Britain, with two legions, while his colleague commanded only one legion together with the auxiliary troops based in the forts of north England. The change was undoubtedly political, to rob the governor of Britain of the command of a three-legion province by dividing it. Its effect on the northern frontier was to remove much of the initiative for direct independent action from the governor immediately responsible for the defence of the province's most vulnerable frontier. However, throughout the third century the governors of Lower Britain, based at York, were not tested, for peace seems to have reigned on the northern frontier. In contrast with the great governors of an undivided Britain in the first two centuries the governors of Lower Britain seem of mediocre quality. There is no hint of any disturbance in this area until the 270s, when Aurelian took the title of Britannicus, suggestive of a British victory, or simply of the recovery of the provinces after the fall of the secessionist Gallic empire. The units in the Pennine forts were removed, probably in the later years of the third century, and, as we shall see, some of the Wall forts themselves run down. The system of frontier defence and control does not by itself seem to have been responsible for this era of peace: in its embryonic state it had not prevented the invasion of the early 180s, nor when fully grown the disturbances of the early 200s. Perhaps the reason is more in the enemy it faced. Possibly the northern tribes tired of incessant war, possibly Severus and Caracalla had given them a thrashing which cowed them for several generations. It is more likely that they were kept happy, and therefore under control, by Roman diplomacy, including not just effective supervision of the meeting-places, but also perhaps subsidies to the northern tribes. When there is a renewal of disturbance, it is marked by the emergence of the Picts and of a threat to the whole of the coastline of Britain.

5

THE ARMY OF THE WALL

THE LEGIONS

At the time of the building of Hadrian's Wall the Roman army was perhaps at the peak of its efficiency. The backbone of the army remained the legion, approximately 5000 heavy infantrymen trained and disciplined to break the enemy in hand-to-hand fighting in set-piece battles. From the citizen body of Rome in arms, with the weapons and armour that each could afford (the richest on horseback), fighting campaigns between seed-time and harvest, the legion had evolved into a body of infantry, with a very small cavalry contingent, armed and armoured in a standard fashion, trained to the highest standards of single combat and disciplined to react to orders and carry out manoeuvres even in the midst of battle. Some of these men were volunteers even before the end of the Republic, following the reputation of individual generals. As a fighting force the legions had reached perfection under Caesar. The first emperor, Augustus, gave the legions permanent existence as units (previously they had been disbanded after campaigns) and recognized that soldiering had become a profession by providing a grant on retirement, in land or money, which under the Republic had been done only by individual generals. The length of service was laid down, and by the time of Hadrian it was twenty-five or twenty-six years (legionaries were only discharged in alternate years). Although the right to levy men compulsorily was retained, there seems normally to have been an ample supply of volunteers. The extension of the areas of recruitment helped to provide this.

Recruiting was still limited in theory to Roman citizens. In the West apart from Italy many of the inhabitants of Gallia Narbonensis (Provence) and Baetica (southern Spain) were Roman citizens, and as the citizenship spread through various means (the settlement of legionary veterans in the provinces, grants of citizenship to groups and to individuals, particularly auxiliaries on or before discharge) so did the sources of recruits multiply. In Britain there was only one early colony of veterans settled as a group, Colchester, and only two other such colonies, at Lincoln and Gloucester, in the late first century; also probably few early grants to towns (Verulamium may be an exception). British-born auxiliaries are first attested serving in their home province in the 80s. Only in the second century would there be many British-born Roman citizens eligible for the legions. In the second and third centuries all legions tended to recruit from their own provinces, especially the areas close to forts and fortresses; auxiliaries and legionaries alike usually settled close to the stations where they had served for twenty-five years, and their sons often joined the army. This almost certainly happened in Britain also, though the evidence is not so clear as elsewhere. Certainly the legions were not mainly composed of Italians, still less of 'Romans' in the sense of inhabitants of Rome (a sense in which Roman citizen had long ceased to be used), after A.D. 100 at the very latest.

The legion was organized into ten cohorts. Originally these were the same size, but at some time not later than the mid 80s, in all probability under the Flavian emperors, the first cohort had been doubled in size for reasons which are obscure. Cohorts II–X comprised six centuries each, cohort I five centuries each of double strength. The century, according to a Roman writer, probably of the second half of the second century A.D., was eighty men strong, despite its name. On this basis cohorts II–X represent approximately 480 men each, cohort I 800, 5120 men in all, including 120 cavalrymen, who were carried on the books of the centuries. These figures are establishment strengths, and the true number must have fluctuated.

The officers of the legions need sufficient attention to explain their mention on Wall inscriptions. The supreme commander within the province was the governor, the *legatus Augusti pro praetore*, who commanded the army as well as being head of the civil administration (excluding finance, separately controlled by the procurator, who reported directly to the emperor) and supreme civil and criminal judge under the emperor. The governor of Britain, which had the largest provincial army, would normally be a man of proven military ability, though the system of selection and the career were geared to administrators rather than generals. Such a man would command a legion (*legatus Augusti legionis*) in his early thirties, with his only prior military experience being as senior tribune on a legionary commander's staff (*tribunus militum legionis laticlavius*) in his late teens or early twenties. The five junior tribunes were from a different social class and are discussed in connection with the auxiliary commands which were entrusted to them (see pp. 207ff.). The legionary cohorts had no commanding officers. The grouping of centuries into cohorts had as its goal tactical purposes only. The only men exercising command under the legionary legate were the centurions. Probably it was the senior centurion in a cohort who took command in battle or on duty on detachment. There was no administration at cohort level, though the cohort was useful for the division of work, as when building the Wall. The cohorts bore their numbers, but the centuries were normally known by the names of their centurions.

The senior centurion of the legion was called the *primus pilus*, and his century *centuria p.p.* From the *primipili* were recruited the prefects of the camp. Each legion had a prefect (*praefectus castrorum legionis*), who ranked third in the legionary hierarchy, after the legate and the senior tribune, had heavy administrative responsibilities, and was the only officer above centurion level with a long career in the army behind him, normally more than thirty years. As an officer frequently in charge of construction gangs he is mentioned occasionally on inscriptions from the Wall area.

The legions were not stationed on Hadrian's Wall. Nevertheless many inscriptions testify to their presence when they built it and played some part in the rebuilding in the 160s. During the troubled second century detachments of the legions, vexillations 500 or 1000 strong, and often the whole fighting force of II Augusta, that is all but the administration and training sections, were up in the north. Detachments of the Sixth and Twentieth seem to have moved to Corbridge in the 160s, though not to fight but to undertake the industrial activities that were carried out there in the third century by detachments of legions II and X, transferred from the southern province of the now-divided Britain. Legionary centurions

Plate 19 Trajan's Column. The legions build: bridge-building, turf-cutting and carrying, ditch-digging. Ready-cut turves lie not far from stacked arms.

appear on the Wall not infrequently, particularly as temporary commanders of auxiliary units, as do the *beneficiarii consularis*, men drawn from the legions but on the staff of the governor.

THE AUXILIARY TROOPS

It was the regiments of the *auxilia* that occupied the forts on the Wall. The legions had developed into almost exclusively infantry units, trained primarily for the set-piece battle. But this left a variety of essential tasks to other troops. The great lack was cavalry. Although the cavalry of Rome and her enemies, as is true of all cavalry down the ages, was not able to break disciplined infantry, it was of inestimable value in the pursuit after victory, when the highest casualties were inflicted, or when the opportunity to outflank the enemy or to attack him from the rear occurred as it did at Mons Graupius. It was invaluable also for scouting. Cavalry was drawn from non-citizens inside and outside the Empire, in the first century A.D.

especially from the Gauls and Spaniards, later from the Danube lands. Other specialists were slingers and archers. The slingers from the Balearic Islands were particularly noted, and the archers from Crete and the Middle East. Finally there was a need for infantry, to patrol, scout, take prisoners, plunder and burn (to name some of the activities shown on Trajan's Column).

These 'aids' to the legions had originally been recruited and officered in a variety of ways, fighting in their national costume with their traditional weapons under their own leaders or Roman officers. As early as the late Republic there are signs, however, that the cavalry was being formed into stable units, and from the time of the emperor Tiberius (A.D. 14–37) the names of cavalry units appear as regularly on inscriptions as those of the legions. On Trajan's Column the cavalry appears in more or less standard uniform and equipment, in contrast to the Moorish light horse, who are distinctive in appearance and dress, representing the old-style type of *auxilia*, now distinguished as *numeri*, units which were neither regular *alae* (cavalry regiments) nor *cohortes* (infantry units). The infantry regiments were formed into regular named units with standard equipment more slowly than the cavalry; again the process is complete by the time of the Column, which is our best guide to the appearance of the first army to garrison Hadrian's Wall. The slingers remain distinct on the Column, as do the archers, and also some clubmen appear, who seem like the Moors to be specially recruited irregulars fighting in their own fashion (Plates 19–20).

Again the Column confirms what is implied by the battle of Mons Graupius in A.D. 83 and earlier battles, that the *auxilia* had reached the stage where they could very adequately fight battles with the legions held in reserve; in contrast they had been relegated to the wings in the battle against Boudica in A.D. 60. On the Column it is the auxiliaries who scout, bring in prisoners, burn villages, and fight most battles. The legionaries build forts, construct bridges, make roads, and come into the fight only for big battles and specialized siege-warfare. The contrast is perhaps too stark; there is evidence from Vindolanda for auxiliaries employing technical skills under Trajan. It holds good nevertheless to some extent for the Wall; the legions build the Wall and its forts (with some assistance from the auxiliaries), but the units in the forts are auxiliary. The legionary fortresses were in the rear, frozen in the positions appropriate for the 70s; the

Plate 20 Trajan's Column. The auxiliaries fight: mail-shirted auxiliary cavalry and infantry secure heads as trophies; one uses a bow. An irregular fights bare-chested with a club.

auxiliaries would be the first troops in action, especially in defence. On land frontiers the legionary fortresses generally lay well back, but on river frontiers they often made use of the rivers for communication and supply, so were sited on their banks.

Who were the auxiliaries, and how were they organized? Detailed discussion of recruiting may be reserved for later. Here the differences between auxiliaries and legionaries may be summarized. From Trajan's time the auxiliaries served for not more than twenty-five years; they were normally non-citizens, though the proportion of citizens tended to grow. Usually they were recruited locally, wherever they happened to be stationed, so any distinctive character derived from the original recruiting-ground rapidly disappeared, though the odd survival may be seen: the curved Dacian sword appears on stones set up by the *cohors I Dacorum* at Birdoswald long after Dacians will have disappeared from the unit. The great reward for the auxiliaries on discharge was the grant of Roman citizenship to themselves and their children. There is still no evidence that they shared in the grants of land or money on discharge received by legionaries, and auxiliary infantrymen received less pay than the legionaries, though perhaps *alae* troopers received as much or more, and cavalrymen in the mixed cohorts as much. On the other hand there were better opportunities for promotion for the citizen who volunteered for an auxiliary unit; the life was less hard and the discipline and training less stringent than that of the legionary; there was more excitement possibly; and local recruiting made it easier for son to follow father into an auxiliary regiment, rather than go off to the legion for which his citizenship, gained through his father, now qualified him. In the course of the second century the distinction between legions and *auxilia* became less and less that between citizen and non-citizen units, and rather simply one of pay and training.

ROMAN ARMY ORGANIZATION

The auxiliary units were organized into six basic types, which seem to owe much to precedents set by the legions. The basic infantry unit was the cohort, which like the legionary cohorts II–X was made up of six centuries. As there is no clear evidence for the strength of centuries, it seems best to assume a paper strength of 80, as in the legion, giving a total of 480, which fits nearly enough the description 'five hundred' (*quingenaria*) applied to these cohorts. Such was the *cohors quingenaria peditata*.

The cavalry regiment was made up on slightly different principles, as the basic sub-unit was not the century but the troop, the *turma*. There were sixteen *turmae* in the *ala*, the cavalry regiment, and its total strength is given by the Roman author and provincial governor Arrian as 512. This gives a strength of 32 men in a *turma*, including apparently the two senior officers under the troop commander, the *decurio*, but not the decurion himself, who like the centurion is on a different level entirely from the men. If these two senior officers in each *turma* are ignored the total strength is 480, the equivalent of the infantry cohort in legion and *auxilia* alike, and four times the number of cavalry attached to a legion.

There was a third type of unit, the *cohors equitata*, containing both infantry and cavalry. The term 'mounted infantry' must be avoided; mounted infantry dismount to fight, and it is clear that the horsemen in these units were trained to fight as cavalry, albeit second-class cavalry. These cohorts were made up of six centuries of infantry and four *turmae* of cavalry. If the same strengths applied as in the legion, *ala* and *cohors*, this would be 480 infantry plus 128 cavalry, 608 in all. Some have felt that as this mixed unit is called *quingenaria* also the numbers should be adjusted to produce this figure; perhaps centuries were 60 strong, producing 360 infantry plus 128 cavalry, 488 in all. Documents give a total of 546, including 417 infantry and 119 cavalry, in the *cohors I Hispanorum veterana quingenaria* in A.D. 106; 505, including 363 infantry and 114 cavalry, in the *cohors I Augusta praetoria Lusitanorum equitata* in A.D. 156; and 487, including 350 infantry and 111 cavalry for an unknown *cohors equitata* in c. A.D. 215. The cavalry number is consistent with an establishment strength of 120. The infantry numbers would mean either two out of three were above establishment strength for a 60-man century, 360, or all three were below establishment strength for an 80-man century, 480; the latter seems more likely. The figures clearly demonstrate that actual numbers could differ widely from theoretical strength.

Larger versions of all three types appeared under the Flavian emperors, between A.D. 69 and 96 or perhaps a little earlier. It is tempting to suppose that they were modelled on the changed organization of the first cohort of the legion; for the first cohort of the legion had five double centuries by the mid 80s at latest, and the new infantry unit, the *cohors peditata milliaria*, ten centuries. Should we suppose that the centuries in the auxiliary unit were now one hundred strong, so ten centuries would justify the title *milliaria*, one thousand strong? But the legionary first cohort is also called *milliaria*, although the legionary centuries in the first cohort were not altered to one hundred strong. A unit with ten centuries might be called milliary whatever its numbers; the auxiliary unit of six centuries was called *quingenaria*. The *cohors milliaria equitata* also had ten centuries of infantry, and in addition eight *turmae* of cavalry. With a century strength of 80 and a *turma* strength of 32 the total approximates well enough to one thousand, 1056.

The *ala milliaria* is an interesting problem. Possibly the last of the six to be established, it had 24 *turmae* instead of 16. This may have seemed the right combination, like 10 centuries for 6, but equally one-and-a-half is a recurring fraction in Roman affairs (among other things it is a recognized pay-grade) and five-thirds is sometimes used in its stead. Milliary units may have been intended not as double-size units but as one-and-a-halfers. This would explain why 10 not 12 centuries and 24 not 32 *turmae* were the bases of the new milliary units.

Table 12 Paper strength of Roman army units

Unit	Number of centuries	Men per century	Total infantry	Number of turmae	Men per turma	Total cavalry	Total
cobors legionis (II–X)	6	80	480				480
cobors peditata quingenaria	6	80 (100)	480 (600)				480 (600)
cobors equitata quingenaria	6	80 (60)	480 (360)	4	32	128	608 (488)
equites legionis				no turmae		120	120
ala quingenaria				16	32	512	512
cobors I legionis milliaria	5 double	80	800				800
cobors peditata milliaria	10	80 (100)	800 (1000)				800 (1000)
cobors equitata milliaria	10	80	800	8	32	256	1056
ala milliaria				24	32 (42)	768 (1008)	768 (1008)

The milliary *ala* with its 24 *turmae* each of 32 men would then be 768 men. To make the title *milliaria* accurate a new *turma* paper strength of 42 must be supposed, giving a total of 1008.

In summary, it is the contention here that the six-century auxiliary *cohors* was formed on the analogy of the legionary cohort, and the *ala* was given sixteen *turmae* to produce a strength more or less the equivalent, and incidentally a multiple of the strength of the legionary cavalry. A mixed unit, a *cohors equitata*, was formed by adding a cavalry force one-quarter of an *ala*, and the equivalent of legionary cavalry strength. It was decided during the Flavian period or perhaps a little earlier to increase the centuries in the first cohort of a legion from six to ten, five double centuries under the five centurions of the first cohort (the sixth centurion post probably disappeared at this time). This increase of roughly 50 per cent was made also for the *cohors peditata* and the *cohors equitata*, and in the latter case the cavalry was doubled up to half-*ala* strength. The *ala* was increased by 50 per cent also, in numbers of *turmae*. It seems most likely that the paper strength of century and *turma* remained the same in all units, rather than that there were three different sizes of century (60, 80 and 100) and two of *turma* (32 and 42). The terms *quingenaria* and *milliaria* were used imprecisely, as the case of the *cohors milliaria legionis* shows. As the evidence available is indecisive both the view put forward here and the alternative, bracketed in Table 12 (p. 161.), are tenable.

A new difficulty has arisen over a recently discovered document from Vindolanda, *c.* A.D. 92–7, showing *cohors I Tungrorum* with six centurions and 752 men, five centurions and 456 men being away from the fort, including 337 men and two(?) centurions at Coria, which may be Corbridge. The shortage of centurions is noteworthy, six instead of the expected ten. It should be emphasized, however, that quite substantial variations from establishment strength are commonplace for armies, ancient and modern, and need no elaborate explanations nor warrant suggestions that establishment strengths are totally meaningless.

THE ARMY IN BRITAIN

Varying numbers of each of these six types of auxiliary unit were available to garrison Hadrian's Wall. There was only one *ala milliaria* in Britain, indeed no province had more than one. There are only two *cohortes milliariae peditatae* and five *cohortes milliariae equitatae* attested. There were at least fifteen quingenary *alae* in Britain at one time or another, and in A.D. 122 there were twelve at least, which emphasizes how few of those available were stationed on the Wall itself. Quingenary cohorts as one might expect were more numerous, thirty-six in the time of Hadrian, of which twenty-four, two-thirds, were *equitatae*, emphasizing how useful this composite unit proved to be.

In addition to the *alae* and *cohortes* there were the *numeri*. The term *numerus* originally meant a unit of any type. It has become conventional to use this term for units in the second century and later, which were neither *ala* nor *cohors*, and were more akin to the old form of auxiliary troops. They appear to have been recruited from non-citizens, generally with little or no tincture of civilization. They did not receive Roman citizenship on discharge; they may not have served for a specified term. They fought in their own fashion, in their own style of dress. It is probably dangerous to ascribe to such units one form of organization, for they are essentially irregulars. There does, however, appear to be a number of units on the German frontier which have a similar organization. Their posts below the centurionate seem to correspond to the basic organization of the Roman army. *Numeri* appear on the frontiers of the Empire, particularly those without clear river-boundaries, and these units may perhaps have been more frontier guards than fighting troops.

THE ROMAN FORT

By the second century each of these units occupied a separate fort, though this may have been a short-lived phase, as there appears to be, earlier and in Scotland in the mid second century, brigading of units together and dividing them between forts. The ancestor of the Roman fort was the Roman camp and its main features were common to both. The forts on the Wall retained their basic form throughout their history, even though changes in army organization in the fourth century affected the internal arrangement of certain buildings. The basic form was a defensive enclosure sufficient to protect troops resting or eating. In the marching camp for one night's rest a shallow ditch and bank with stakes planted in it sufficed. A large number of simple gaps in the enclosure served as entrances. Ditches could be widened, deepened, multiplied, banks raised and widened till they became true ramparts, surmounted by crenellated timber breastworks. The large numbers of gates remained as the essential characteristic of bases for troops accustomed to fight in the open. The siting of camps and forts is also characteristic. Impregnable and inaccessible positions are of no advantage to troops whose aim is to fight in the open, and flat or gently sloping sites with good access to water were preferred. It was no hardship to be overlooked from higher ground (as Risingham and Vindolanda were), as long as you were out of range of missiles. Forts tend to be about a day's journey apart, giving overnight protection to convoys and mutual support, and siting follows this almost mechanical spacing rather than local conditions; it is strategic rather than tactical. It probably also simplified the problem of supplying food to the forts, each being able in normal circumstances to draw partly at least from the area immediately around it. Movement of supplies by ox-cart was slow, so where possible advantage was taken of supply by water.

The forts on the line of the Wall were only unusual in having all the main gates double-portal and an extra pair of single-portal gates south of the Wall, if they lay astride it. Their walls were stone from the beginning in most cases, backed by an earth rampart, though some on the turf wall began life in turf and timber, implying perhaps a permanence that was to prove illusory. Apart from some rebuilding in stone under Trajan, mainly affecting the legionary fortresses, auxiliary forts in Britain had been built with earth and turf ramparts, reflecting perhaps the fluidity of the military situation. If the unit had to defend itself from its walls the earth rampart, with or without a stone wall in front, would form an adequate fighting platform. At the angles, and between the gates and the angles, rose towers. These were again translations into stone of the look-out towers on timber forts, which were simply platforms on stilts. Replacing timber posts by stone walls created ground floors, but there was no special use for them. The gates themselves were either flanked by towers or as at Housesteads were crowned

Plate 21 Chesters from the air looking west. Five of the six gates may be seen. In the centre of the fort lies the headquarters building, flanked by the commanding officer's house and bath-suite, to the right of which parts of three barrack-blocks are visible.

by a massive gatehouse. It seems probable that the towers around the perimeter, including the gate towers, had ridge roofs rather than flat tops.

The fort gates on the Wall repay study (Plate 37). In their original form the four main gates were twin-portal, each with two doors opening inwards and closing against a raised threshold, with a central block. The doors were probably of oak, not hinged but pivoted, turning in iron collars let into holes top and bottom. Often there is a channel in the lower pivot stone, so that the upper door pivot can be thrust up into its hole, and the lower pivot can be guided in and dropped into position. Lead could then be run into the channel and around the collar, loose till this point, to make the door virtually irremovable. The doors occupied the front arches of the gateway, which was arched front and rear, with central piers between the two portals. The doors were secured by bars, their bottom edges screened by the raised threshold, and their sides concealed by projections of the side walls or central pier. They could only be broken down by an onslaught on the middle, the most difficult method. The doors lacked elaborate

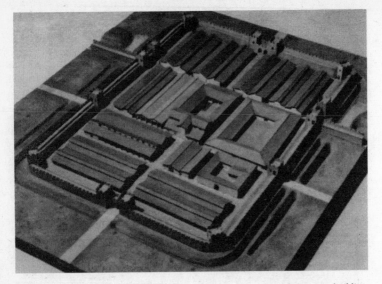

Plate 22 Benwell fort lies astride Hadrian's Wall. In the centre is the headquarters building, to its right the courtyard house of the commanding officer and to its left a pair of granaries. To this side of the commanding officer's house is the hospital. The other buildings are barrack-blocks, storehouses, probably stables and a workshop.

protection as they were not designed for passive defence, but were nevertheless no easy prey.

The gates and the internal roads of the fort were laid out according to a pattern that again derived from the old camp. The fort faced the enemy or the east. Its front gate was the *porta praetoria*, from which the *via praetoria* ran to the front of the headquarters building, the *principia*. In the camp the headquarters had been the commander's tent, the *praetorium*, but in the fort the commanding officer had separate quarters, in a spacious house, the *praetorium* still, with accommodation for himself, his family and slave household, flanking the headquarters building. On the other side of the headquarters building are generally found the granaries (*horrea*). Along the front of these principal buildings ran the *via principalis*, at right angles to the *via praetoria*, joining the main side gates, the *porta principalis sinistra* and the *porta principalis dextra*. Behind the principal buildings and parallel to the *via principalis* ran the *via quintana*, which in six-gate forts served minor side gates, the *porta quintana sinistra* and the *porta quintana dextra*. From the

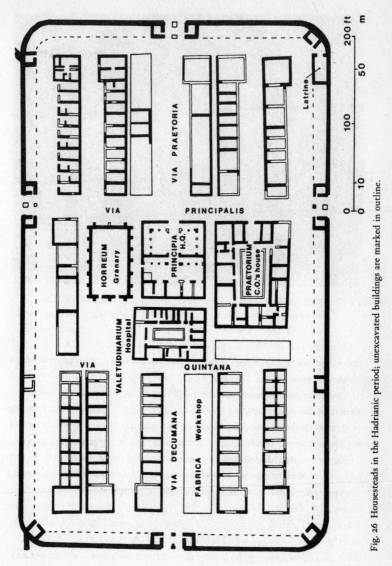

Fig. 26 Housesteads in the Hadrianic period; unexcavated buildings are marked in outline.

Plate 23 The headquarters building at Chesters, looking across the courtyard towards the cross-hall, with the tribunal to the right, and the range of five rooms at the rear.

back of the principal buildings, continuing the line of the *via praetoria*, ran the *via decumana*, ending at the *porta decumana*, the back gate, through which in ancient times soldiers were led out to execution. Between the buildings and rampart on all sides there was a wide space, the *intervallum*, which lengthened the range for anyone attempting to fire the buildings with missiles from outside. It also facilitated movement and assembly, and was occupied by a road, the *via sagularis*, running round the inside of the rampart.

An interesting dimension has been added to the investigation of fort plans by the application of archaeomagnetic methods at certain forts, though interpretation without excavation is hazardous.

FORT BUILDINGS

The buildings may now be described in more detail. The headquarters building combined a number of features from the camp, notably the tribunal on which the commanding officer took his place, flanked by the standards,

Plate 24 The tribunal in the cross-hall of the headquarters building at Vindolanda. The lower two of a flight of steps can be seen to the left of the dais.

and the open space for assembly. It had developed into three main divisions, a courtyard, surrounded by verandahs, which were open under Hadrian, but later often divided into small rooms, a cross-hall (*basilica*), generally a nave with one aisle, lit by clerestory windows, and a rear range of rooms, the central one being the shrine of the standards. There was often a well in the courtyard. The cross-hall and courtyard combined could hold the whole unit. At one end of the nave stood a platform, on the left-hand side facing the front of the building, in the correct position for the tribunal in the old camp. This would be used by the commanding officer. The aisle gave access to side-entrances to the building. At the back were generally five rooms, the central one being the shrine (*aedes*) where stood the emperor's statue, the standards and other objects associated with the army's official religious activities. On either side were two rooms, normally interpreted as offices, on the tribunal side those of the *cornicularius*, the adjutant of the unit, and his clerks, on the other those used by the *signiferi*, the standard-bearers, who were also responsible for pay and savings. From the shrine there was often access to a strongroom where the money was kept,

Plate 25 One of the rear rooms in the headquarters building at Vindolanda. The screen to one side of the entrance would have been balanced by a second, the groove for which is visible.

a feature which was sometimes original, sometimes a later insertion. The shrine and the two rooms flanking it were open-fronted, with central entrances flanked by low stone screens into which iron grilles were fixed. Through these grilles the standards and images could be seen and business with the soldiers could be carried out in the flanking offices across counters. The latter would have obvious advantages as their widespread use today shows. The offices at the extreme ends of the range, which could only be entered from the offices flanking the shrine, offered greater privacy (Plates 24 and 25). Later, headquarters buildings were modified in two ways, either by the division of the verandahs into rooms (Housesteads, Carrawburgh and Vindolanda) or by the insertion of hypocausts into the rooms used by administrative staff (Carrawburgh and Vindolanda). There is no evidence that these changes were related.

The commanding officer's house, like so many of the buildings of the fort – headquarters, hospital, facing barracks – was built on the courtyard principle, a practice of the Mediterranean world to give shade. It was laid out on spacious lines, with four ranges of rooms, providing accommodation

Plate 26 The east granary at Corbridge. The floor of stone slabs is supported on dwarf walls to allow the free circulation of air below it.

for the officer, his family and slaves, and for guests, who as Vindolanda has shown might include the governor of the province, on a scale which compares with a villa or town-house of the land-owning gentry to which the officer would belong. It often would include a separate bathing suite, so that the officer and his family did not need to use the men's baths.

The granaries, normally a pair, were buttressed buildings with under-floor ventilation. The floors were raised on single piers or dwarf walls to form channels ventilated through holes in the walls. It is not clear how these buildings were completed at the top; perhaps there were wooden louvres at the top, with the roof's weight carried by buttresses, but this is not certain. The most plausible reconstruction of the internal arrangements is perhaps rows of bins on either side of a central gangway, though sacks may also have been used. There was a covered loading bay, generally on the *via quintana* (Plate 26).

It is generally assumed that a hospital (*valetudinarium*) was a normal provision, certainly in *ala* forts and milliary cohort forts. Buildings identified as hospitals are either in the row of buildings fronting on to the *via principalis*, or tucked in behind, communicating with the *via quintana*. In some the courtyard principle appears in ranges of rooms around a central courtyard.

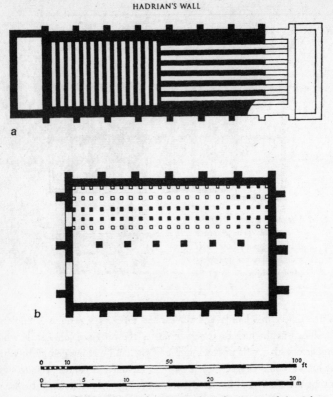

Fig. 27 Granaries. a. Halton Chesters; b. Housesteads. Scale 1 in. = 40 ft (1:480).

Others have a central corridor, though these may well be workshops rather than hospitals. None of the buildings suggested as hospitals in auxiliary forts is proven to be a hospital, though medical personnel are undoubtedly attested in some forts.

The rest of the fort, the *praetentura* in front of the principal buildings, the *retentura* behind, was given over to barracks and stables, though at Birdoswald a building of basilica type, i.e. with a nave and aisles, has been discovered in the *praetentura*. It is possible that this was a *basilica exercitatoria*, a drill hall, a building known from inscriptions but not identified archaeologically, but caution is required till more are identified. The barrack takes us back vividly to the old tented camps. Instead of a row of bivouac tents, with a large box tent at the rampart end for the centurion, there is a long

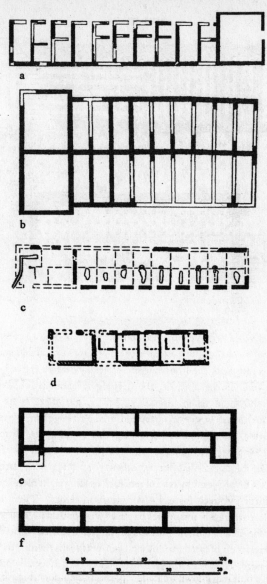

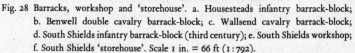

Fig. 28 Barracks, workshop and 'storehouse'. a. Housesteads infantry barrack-block;
b. Benwell double cavalry barrack-block; c. Wallsend cavalry barrack-block;
d. South Shields infantry barrack-block (third century); e. South Shields workshop;
f. South Shields 'storehouse'. Scale 1 in. = 66 ft (1 : 792).

Plate 27 A pair of barrack-blocks at Chesters looking towards the officers' quarters.

building, divided transversely into rooms corresponding to the old tents and holding a tent-group (*contubernium*). Each room available was in fact subdivided into two, the front roughly corresponding to the old space for arms, the back to the tent, i.e. the sleeping accommodation. Bunk beds are often shown in reconstruction drawings, but there is no positive evidence for them. At the rampart end a larger projecting block formed the centurion's accommodation, giving the building its characteristic L-shape. It is generally assumed that two *turmae* of cavalry were housed in a similar block to that for an infantry century, with rather more elbow-room, eight rooms instead of ten, each holding eight men (two *turmae* each of thirty-two men instead of a century of eighty). There were two *turmae* officers to house; sometimes barracks were built with two projecting ends, one for each decurion – elsewhere the two decurions shared the end block. Barracks often faced each other, their verandahs divided by a central drain and path, again searching for shade. They backed usually on to other barracks or buildings, with so little space between that there must have been little light in the sleeping quarters, unless they were clerestory windows (Plate 27).

Stables are something of a mystery. A number of buildings have been

Plate 28 The latrines at Housesteads. Wooden seating would have been placed over the main sewer channel, which was fed by drains leading from water tanks. The smaller channel on the central platform was probably used for washing the sponges that were used instead of toilet paper.

identified as stables, some more convincingly than others, but no one type of stable has emerged and no stable's internal arrangements are fully known. There would be extra horses for the officers in cavalry regiments, which would also need remounts, probably one to every two troopers. Were all these accommodated in the fort? A reasonable estimate is that the horses of two *turmae* would require as much space as the men, i.e. the equivalent of one century barrack-block. New light may be shed by excavations at Wallsend, in progress as this is being written. Here barracks and stables appear to be combined, backing on to one another, in a manner found in Germany at Dormagen and Oberstimm. A slightly smaller size for the *turma* has been suggested on the basis of the excavations, twenty-seven rather than thirty or thirty-two, but further discussion must await full publication (Figure 28c).

There were probably stables in all forts, for even in infantry forts the commander and the centurions would have horses. There must have been accommodation for baggage animals, probably mules, and for oxen for

Plate 29 An oven tucked into the back of the rampart at Chesters.

drawing carts, and for the carts themselves. Chariots, incidentally, were not in general use in the Roman world, except for racing, but there would be plenty of other wheeled vehicles, from heavy wagons to gigs. Other buildings must have existed but are not yet easily identifiable. At some forts workshops and arms stores have been recognized. There was no central mess-hall; it is not clear where the men ate. Latrines were generally tucked into the back of the rampart. Also in the back of the rampart and in the guard-chambers of the gates and the lower storeys of towers (which had no essential function) were placed bread-ovens. In some forts, though by no means all, water was brought in by an aqueduct; large storage tanks were also used, and an elaborate system of channels carried off waste and surface water.

BUILDING METHODS

Building techniques varied within each fort. For convenience buildings with stone foundations are called stone. Many of these even in a stone fort were half-timbered; a stone sill-wall carried a horizontal timber beam into which vertical timbers were slotted. The vertical timbers supported wattle-and-daub walls. Only perhaps the granaries and the bath-house were entirely built of stone and over the first there is a question-mark, as has been seen. Though often assumed, it is by no means clear that Wall forts' internal buildings were of stone and not timber in the Hadrianic period. The major difference between timber forts and stone forts is the addition of the stone wall to the rampart. Hadrian's Wall forts, unusually, had a stone wall combined with an earth rampart from the beginning.

THE BATH-HOUSE

Outside the fort but emphatically of it was the bath-house. Though later forts occasionally accommodated an internal bath-house, the idea of the bath-house arrived relatively late; there was no room for it in the fort, and it presented a fire-risk. It did become standard provision, though, with its two sets of baths, the steam baths (which we label Turkish, as they came to us via the eastern Roman Empire), the other the dry heat baths which have come to us more recently as saunas.

In the steam baths the bather left his clothes in the undressing-room (*apodyterium*) and after using the adjacent latrine, and perhaps visiting the cold room (*frigidarium*), moved through successively warmer rooms filled with steam (*tepidaria*) to the hot room fed directly from the boiler (*caldarium*). On the way he rubbed oil into his skin (the Romans had no soap) and in the hot room he could get into a bath of very hot water. Steam was the essential treatment and when the man had perspired sufficiently and scraped off the dirt he made his way back, closing his pores by going into the cold room and splashing himself vigorously from a basin or plunging into a cold bath. The alternative treatment was to go into the *sudatorium* (or *laconicum*), the sweating-room, where the room was heated to a high temperature without any water or steam.

Bath-houses incorporated furnaces, with brushwood or charcoal fuel. They heated bronze or lead boilers supplying steam and hot water, and circulated hot air underneath the floor (raised on pillars) and up through cavities in the walls. The hot air was discharged into the open from just below the roof, in all probability. These bath buildings must be distinguished from the hypocausts for underfloor heating, which appear

Plate 30 Chesters bath-house seen from the north-east with the changing-room in the foreground.

for instance in the commander's house. Hypocausts required fewer box tiles as the temperature aimed at was lower; condensation was not a problem, so complete wall jacketing was unnecessary. The granaries also have underfloor passages, but for ventilation, not heating.

The other military feature outside the walls was, it is generally thought, the parade-ground. Not many have been located The best-known is at Hardknott, where an artificially levelled area is interpreted as a parade-ground. All else – temples, inns, shops, brothels, private houses – though intended for and very largely financed by the fort's inmates, had no official status, although the commanding officer would exercise jurisdiction over them as they fell within the fort's territory. This was an area around the fort assigned for use by the unit. Animals could be grazed on it. In the case of legions quite large areas were involved.

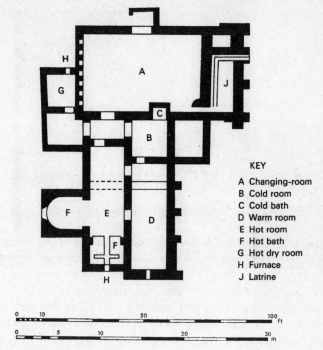

KEY

A Changing-room
B Cold room
C Cold bath
D Warm room
E Hot room
F Hot bath
G Hot dry room
H Furnace
J Latrine

Fig. 29 Chesters bath-house. Scale 1 in. = 40 ft (1 : 480).

6

LIFE ON THE WALL

What has been described is the bare structure of the fort. What was life like within and without its walls? In discussing this there are two major difficulties. Firstly, although we are concerned here with auxiliary regiments, many of the literary and other documentary sources refer to legions. It is not always clear how far they apply to auxiliaries, who had lower standards of discipline and training and rather different functions. This point is re-emphasized in the chapter wherever it seems particularly relevant.

The second difficulty is that the *auxilia* were not as homogeneous as the legions. There were three distinct groups: the infantry, both of the purely infantry and the mixed cohorts; the cavalry of the mixed cohorts; and the troopers of the *alae*. The infantry, the lowest-paid, had the simplest training and the lowest qualifications. All cohorts had a similar basic organization, but sometimes used specialized arms and armour, the outstanding example being the units of Oriental archers. The cavalry of the mixed cohorts were paid more than the infantry, less than the men of the *alae*. They were generally selected from the infantrymen of their cohort. On the march and in battle they were grouped with the *alae*; they did not fight with their cohort. The *alae* had a height qualification for entry, and were the best paid of all the *auxilia*. Their training was probably almost as exacting as that of the legionary. Their arms, equipment and clothing were elaborate, including the splendid sports helmets used by a number of senior troopers. Their status improved steadily till they replaced the legions as the striking force of the army in the third century.

RECRUITMENT

The Roman army recruited auxiliaries locally from the very beginning except perhaps into the specialized units of Oriental archers. The legions did so more slowly in the West, where Italy, Provence and southern Spain provided a good reservoir of Roman citizens; in the East where there were fewer citizens men were recruited locally and given the citizenship on enrolment. As time went on, local recruitment meant not simply recruitment from the province but from the frontier region of the province. So a typical auxiliary on the Wall was born in the province, probably in the frontier region, possibly if not probably in the village outside the fort and fathered by a soldier of the regiment. Normally he would be a volunteer. The forced levy remained as a reserve power, but only in time of crisis or to remove the fighting force of a defeated tribe to a remote part of the Empire. The volunteer for auxiliary units would normally be a non-citizen, for a citizen could apply to the legions. By the middle of the second century more and more citizens, particularly the sons of auxiliaries, were entering the auxiliary regiments, which offered better opportunities for promotion, as long as citizens were in the minority in them, less exacting training and perhaps a more exciting life. The legionaries, kept out of the fighting line except in crises, experienced intensive training, heavier equipment, more numerous fatigues, stricter discipline and unexciting toil. It would be some time, however, before the number of citizens in the Wall area became considerable, the main source being the sons of veterans who by their service in the auxiliaries had gained the citizenship for themselves and their children.

TRAINING

The volunteer signed on for twenty-five years. Like the legionary recruit he was aged between eighteen and twenty-three in the majority of cases. He was given a medical examination and required to prove that he was free-born, neither a slave nor a freed slave, and of good character. He then took the military oath and was assigned to a unit where he underwent basic training for, according to the Roman writer Vegetius, a minimum of four months. Vegetius probably had legionaries in mind but something similar though perhaps not quite so exacting would be required for auxiliaries. The men had to be physically fit, so they ran, jumped, learnt to swim, felled trees and carried packs weighing up to 60 Roman pounds (about 3 stones or 19 kilos). Cross-country marches were also on the training programme. The soldier learnt his foot drill, the military double pace of 60 inches not unknown to British infantrymen, and how to march in step six abreast maintaining correct dressing. Weapon drill and training involved practice with dummy weapons against wooden posts, working up to practising with covered points against human opponents. The recruits sweated away morning and afternoon, while the qualified soldiers only trained in the morning session. Double-weight wooden swords and shields helped to toughen the legionaries for the exhausting hand-to-hand fighting in which they specialized: auxiliaries did not escape similar training though perhaps less strenuous. Much of this training may have taken place on the parade-ground, though there were covered exercise-halls for bad weather.

The recruits had to reach the required standards; failure might be punished by barley rations instead of wheat. Camp construction was probably included in their advanced training, though Trajan's Column shows legionaries doing all the camp construction and of course the building of roads and bridges. On campaign the auxiliaries were brigaded together with the legionaries, and camped with them. Training did not cease, at least in theory, on completion of basic training. Three times a month route marches of 20 Roman miles had to be completed. The recruit had been trained to march this distance in five hours, which is about the British army pace of 3 miles to the hour, including a ten-minute rest. Apart from route marches all soldiers were expected to keep up their basic weapon skills by daily training. Field exercises might also be conducted. The siege camps flanking the Iron Age hill-fort at Burnswark seem to be best interpreted as semi-permanent accommodation for troops practising siege-warfare.

CAVALRY RECRUITMENT AND TRAINING

The soldier in an *ala*, a cavalry regiment, had also to master the skills of horsemanship. The basic height qualification for entry to an *ala* was 5 feet 10 inches Roman. On the whole men were not recruited directly into the cavalry contingents of the *cohortes equitatae*. They generally entered as infantry and were later selected for the better-paid cavalry section. The trooper was trained to mount, ride, jump ditches and walls, and to swim with his horse – all while wearing armour. He had to use his weapons, the spear (to throw or to thrust) and the sword, without the assistance of stirrups, it must be remembered. The *alae* practised close-order manoeuvres, and the sight of a regiment of 500 wheeling, with the elaborate trappings of men and horses, was a fine one. This was brought out by Hadrian in his speech to the *equites* of a mixed cohort when he reviewed the Roman army in Africa. It was difficult, he said, for the small body of *equites* of a cohort to impress when they appeared on display after an *ala*. Nevertheless it was an *eques* from a *cohors equitata* who swam the Danube in full battle kit in Hadrian's presence, and hit an arrow still in the air with a second one.

PAY

Basic training over, the soldier might reflect on his pay and prospects. As well as the basic requirements listed earlier, he needed letters of commendation to secure the unit he wanted and perhaps speedy promotion in it. The Roman world, like most societies, ran on a system of references, and commending men at every level for posts was not merely tolerated, it was part of the social fabric. All but the greatest and the humblest were both patrons and clients, looking after the interests of those who depended on them and expecting their support in return. To know someone who would speak or write for you, perhaps even just a soldier on an officer's staff, was worth much. Here again was a reason for soldiers' sons to do well in the army, especially in father's old unit. The hopes and fears of soldiers 'joining-up' are vividly portrayed in a number of letters that have survived.

The distinction between the men of the legions and the men of the *auxilia*, and among the *auxilia* between cavalrymen of the *alae*, cavalrymen of the mixed cohorts, and infantry of the cohorts, showed in pay scales. The legionary was at the top of the scale, the auxiliary infantryman at the bottom. The only precise figures are for the legionary; estimates of the auxiliary infantryman's pay vary between one-third of a legionary's and two-thirds or five-sixths. The major effects of the latter figures would be,

Table 13 Soldiers' pay rates in the second century

	legionary	legionary cavalry	*ala*	cohort cavalry	infantry
Watson	300		200	150	100
Speidel, E.	300	350	300	250	200
OR	300	400	350	300	250
Speidel, Y.	300	350	300	300	250

as already noted, to have the *ala* trooper paid more than the ordinary legionary and the cavalryman in the cohort the same. This may be balanced out to some extent by expenses linked to the upkeep of the horse.

The pay structure for any unit of the Roman army was based on four divisions but only three pay rates: ordinary pay; ordinary pay with immunity from fatigues; one-and-a-half times ordinary pay; twice ordinary pay. The table gives the likely figures in *denarii* per year from Domitian to Severus, i.e. for the second century A.D. The major estimates are cited.

The ambitious recruit would try to become an *ala* trooper or, failing that, an infantryman in a mixed cohort so that he could apply for selection as an *eques*. In any case he would next try for a job which gave him immunity from fatigues, by learning a trade or as a clerk on his commanding officer's staff.

Pay day was not a weekly event; in the Roman army pay was given out three or four times a year with accompanying splendour at special parades. Not all of it was passed across the table, or more probably the counter, to the soldier. From it was deducted a standard amount to cover bedding and food, for any items of clothing and odd items like camp dinner and burial club. There were charges also for weapons, a share of the cost of the tent each tent-group must have, and the cavalryman's horse, but these probably recurred but rarely after the first fitting-out. The horse made 'kitting-out' deductions particularly heavy for the cavalryman, though the charge seems to have become standard, whatever the horse's age or quality. Any credits or debits to the soldier after the deductions for the 'quarter' had been made were carried forward. The soldier could also save; the standard-bearers, who were in charge of pay, kept a record of his savings as well as his credits or debits. The *viaticum*, the three gold coins which were the equivalent of the 'Queen's shilling', was also retained, and not handed out to the soldier.

The auxiliary could not hope for largesse from the emperor to add to his pay; this was apparently reserved for the citizen troops. The auxiliaryman's great reward was the citizenship, but that lay twenty-five years in the future for the recruit.

PROMOTION

The recruit (*tiro*) was now a soldier (*miles*). He could set about improving his pay and prospects. The first move was to secure a post that carried *immunitas* (exemption from fatigues), such as a clerk (*librarius*) on the staff of the commanding officer (here a literate recruit had an advantage) or by doing general duties on his commander's staff (*beneficiarius*). The recruit could take up duties as a hospital orderly (*medicus* or *capsarius*) and learn simple first-aid and bandaging. The musicians, who signalled in battle or regulated the watches in camp and fort, also had immunity. The *tubicines* blew long straight trumpets and signalled the commander's orders. The *cornicines* with their curved horns picked up the messages and drew the men's attention to the standards, which signalled to centuries or *turmae*. The *bucinatores* were concerned with regulating the watches. The legion of course had many more trades and a number of officers had their own staffs.

For more pay and more responsibility the recruit would need promotion to junior officer (*principalis*) in the century or *turma*. In the century his first post might be *tesserarius*, who appears to have had responsibility for passing on written orders to guard-posts and the like. Above him was the *optio*, the second-in-command of the century, and the centurion's deputy. A completely new type of document found at Vindolanda shows *optiones* with *curatores* certifying that all men and equipment were present and correct. Above him again ranked the standard-bearer, the *signifer*. He was responsible for transmitting orders and could therefore not take over if the centurion fell, but his responsibilities in battle and in administration – the century's finances were his special concern – were onerous. After holding one or more of these posts the soldier might receive a senior post on the commander's staff, that of *cornicularius* or adjutant, or of *actarius*, possibly the man in charge of records. From any of these posts he might reach the dizzy rank of centurion. From there he could advance to senior centurion of the cohort, *centurio princeps*. Only rarely did an auxiliary centurion get a transfer to the legionary centurionate. Nevertheless life as a centurion was a good life, in contrast with even the highest rank below him, as the scale of the centurion's quarters in an auxiliary fort shows. One other post below centurion ought to be mentioned, that of *custos armorum*, the man who kept the arms store, probably one in each century and in rank roughly equal to the *tesserarius*.

CAVALRY PROMOTION

Ranks in the *turma* were rather different. There, it would appear, the *optio* and *tesserarius* were usually termed *duplicarius* and *sesquiplicarius* respectively, literally 'twicer' and 'one-and-a-halfer'. This is a reference to their pay, and corresponds to the presumed pay of *optio* and *tesserarius* in all other units in relation to ordinary soldiers. There is an ancient tradition that the *turma* was originally commanded by three decurions, one being the senior, and this peculiar nomenclature may be an echo of that old situation. There is also a mysterious figure called the *curator*, probably connected with the horses, as well as a *custos armorum*. The prefect of an *ala* also had a *cornicularius* and an *actarius*, and the dream here was to become a *decurio*. The *decurio alae* outranked the *centurio cohortis*. Occasionally young men of rank sought direct commissions as *decuriones* in provinces without legions whose governors therefore had no legionary centurionates in their gift. Even if the *decurio* reached the senior post of *decurio princeps* – more difficult than *centurio princeps*, for there were more decurions in the *ala quingenaria* than centurions in a *cohors milliaria* – there was little chance of making the giant step to *centurio legionis*. So even senior officers generally stayed in the one unit; transfers from unit to unit at any level below the commanding officer seem to have been rare. At least they rarely appear on inscriptions; other documents suggest that transfers of men between auxiliary units did happen from time to time. Occasionally legionaries transferred to become junior officers in the *auxilia*, in the hope of later return to a legion as centurions, but it is difficult to estimate how common this practice was.

One interesting possibility for men from the *alae*, after completing at least four years' service, was to be selected for the emperor's mounted bodyguard, the *equites singulares Augusti*. Decurions in the *equites singulares Augusti* could hope for a legionary centurionate. Less important though

Table 14   Ranks, pay-grades and posts below the centurionate

Rank	Pay-grade	Post
Miles	} Basic	Clerks, musicians and other specialists, some
Immunis		junior staff posts
Principalis	} Pay and a half (*sesquiplicarius*)	*Tesserarius, custos armorum, curator, actarius* and other staff posts
	} Double pay (*duplicarius*)	*Optio*, standard-bearers, *cornicularius* and other senior staff posts

still rewarding was service as guard (*singularis*), infantryman or cavalryman, of the provincial governor. The Vindolanda military strength document shows forty-six men as guards, probably of the governor in London rather than the legionary legate in York.

DUTIES

All this would lie some years in the future for the recruit. To reach a post in the century or *turma* might take seven years, a senior post on the commander's staff ten years, a centurionate or decurionate fifteen years. In the meantime life would be governed by training and duties. It would be comparatively simple to follow his progress if we could recover the individual file, carrying reports on his health and character, which every man had. In it would be filed letters regarding his entry into the unit. His duties would be recorded on a daily basis. In the daily report of the unit, giving the muster strength, he would be counted in. If he varied the tedium of life in the fort by getting on to a party going out for fuel, or on escort duty, his departure would be recorded, and his return if his absence was for more than a day. If he went on detachment duty for some time he appeared on a list of men who had left camp on more than one occasion.

Such detached duty might take a man far afield. Under Trajan, who inveighed against the practice, one unit had men outside its province collecting clothing and on guard-duty at mines, and inside its province men were detached for service in the governor's bodyguard, on the staff of the procurator (the emperor's man in charge of finance), on garrison duty, scouting and convoying animals. Such duties may have been a welcome break to the soldiers but must have played havoc with training. The Vindolanda military strength document shows 456 men away from the fort out of 752, 337 of them at Coria (Corbridge?). Still the records showed where the man was. Annually, and perhaps monthly, the total strength of the unit, with notes of permanent and temporary losses and gains, was sent to the provincial governor. The soldier's pay records were also diligently kept, and if he died in service account would be rendered to his heir.

Where did the recruit spend his time, and for how long was he on duty? How much free time and leave did he receive? These are questions that cannot be answered. There is evidence that things got slack in periods of prolonged peace. On the other hand diligent commanding officers could enforce a training programme. Apart from daily exercises on the parade-ground the men might be taken out for a spell 'under leather' – tents were still standard issue in the third century – and they needed training for operations which would take the unit out into the field. Josephus, a Jewish writer who described the Jewish war of 66–70, lists a man's field-training equipment as saw, basket (for moving earth), axe, pick, strap, reaphook (for foraging), chain and rations: Trajan's Column shows *paterae* (mess-tins), cooking pots and string bags. Various sites have been identified as Roman training areas where practice camps were built, where cavalry could practise manoeuvring in broken country, with banks and ditches, and artillery practice be carried out against long-deserted hill-forts. As a variation 'attackers' could try to dislodge 'defenders' with clods of earth and similar non-lethal missiles.

When Hadrian was touring the armies of the Empire no commanding officer could let his unit neglect training, but few of his successors imitated his example. The Romans were well aware of the maxim that soldiers should be busy to keep them out of mischief, but not every commanding officer took notice. There were routine duties, attested for the legion and presumed for the *auxilia*, including mounting guard at the headquarters building and at the gates, cleaning centurions' kit, bath-house fatigues, including the laborious job of collecting brushwood or making charcoal, and cleaning out latrines. The soldiers also had to clean their own weapons and armour, gather fuel for their own cooking, and gather fodder for the animals. The cavalrymen had to attend to their horses though slaves may have helped. Officers and some soldiers owned slaves and possibly also the unit. Despite this recitation of duties the auxiliaries escaped, for the most part at least, the back-breaking toil of road-building and quarrying that came the legionaries' way, and the laborious alternatives to fighting, such as the canal-digging and mining that some governors invented, again hit the legionaries hardest.

RECREATION

Breaks for meals were taken at regular times as part of the Roman army day, but it is not clear where the soldiers cooked or ate. The ovens could only deal with certain types of food. Some have suggested that there were hearths for cooking on the barrack-block verandahs, but there seems to be no evidence for these; hearths, which may have been used for cooking, have been found inside barracks. Possibly some hearths, like ovens, were placed against the rampart back. The barracks themselves were rather cramped but food would have to be eaten there or on the verandahs. In the British Army in the eighteenth and nineteenth centuries it was the normal practice for the men to eat in their barracks. When free at other times the soldiers no doubt lounged around outside and read the notices. These were probably posted in the verandahs around the headquarters courtyard, which may have been more like the market-place of the Italian town on which it was modelled than a sacred barrack square. The bath-house must have been a good place to skulk, perhaps one of the few warm places. Open fires have been found in the barracks at some forts, and braziers may have been used in others. Braziers may also have warmed offices (hypocausts were later provided there), but no doubt the soldiers were glad of their thick woollen cloaks over tunics and trousers.

The bath-house was outside the fort; and a short step away, once the civilians were no longer kept south of the Vallum, were the delights of the shanty town of the civil settlement, built in a better style in the third and fourth centuries. In the midst of a wilderness Rome set down 500 or 1000 men with money in their pockets. They wanted variety of food, wine or beer beyond the army ration, women and a change from army routine.

That meant inns, shops, brothels, for immediate needs. Beyond that the soldiers wanted to set up homes. The Roman soldier could not marry legally, till the early third century at least, but could and did marry according to local custom, common-law marriages so to speak. On his discharge the children of this union would become Roman citizens by the same document that would grant citizenship to him. In the meantime the soldier, living in the fort, might have a wife and children living outside the fort, or even in the barracks, on evidence from Vindolanda paralleled in the practice of other armies, including the British. The state took no responsibility for them; they might be left abandoned by a movement of the unit (which in practice occurred less and less frequently). He could leave to them what possessions he had by will, orally if he wished, but they had no standing in Roman law till he received the citizenship upon discharge. Movements of units in the second century must have made permanent unions difficult, and it is not till the third and particularly the fourth century that we find settlements of some size outside the Wall forts. Nevertheless at all times some unofficial wives and children lived, perhaps in squalor, outside or even inside the forts, and the soldiers must have been able to spend some time with them. It may be that, as in the army in camp, afternoons were free for the trained soldiers in forts, whereas recruits exercised morning and afternoon.

ARMS AND ARMOUR

Before passing on to other variations in the army routine, leave and the military religious calendar with its festivals and possible holidays, it is time to deal with the major variation in routine, fighting. There are few descriptions of fighting, particularly by auxiliaries; indeed fighting was an abnormal activity and peace the expectation for much of the time. Even under war conditions it is rare for the majority of troops to be actively involved in fighting at any one time. Active campaigning in the second century need not occupy much of a man's service of twenty-five years, perhaps two or three summers in the field with hardly a sight of the enemy. Like the soldier in any other army the Roman soldier had little opportunity to practise the killing for which he was trained. The auxiliary infantryman had as armour a helmet, iron or bronze, a mail or scale shirt, and an oval shield. This shield was flat, made of plywood covered with leather with a circular metal boss and applied metal rim. His offensive weapons were the spear, for throwing or thrusting, and the sword, a version of the *gladius* used by legionaries, two feet long and two inches wide (600 mm by 50 mm), designed for thrusting with its long point, although it had cutting edges also. A dagger was also carried, no doubt useful as a scout-knife, and a last resort if the sword was lost. There are not enough accounts of auxiliaries in action to differentiate clearly their fighting methods from those of the legionaries. They could form a battle line and did so increasingly though this was not their main function. They probably did not have such elaborate battle training as the legionaries, but had a greater variety of roles (p. 156f.).

Variations in weapons and armour often relate to the fighting methods of the tribe from which the unit was originally raised. The most distinctive group was the Oriental archers, who used a composite bow, in the middle wood, on the outside sinew, on the inner side horn. When the bow is bent the sinew is stretched and tries to contract; the horn is compressed and seeks to expand. It was the normal bow of the Graeco-Roman world and the arrow shot was of no great weight and range; this helps to account for the relative ineffectiveness of archery against Roman heavy infantry. Archers sometimes carried axes and swords in case the enemy managed to close with them. Slingers were also used by the Romans, throwing both from hand and using slings, but they do not seem to have formed organized units. According to Vegetius some instruction was given to all soldiers in the technique of slinging.

CAVALRY ARMS AND ARMOUR

The *ala* trooper also wore a bronze or iron helmet and a mail or scale shirt and carried an oval shield like that of the auxiliary infantryman. His offensive weapons were the spear, used for throwing as a javelin or for thrusting as a lance, and the *spatha*, the long slashing sword, described by Tacitus as if it was the characteristic weapon of the *auxilia* but apparently confined to cavalry. Although he lacked stirrups, the design of the Roman saddle allowed him to use the combined weight of man and horse. There was heavy cavalry, notably the armoured cavalry (*cataphractarii*) where both horse and man wore armour. Some units were equipped with a heavy lance, the *contus*. On Trajan's Column the Moors appear as light horse, with apparently no armour, no saddle, simply a spear and shield. Other units were partly or completely made up of mounted archers. One suspects that there may have been considerable variation in arms and armour from cavalry regiment to cavalry regiment. Inspection of weapons is attested now for the first time, of the lances of an *ala* at Carlisle, but it may regularly have been applied to weapons generally for cavalry and infantry alike.

One feature of cavalry armour calls for special attention. These are the sports helmets discovered from time to time. They are of iron or bronze, richly decorated, very light in construction, with face-masks. They were worn without body-armour and with light shields only. This equipment was reserved for special displays of skill, worn only by soldiers who held higher ranks or were accomplished horsemen. The elaborately moulded face-masks, which are of male and female types, may have been used in a version of the Troy Games, pitting Greeks against Amazons in mock battle.

The horses seem to have been on the small side. The biggest horses from Newstead, the Roman fort on the Tweed, measure nearly fifteen hands, but the majority are below fourteen hands. The military saddle, made of goatskin stretched over a rigid tree with four horns, gave the rider a secure seat. A version with larger bronze-faced horns was probably used for shock tactics. There was probably a cushion to protect the horse's back beneath the saddle. Saddle cloths, both over and under saddles, added colour and richness, and the harness was richly decorated with bronze medallions and pendants, as can be deduced from finds and sculptured representations. Here the cavalryman from the cohorts could not compete; he could not afford to. As Hadrian remarked, the quality of the horse and the arms, which may be taken to include trappings also, were in proportion to the pay.

ARTILLERY

The use of catapults by the *auxilia* is not clearly attested; on Trajan's Column they are in the hands of the legions. They were used in defending camps, presumably by legionaries. It is disputed whether the *ballistaria* erected at High Rochester in 220 were platforms or sheds for catapults; the archaeological evidence for catapult platforms has been rejected. Discussion continues; until further evidence emerges it is best to regard the *auxilia* as normally operating without catapults; these when required in field or siege operations were provided by the legions in a combined force of legions and *auxilia*.

REWARDS AND PUNISHMENTS

Military decorations were not available for the auxiliaryman or, to be more precise, for the non-citizen. They were reserved for citizens. Decorations could only be awarded to the auxiliary unit as a whole. Thus the *ala Petriana* was *bis torquata*, meaning that the *torques* that formed part of the standard decorations to the citizen soldier, legionary or praetorian, had been awarded twice to the unit as a whole, and may have been carried on its standards. Another award for bravery was to give citizenship to the soldiers of the unit; they continued to serve, and future recruits reaped no benefit from the award, but the decoration became part of the title of the unit, as, for example, the *ala Petriana civium Ramanorum bis torquata*.

Roman military discipline was famous, draconian in its severity. But it is only fair to look at fact as well as theory. It was vital in the interests of all that the severest penalties be visited on men who endangered their fellows by running away, sleeping on sentry duty or other negligence in the presence of the enemy. Under peacetime conditions lesser penalties might be substituted for the full rigours of the law. When an army that had softened under such conditions had to be licked into shape one method was the old-time discipline, the famous instance being that of Domitius Corbulo, who had a man put to death for laying aside his sword while digging a ditch. More relevant to our soldier would be the beating, or flogging with a centurion's vine-stick, that awaited minor offences, or fines or extra duties. A centurion might find himself standing outside headquarters for hours unbelted or holding a measuring-rod. Reduction in rank or transfer to a position of inferior status, such as from *ala* to cohort, cohort to fleet, punished serious offences, and worst of all was *missio ignominiosa*, dishonourable discharge, with the loss of the veteran's privileges (see below), and of the prize of Roman citizenship. The death penalty could be exacted for desertion, mutiny or insubordination, but extenuating circumstances even for desertion were normally allowed. Soldiers were valuable, and it was hard to see a comrade put to death. The most famous Roman punishment is decimation, the execution of every tenth man drawn by lot from a group guilty of cowardice in the face of the enemy; the 'by lot' emphasizes the man's responsibility for the conduct not only of himself, but of his unit. Though the word has passed into our language, with an exaggerated meaning, instances of decimation are rare. There were lesser punishments for such behaviour, such as compulsion to camp outside the ramparts, and barley rations.

LEAVE

Fighting and its rewards and punishments might have had little relevance for our recruit. He came in for the odd cudgelling by the centurion and extra duties, and survived. But if he rarely left the fort on campaign, and only occasionally on odd duties, did he get away on leave? Leave was a privilege and at one time centurions, in the legions at least, expected payment for granting it, till the emperors took over the responsibility of paying the centurions to waive this 'right'. Leave was granted, but how regularly and how it was arranged we do not know; there are leave applications now attested at Vindolanda. One thing is clear; there was no help with fares home. At the end of his service a man, who had perhaps been recruited in another province, had to find his own way home; most men preferred to stay near where they had served rather than travel home at their own expense after so long away (much might have happened in twenty-five years). All the pressures were to stay, so that even those who had not been recruited locally might make a home for themselves and their citizen children close to the unit and their old comrades.

ROMAN MILITARY RELIGION

The British soldier's life in peacetime is closely related to the week-end and the 48-hour pass. The Roman soldier had no week-ends, but he did follow a set religious calendar with festival days. It is likely but not certain that they brought him free time after the special parades. Otherwise one must conclude that there were no free days whatsoever. Rome was completely tolerant of all religions, provided that they were not inhumane in their practices (Druidism) or suspect in their political loyalties (Christianity). It took no account of a man's private religious practice, but expected a soldier to join in imploring the blessing of the gods on the emperor and Empire. A unit of the Roman army collectively kept the festivals of the protecting gods of Rome, the ancient festivals of the city of Rome, remembered the birthdays, accession days and victories of the divine and living emperors and celebrated the festivals of the unit itself, those associated with the worship of the standards, which, even more than the standards of regiments today, had a mystical importance and sanctity. Rome had only the three centres of loyalty. The first was the city, nearly nine hundred years old in men's reckoning when the Wall was built. The second was the emperors, super-men whose achievements cast reflected light on their living successor, and some of whom had won a special place in the affections of the army. Germanicus, indeed, a member of the imperial family though never emperor (he died in A.D. 19) was still remembered on his birthday over two centuries later. Thirdly and finally, all the affection and loyalty that was associated with the unit itself was represented also. Great parades and festivities were associated with the calendar, which was observed by all units, with presumably little variation, and on some of these days the soldiers might hope for rest.

Many ceremonies may have taken place on a parade-ground. Some were perhaps connected with the shrine, at the heart of the headquarters building and therefore of the fort, where the image of the emperor stood surrounded by the standards. Each century had a standard, similar to that of the legionary century, a tall staff decorated with flat discs, a cross-bar at the top and above it a hand or a spear-point in a wreath. The standard of the auxiliary cohort appears to have combined elements of the century standard and the flag. (A legionary cohort may have had a special standard, but nothing certain is known about it.) The animals on staves carried by soldiers, depicted on reliefs or found detached on military sites, may be emblems like those of the legions. The cavalry *turma* had a rather different and unusual standard, adapted for horseback, and the standard for the whole *ala* was a *vexillum*, a cloth flag. Also in the shrine perhaps stood statues of the guardian gods of Rome, and altars dedicated to them.

Plate 31 The temple of the god Antenociticus at Benwell.

PERSONAL RELIGION

Outside the official religion the soldier had a bewildering variety of deities to respect, for while it was impossible to worship all actively, none could be disdained. Native gods were not despised, far from it, for they were the local manifestations of divinities known elsewhere. Here only a brief catalogue can be given of the varieties of religion available; there is more detail in Appendix 3 (pp. 277–90). There were, first of all, the gods of Greece and Rome, familiar to the soldier from the official calendar. There were the native gods, familiar to the soldier if he was a native or respected by him as powerful in their home territory. There were gods from overseas, similar in their basic characteristics to the native or Roman gods. Some came with units. Mars Thincsus was brought to Housesteads by German units; Dea Syria to Carvoran by a unit of Hamian archers, a specialist unit that, it is thought, did recruit from the original recruiting ground; the notion has been challenged. Some order was brought into this galaxy by the process of syncretism, which saw in the native gods local manifestations

Plate 32 The head of the god Antenociticus.

of the gods known to Rome; thus Thincsus is known as Mars Thincsus, in his sculptured representation he looks like Mars, and his fierce goddess companions become mild Victories. On the whole the native gods got the better of the bargain; their distinctive characteristics still remained, even though their features became classical, and they gained new worshippers without losing the old. Native gods like Coventina at Carrawburgh probably had a stronger grip than the gods of Greece and Rome, but men were asking for more, for a deeper knowledge of the gods, for a real hope of immortality and a strong ethical code, left mainly to the philosophers by the old gods. Religions moved in from the East, helped by the freedom of movement in the Empire. Gods like Jupiter Dolichenus and Cybele found favour in this north-west corner of the Empire, and after them came Mithraism and finally Christianity.

Plate 33 The temple to the eastern god Mithras lies in the valley to the west of the fort at Carrawburgh. The altars were dedicated by prefects of the local unit on duty here in the early third century.

HEALTH

What chance had the soldier in the auxiliary units of surviving for his twenty-five years and retiring? It has been estimated that perhaps 60 per cent of recruits to the legions survived till discharge. Insufficient evidence is available to make a detailed comparison for auxiliaries, but a number of points may be borne in mind.

The auxiliary fed reasonably well. Troops stationed in forts, not on active service, had a greater variety of food than is sometimes realized. The basic food carried on campaign was bacon fat, biscuit, poor-quality wine (the 'vinegar' offered to Christ on the cross), wheat (generally made into wholemeal bread or porridge) and also cheese. Meat was eaten when available. There was no prejudice against it but it was difficult to transport, alive or dead, along with the food for the march that could be carried, foraged, or supplied.

The diet in the fort would probably still be based on wheat, though it could be varied, as animals could be kept on the land assigned to the fort, bought, or hunted. Ox, sheep, goat and pig all seem to have been popular. Milk and cheese could again be obtained from the unit's own herds, exacted or purchased. Oyster shells have been found on many sites, and there are remains of other shellfish, fish, chickens and other fowls and eggs. More expensive wines than standard-issue sour wine were brought in. A variety of local fruit was eaten. Soldiers' letters are often concerned with food, relations and friends being asked to provide further variety. It is a remarkable fact that there is no recorded complaint about the quality of the Roman military diet; the soldier fed better than or at least as well as many civilians of a similar social background. And the army is always the last to go hungry. New detailed evidence for the issue of wheat and barley to the men and horses of an *ala* comes from Carlisle.

The auxiliary was reasonably clothed and housed. A leather tunic and leather trousers, with a heavy woollen military cloak, gave him adequate protection, and his footwear, the *caliga* or military boot, had points of superiority over the modern army boot. Socks and underpants are requested in a letter from a soldier at Vindolanda, so such useful items were presumably worn. The barracks were at least comparable with the average civilian dwelling in town and superior to the stone houses of the native settlements around. They were unheated, unless braziers of charcoal were used, but the bath-house at least was warm. The water supply to the fort was well taken care of, surface water was carried away by an elaborate system of drains, and the bath-house and latrines helped to keep the army healthy.

Nevertheless men living in such large numbers were liable to epidemics, and disease always has been the great enemy of armies, far more than wounds. If the soldier did fall ill or was wounded there was a hospital at his own fort or perhaps at another not far away. Medical attention was available at three levels. There were medical officers, doctors who took the equivalent of a short-service commission. There were doctors of centurion rank, who made a career of the army; there is one recorded at Housesteads. Finally there were bandagers (*capsarii*) and orderlies (*medici*) who took care of the sick and did first-aid on the battlefield, ordinary soldiers who received some training and were immune from fatigue duty because of their trade. There were equivalents on the veterinary side, who were classed under hospital staff. A legionary hospital came under two *optiones valetudinarii*, and was a special responsibility of the prefect of the camp. Army doctors were particularly skilled in their treatment of wounds and surgery, as is shown by surviving descriptions, and the variety and quality of instruments that have been found. The richest evidence is for the legionary hospitals; there are doubts regarding the occurrence of hospitals in auxiliary forts (cf. p. 170f. above) though there were medical staff in auxiliary units. The good general visited the sick and inspected the sick quarters, and there is evidence of a special diet for the sick and convalescents. There is also some evidence that medicinal herbs were grown in the hospital courtyards.

A soldier might need to be invalided out. If he was, with what was called a *missio causaria*, he did not automatically receive the privileges due to the man who served for twenty-five years; this was a matter for discretion.

DEATH

What if our soldier died? If he died on service his last resting-place was in a cemetery outside the fort, perhaps along one of the roads leading from it. Roman law strictly forbade the burial of the dead within an inhabited area. Though the location of some cemeteries on the Wall is approximately known, there has been little investigation. The soldier was cremated, or perhaps, from late in the second century, inhumed. Both rites continued side by side in the third century but after the late third century cremation tended to disappear. However, a cremation cemetery surprisingly of third–fourth-century date lies west of the fort at Birdoswald. The ashes were placed in a container (urns, *amphorae*, glass jars, lead canisters, stone coffins and tiled tombs are all attested). The ashes of a legionary centurion might be carried home. The coffin for an interment was normally of wood, but stone, brick, tile or lead were also used. The funeral arrangements were a private matter for the dead man's heir or heirs. Inscriptions in stone giving the name of the deceased and possibly some details of his career were expensive, so there are far more for legionaries than for auxiliaries, and among auxiliaries the higher paid are disproportionately represented. A man should not fear that his body be left unburied, a fate which practically every religion in the Roman world held in abhorrence.

Special arrangements to ensure decent burial are known in the legions; they probably applied to the *auxilia*, although this is not attested. Christians too believed in proper disposal of the dead, by inhumation, not cremation, but they required nothing else in the grave, no goods for the next world, and on their inscriptions showed an indifference to their exact age, which on pagan inscriptions was sometimes calculated to the hour under the influence of horoscopes. The orientation of the body may also hint at a Christian burial.

DISCHARGE AND RETIREMENT

In his twenty-five years the soldiers whose fortunes we have been following rarely left the vicinity of his own fort, apart from a few skirmishes, practice marches and an escort or two; in the second century he might have seen a year or two's campaigning. Now an unusual honour awaited him. He was honourably discharged, and might ask for a record, in the form of a pair of bronze tablets, to be sent from Rome, listing the privileges now granted to him. That copy was taken from a great bronze tablet, set up in the heart of Rome, Rome that he had never seen but whose gods and god-emperors he worshipped and whose traditions and traditional festivals he inherited. On it his name duly appeared, along with all the others who were discharged that year in Britain. The copy said that he was given Roman citizenship and *conubium*, the right to marry a woman and raise Roman citizens. If he already had an unofficial wife she became official. Any children born to him during service also received the citizenship. His wife did not receive the citizenship; if divorce or death ended the marriage she could not raise Roman citizens of her own account (a child derived its status from its mother). The privilege was limited to one union, that existing at the time of discharge or the first one thereafter. A further limitation was made in A.D. 140: children born during service were not made Roman citizens, only those born after discharge. In this respect they were only being reduced to the same status as the children born to legionaries during service, for whom there was no retrospective provision. Legionaries once discharged had every right as citizens to contract formal unions, though they would have to marry citizens to beget citizen children, but nothing was done for their children born during service, who were thus obliged to join the army to become citizens. There was no altruism for legionary or auxiliary, though it must be said that in granting citizenship to auxiliaries and their children Rome was more generous than any other ancient state — even if the privileges were to some extent limited and conditional (Plate 12).

In any case the number of citizens joining the *auxilia* steadily increased. From this same period of the 140s the wording of grants of privileges to auxiliaries made clear that citizenship was being given to those who did not already have it. The auxiliaries rapidly became citizen soldiers, and a decree under Caracalla in the early third century making all but a few groups in the Empire citizens probably hardly affected the auxiliary recruiting grounds. Some time before (the last recorded example is A.D. 203) the issue of copies of a decree set up in Rome had ceased; probably non-citizens were now so rare in the *auxilia* that individual grants were made as and when necessary.

There was no grant of money or land to auxiliaries; that was reserved for the legions. Nevertheless the auxiliary had the prized gift of citizenship and the privileges given to army veterans, immunity from taxation and from the expensive honour of municipal office. He had raised his family and descendants an important rung in the social ladder, and his sons would be well placed for a military career, which offered the best chances of advancement materially and socially. The veteran himself might not have much expectation of life, if the pattern for legionaries holds good for auxiliaries also. His savings might not amount to much, lacking the legionary's grant and extra donatives from the emperor; he would miss the regular food, standards of hygiene and medical care the army had given him. The figures for legionaries suggest that the veteran had a poorer expectation of life than the civilian, though while serving he had had a better one. The lack of inscriptions of veterans has led to the suggestion that veterans did not settle on the British frontier. As there is little positive evidence that they settled elsewhere, however, it seems best to suppose the same pattern was followed here as on other frontiers, where veterans settled close to their forts.

THE CIVIL SETTLEMENTS

If the veteran did settle close to his fort he lived in the *vicus* with his wife and family, if he already possessed them. It is still very difficult to say much about the civil settlements. They existed because of the forts. During the second century the Vallum may have kept civilians at a distance, though this is uncertain. Its abandonment in the third century certainly allowed dependants of the unit and traders to build homes and shops right up to fort walls. There seem to be signs in the third century of the regular laying-out of civil settlements, with well-made structures, presumably half-timbered with stone sill walls. No such settlement has reached the stage of excavation where anything like a complete plan is available, although aerial photographs of Housesteads reveal a large settlement and Vindolanda seems extensive. In particular, little is known of second-century civil settlements, but they must have existed. A significant new development has been the discovery at Wallsend and Birdoswald of buildings, presumably civilian, north of the Wall. The presence of these buildings should not occasion surprise. The popular notion that danger lurked immediately north of the Wall is ill-conceived. The fort at Great Chesters was supplied from a spring north of the Wall by its aqueduct.

Of the buildings in the civil settlements, the bath-house was military and official. The temples, on the other hand, although created primarily for the officers and men of the forts, had no official position. They were privately financed. Attention has been drawn to the difficulty of identifying religious dedications by members of the civilian community, as opposed to soldiers or the families of fort commanders. The so-called '*mansiones*' found at Corbridge, Benwell and Vindolanda raise problems. Are they overnight stopping-places for people travelling by the imperial post, a relay system of horses for official purposes, or are these merely inns, set up by private enterprise? Corbridge and Vindolanda, a day's journey apart on the Stanegate, both have such buildings, but either explanation would apply here. The other buildings, classed as shops and/or houses, give us fragmentary information, but as yet no chance of seeing the settlement as a whole.

There is often evidence for industrial activity in the villages, but

Plate 34 Vindolanda from the air looking east. The fort platform, with the headquarters building in the centre, is clearly visible. In the foreground the buildings of the civil settlement line the road leading out of the west gate. To the left lies the fort's bath-house and to the right the reconstructions of Hadrian's Wall.

generally on a small scale, sufficient probably for the needs of the community and no more. Specialized manufactures such as bronze *paterae* (soldiers' mess-tins), fine footwear, glass and some mass-produced pottery were brought to the civil settlements, but iron was smelted locally at Corbridge, Housesteads and Vindolanda. The wealth of iron objects shows the extent of the demand. Leather was another local material with plenty of uses. A cobbler's shop was identified in the village at Housesteads, and a rich variety of shoes and other leather goods has been found where conditions have preserved them, as at Vindolanda. Pottery could be produced locally, sometimes on a large scale as at Corbridge, and marketed widely. But in general it is difficult to demonstrate that industry supplying more than the local market existed. Even the military workshops at Corbridge, often described as supplying the Wall, cannot be demonstrated to have supplied more than the legionaries stationed there, though they may well have done so.

The legal status of these civil settlements and the people living in them

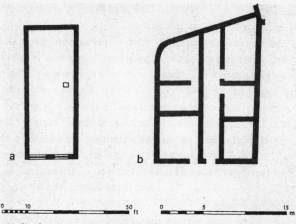

Fig. 30 Civilian houses. a. Housesteads; b. Vindolanda. Scale 1 in. = 40 ft (1:480).

requires attention. Some generalities may help. Roman citizens were a privileged body of people, possessing rights and responsibilities. Citizenship was never a mere matter of where you lived, and Rome showed genius in making its citizenship a privilege accessible and even desirable to its former enemies. The people of Britain, like others who submitted to Rome, were regarded as persons who had surrendered unconditionally, with no rights at all (*dediticii*) at first, but almost immediately they became *peregrini*, the normal word for non-citizens. They were not slaves or freed slaves. Though a freed slave could be a Roman citizen he was not eligible for service in the legions or *auxilia* and might be despised by the non-citizen freeman. Citizenship and social status passed through the mother, and must not be confused with legitimacy. The son of a Roman citizen mother was a citizen, if the father was free at least, whether or not they were married. This explains the cautious attitude of the Roman government to (non-citizen) wives of auxiliaries; it preferred to make her children citizens while denying the right to her. As the number of citizen men and even more of citizen women (daughters of auxiliaries) grew steadily situations must have become complicated, especially in the civil settlements, the greatest concentration of Roman citizens in the province, apart from colonies and towns that had managed to obtain citizenship. It was probably a relief to all when the Constitutio Antoniniana under Caracalla made practically everybody citizens, though it is by no means clear that marriage during service for soldiers had become legal by this time.

The civil settlements contained citizen veterans, their citizen children, and normally non-citizen wives (an increasing proportion of wives were citizens as the number of citizen women in the area rose). Their main industry would be the production of children for the army, with some return of money from serving members of the family. The veteran could hardly afford to buy land, unless he had done well with savings. The civil settlement normally stood on the fort's territory (*territorium*); such land could only be leased. Army herds also grazed on the *territorium*; the veteran may have been allowed to feed his few animals on it. Alternatively he could turn his hand to supplying the needs of the community by working in metal, wood or leather.

The basic source of recruits was presumably the local population, though soldiering tended to become almost a hereditary occupation, so the army was to some extent self-reproducing. Traders and shop-keepers may have come from further afield, though this is clear only for the big towns at present, as the civil settlements have still to yield much in the way of inscriptions.

These mixed communities of citizens and non-citizens came directly under the jurisdiction of the fort commander, who acted as a sort of district officer. In the true Roman tradition these communities were encouraged to be self-governing. The community at Vindolanda was able to dedicate an altar as a body (to Vulcan the smith god), and the community at Housesteads made decrees. At Carriden, on the Antonine Wall, where the civil settlement had a life of no more than twenty years on present theories, the community also acted in a corporate way to set up a dedication. Thus some sort of organized communal life under magistrates flourished in these communities of in some cases hundreds of inhabitants.

The towns of the Wall, Corbridge and Carlisle, and its port, South Shields, have yielded enough finds to hint at the variety and richness of life there, but we have hardly begun to see these settlements in plan. The buildings excavated at Corbridge before the First World War have not been touched since, apart from the area under guardianship, where in fact much of the later centuries has been removed, and our knowledge of the other two sites is fragmentary. They had presumably reached some level of self-government; Corbridge had walls, for which a special grant was needed, and from the third century Carlisle may have been a city in its own right, or the city-state of the Carvetii. The sculptures and inscriptions hint at a more cosmopolitan life than that of the villages. Gods are worshipped there which are not so far recorded in the settlements. Corbridge in particular had devotees of eastern religions who set up altars in Greek, and shares with South Shields records of a man from Palmyra, a city at the eastern end of the Roman world.

THE COMMANDING OFFICERS

Rather outside the busy life of fort and civil settlement stood the commanding officers, though their word was law in both worlds. In the second and third centuries these men were largely drawn from the equestrian order, made up of men just below senatorial rank with a property qualification and free birth. In the third century they were supplemented by men from the praetorian guard and legions who had held senior posts just below centurion level, men who might have gone on to the centurionate but who had entered the posts previously reserved for the equestrians. There should have been no shortage of equestrians, so it would seem that the army life was becoming unattractive for them, a phenomenon for which there is other evidence. The equestrian in the second or third century entered the army by assuming command of a quingenary cohort, *peditata* or *equitata*, his first military experience. His only preceding public service, if any, was as a town magistrate at thirty, on the staff of a governor without troops under his command, or of a senior magistrate at Rome. In Roman eyes an officer was an administrator first and foremost, and a man who could run a city could run a unit too.

The officer, in his twenties or thirties, held his quingenary cohort for three or four years on average. He had obtained his post from the governor of Britain by a direct approach or more likely through an influential relation or friend. When relieved of his command by the arrival of his successor he would hope to be appointed by the same governor or a governor in another province to a tribunate in a legion, a pleasant change from the isolated cohort command, or if highly thought of he might be appointed to command a milliary cohort. There were fewer such commands than legionary tribunates. In any case a minor legionary tribune, one of five on the legionary commander's staff, could do less damage than a man in sole command of a milliary cohort; with the system of selection damage is what many officers may have done. There was also a substantial drop-out, for the approximate numbers of posts in the *militiae* (the different steps in the career) varied. There were about 270 as prefect of a quingenary cohort, but only about 30–40 as tribune of a milliary cohort and 141 as legionary tribune, so about one-third of the cohort prefects received no second appointment and gracefully returned to civilian life. The legionary tribune or tribune of a milliary cohort would hope to be appointed to a cavalry regiment as one of the 90 prefects of quingenary *alae*. At this stage if not before he certainly changed provinces.

Such appointments were made by the emperor, not the governor, and no equestrian officer held all three grades (*militiae*) in the same province, because of the political danger of a governor monopolizing the appointment of his officers and the desirability of broadening the military experience of equestrian officers. Again there was a heavy drop-out, perhaps another 90 to whom no cavalry prefectures were offered. The pinnacle of the equestrian *militiae* was the prefecture of a milliary *ala*, only about ten such posts existing in the Empire. Hadrian made this a fourth *militia*. In Britain there was only one such *ala*, the *ala Petriana* at Stanwix. The equestrian made his whole career in the army or went on to one of the posts in administration reserved for equestrians. Most of these posts were as financial heads in the provinces or departmental heads in Rome, or of branches of these departments responsible for a group of provinces; the only military posts were some governorships of provinces with auxiliary troops but no legionaries, and the command of the various fleets, including the British fleet. The Roman fleets were of minor importance, mainly concerned with convoying and supply of armies, and the suppression of piracy; only in the third century did attack by sea become a real possibility.

This means that any equestrian officer was unlikely to hold more than one command on the Wall itself, and unlikely to hold more than two posts in Britain. Equestrian officers were men on the move, only staying three or four years, separated socially by an immense gulf from their non-citizen men; even their officers, centurions and decurions, were overwhelmingly men promoted from the ranks. The commanding officers could have their wives and families and slaves with them, and though they might insist on thorough training for their unit they might have been little seen when off-duty. Hunting was probably their main recreation, unless they were fortunate enough to see some active service.

It is often suggested that there 'must have been' an officer in overall command of the Wall. No officer regularly commanding more than one auxiliary unit is attested for the Roman army anywhere in the first two-and-a-half centuries A.D., though *numeri* were occasionally subordinated to the auxiliary unit commander at the fort to which they were attached. The Roman army hierarchy cannot simply be assimilated to modern ones; note the absence of a regular commander for the legionary cohort. The prefect of the milliary *ala* at Stanwix outranked the other commanders on the Wall, but there is no evidence that he exercised any special powers over them.

THE LATE ROMAN ARMY

Changes in the late Roman army affected the Wall units. Information on the late army is far less than on the army of the Principate, a convenient term for the period from the first emperor Augustus, whose sole effective power dates from 31 B.C., to the late third century A.D. The changes in command (described in detail later) removed the units in the forts on the Wall from the power of the governor, and placed them under a general, the Duke of the Britains. This probably happened at a date between 296 and 306, when the governor still appears on a military building inscription, and 337, when the emperor Constantine died. The only military duty then remaining to the civil governor was the supply of food to the troops.

The units in the Wall forts retained their names and identities throughout these changes, so that the *Notitia Dignitatum*, the last official document covering Roman Britain, lists them as they had been in the late second or early third century and apparently were still in or around 411, the date when Rome may be seen to have lost control of Britain. How far their internal organization was the same cannot be determined; there are no documents and insufficient archaeological knowledge of the fourth-century layout of the forts. There are, however, some clues.

In 298 there were apparently only 116 men in one *ala*, 121 in a unit of *equites sagittarii* and 164 men in an auxiliary cohort, and about 1000 in each of two legions. High figures exist for Diocletian's army: 389,704 men, but perhaps these were derived from paper strengths which had lost any relationship to reality (the figure comes from the sixth century). Certainly if frontier troops in particular contained only just over one hundred men it is easier to understand both the reduced barrack accommodation in the late third- and early fourth-century forts and the small size of the field armies sent to Britain in 360 and 367, four units in each year. If the number of serving soldiers in Britain had been drastically reduced, a few crack units would make a considerable difference. It is noticeable that when Britain does receive her own field army under the Count of the Britains it contains only nine units. Evidence from South Shields may show a large unit in the fort in the fourth century, and it has been suggested that the newer units in the hinterland were large, but firm evidence is lacking.

All commanding officers of cohorts now bore the title tribune. The commanding officers of the *alae* and *cohortes* were directly commissioned from civilian life or had risen from the ranks, more probably from the new field armies than from the frontier troops. The division in the army was no longer between legions and *auxilia* but between frontier troops and field armies. Legions and *auxilia* alike had become tied to the frontiers and the differences between them had dwindled; now the Roman army recovered its lost mobility in field armies in which the dominant arm was cavalry. There was no field army proper in Britain, though the new units brought into the hinterland south of the Wall some time between the 260s and 411 (the most likely times being either the early fourth century or after 368), while still frontier troops (*limitanei*), may have had greater mobility than the Wall garrisons. A small field army was created in Britain under the Count of the Britains, apparently in the very late fourth or early fifth century. Till then field troops were brought over from the continent when they were needed, as they were in 360 and 367.

The later army was made up of conscripts, and sons of soldiers and veterans were legally obliged to serve. Attempts to evade military service were on the increase, but perhaps less in Britain than elsewhere. There may well have been more volunteers here, less resistance to conscription, and less danger. Pay was still received, and donatives from the emperor on accession and at five-yearly intervals thereafter. The old distinctions between citizen and non-citizen troops were dead; the rewards of legionaries and auxiliaries were alike. Allowances were good, for uniforms, boots and arms were supplied by the state; so were horses at first, though this privilege was soon commuted for extra pay. Rations of bread, wine, meat and oil were provided by the praetorian prefect for the Gauls acting through the *vicarius* of Britain and the governor of Britannia Secunda (later perhaps of Valentia). Promotion was by seniority. Decurions and centurions survived as posts in the old *alae* and *cohortes*; in the *vexillationes* and *auxilia* south of the Wall new names for posts emerged. Soldiers could marry during service; veterans had much the same privileges as under the Principate.

Life was probably little different on the Wall itself; perhaps only different in names of units in the hinterland. Citizenship and legal marriage were taken for granted; the former had cheapened in value as it had spread. Recruitment was compulsory and hereditary instead of being voluntary and virtually hereditary. The trend towards closer identification of unit and fort continued, and the civil settlements flourished. The soldiers were still better off than the peasantry from which they came. Corrupt practices on the part of their officers might mean the sale of prolonged or indefinite leave to soldiers, and the collection of dead men's pay; discipline tended to become slack on the frontiers. Nevertheless the frontiers had to be defended, and the evidence is that the northern frontier was not broken, though it may have been bypassed. There is no general evidence for cultivation around the forts by serving soldiers till the fifth century, so descriptions of the Wall forts as manned by a farmer militia are unsubstantiated.

It must also be said that nothing suggests the presence of *foederati*, who bulk large in attempts to reconstruct the last days of Roman Britain. The first settlement of *foederati* was in 417, and it is an abuse of terminology to use the term earlier. These were whole tribes enrolled as allies of Rome, and living inside the frontiers. Small groups of barbarian prisoners of war, called *laeti*, were settled in the Empire as a source of recruits; none are known in Britain, but they may have been listed on a missing page of the *Notitia*. A number of men who call themselves Germans appear on the Wall, mostly on undated inscriptions, but these may have been volunteers enlisted in the regular units.

The units, then, may have changed little in organization since the period when they came into being, but they had become even more permanently identified with their forts, recruiting on a hereditary basis, but still an efficient fighting force. The squalid living conditions in certain fort buildings may reflect change of use, probably in the days after the fort's regular garrison had ceased to function, and need not be interpreted as a sign of a catastrophic decline in the army's basic fighting efficiency.

THE LOCAL POPULATION

Virtually nothing has been said or can be said about the people living in the immediate area of the Wall but outside the civil settlements. It can be assumed but not proved that on the east the Wall ran through the territory of the Votadini, on the west that of the Brigantes. Their attitude to the Wall is not known, though the building of the Vallum implies that Rome had found belated reason to distrust the people to the south, the Brigantes. Most of our ideas about the attitudes of the tribes are founded on the pattern of forts occupied; this seems to imply south of the Wall little threat east of the Pennines, more in Cumbria. The Votadini north of the Wall seem to have been friendly on similar evidence, and because their major hill-fort was apparently allowed to continue to be occupied. The Selgovae and the Dannonii are considered not to have been so well disposed to Rome.

There was a substantial farming population in the north when the Romans arrived. This spread into areas no longer considered so profitable to farm (though the climate was similar to today's). Farming was mainly pastoral, with cattle predominating, though some cereals were grown. Considerable clearance of woodland had already taken place, though there were more trees than now. Patterns in the life of the area were changing. Hill-forts were abandoned, and in the east modern research has identified a characteristic settlement of stone-built huts defended by no more than a ditch and fence to keep out wild animals. This might reflect the imposition of the *pax Romana*. The size of settlements seems to have increased in the Roman period. The sub-rectangular form of these sites in south Northumberland, however, owes nothing to Roman example and precept. No attempt was made apparently to establish an empty zone in front of the frontier. It has been suggested that the second-century settlement at

Plate 35 A model of the native farm at Riding Wood. A low wall and ditch surround the houses and the farmyard.

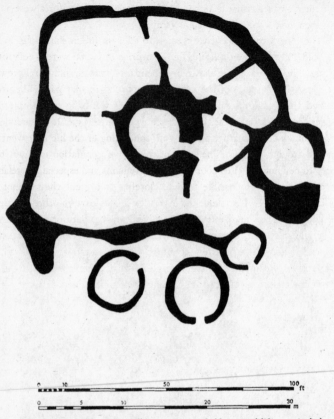

Fig. 31 The native settlement at Milking Gap. It probably started life as a single house
within a walled enclosure and later expanded into a settlement of five houses. Scale
1 in. = 40 ft (1:480).

Milking Gap near Housesteads was forcibly evacuated because it lay
between the Wall and the Vallum, but the discovery of another native
settlement close by casts doubt on this thesis.

Rome built roads for military purposes which also opened up communications. The army was a voracious customer for meat, corn (there is
evidence for ploughing in the Wall area) and leather, and some would be
paid for above the quotas supplied as tribute. The army offered food,
clothing, shelter and pay with security. It honoured local gods, providing

for them shrines richer than had ever been seen. And the forts were a lure for men, and women, who had anything to sell.

These paragraphs are little enough to offer on life in the north. In the age-old toil of making a living four centuries of Rome were a very little thing. The fort garrisons and their dependants were an unnatural growth, only possible because of the external support of regular pay. When that ceased they withered and died. The peasants were the real people, the others only shadows. But the evidence works in reverse. It is possible to know much of the history of the Wall, something of the life that went on in and around its forts. The story of the native population is unwritten, only to be found on sites poor in material remains and especially artefacts, sites which it is impossible to date closely. At present they cannot be linked with the civil settlements, except by analogies with other frontiers, or with the tribes known from geographical sources but not named in the surviving historical documents. Our attention is therefore concentrated on the Wall as it can be known through written and unwritten evidence, while acknowledging that its story will never be complete until it can be set in the context of the peoples it controlled and divided.

7

THE THIRD AND FOURTH CENTURIES

The third century was a difficult time for the inhabitants of the Roman Empire. Inflation raged; civil war was endemic; the frontiers of the Empire came under increasing pressure from the barbarian peoples beyond. Britain, however, only suffered the first of these ills. The civil wars passed her by and the frontier remained peaceful. One result of the civil wars, and the invasions from outside, was the remodelling of the army, though this may not have affected Britain much until the end of the century. In many ways in the third century her position as an island on the boundary of the Empire served her well; she slumbered and her army relaxed while the rest of the Empire suffered.

There was little sign of trouble on the northern frontier. From the beginning of the third century, if not before, the units in the outpost forts together with scouts and irregular troops, supported by the 12,000 men stationed in the Wall forts, patrolled the lands beyond the Wall. The reasons for peace in the third century are not easy to define, but peace there seems to have been.

THE EARLY THIRD CENTURY

The first decades of the third century saw various improvements and repairs to the forts of the north of England. At Chester-le-Street in 216 and at South Shields six years later new aqueducts were constructed to bring a fresh supply of water into the fort. Netherby saw the construction of a cavalry exercise hall in 222, and Great Chesters the rebuilding of a granary in 225. At Vindolanda a gate with its towers was restored from its foundations at about the same time, while at High Rochester *ballistaria* (catapult platforms or sheds to house them) were constructed. These repairs and renovations were carried out at many sites throughout the first half of the third century: Old Carlisle, Old Penrith and Whitley Castle in the hinterland; Birdoswald, Carrawburgh, Chesters, Vindolanda, Great Chesters on the Wall; and Netherby, Risingham and High Rochester to the north. Several sites have produced more than one inscription: at High Rochester building work was going on in 216, 220 and about 230 when two dedication slabs were erected; at Chesters in 205–7, in 221 and again a few years later; and at Carrawburgh in 211–17 and in 237. Some years later, probably in the early 240s, the headquarters building and the armoury, perhaps part of the same building, were restored at Lanchester after they had fallen down. At the same time another inscription from the same site records the rebuilding of the bath-house and *basilica* from the ground. The last inscription of this series is one at Lancaster of 262–6 attesting the restoration from the foundations of the bath-house and *basilica*, which had fallen down through old age.

No inscription recording work on the curtain is clearly dated to this time, but certain repairs are generally attributed to the reign of Severus. This work is distinguished by the use of hard white mortar. This seems to have been applied liberally to the Wall, spreading over the Wall face, and almost creating a mortar-rendered effect. (A whitening of outside walls with plaster, sometimes with picking out of coursing in red, is attested for some buildings and towers, and it may be the Wall was 'finished off' in this way.) In places in the crags sector the rebuilding of the Wall was extensive and it probably included the demolition of many turrets and the building up of their recesses. It seems that it was also in the early third century – if not earlier – that the bridges at Chesters and Willowford were rebuilt. In both cases the new bridges were larger than their predecessors, now carrying a road and not just a walk. Most of the inscriptions date to the first thirty years of the third century and demonstrate clearly a time of great activity for the army – the soldiers were hardly being allowed to rest in their barracks.

Important new evidence has come to light in recent years to suggest

Plate 36 The eastern bridge abutment at Chesters. This appears to have been reconstructed in the late second century, probably to help carry the Military Way across the river. To the left can be seen the outline of a hexagonal pier of the earlier bridge incorporated into the later structure.

that even these barracks were changing. New barrack-blocks at Vindolanda, built about 235, were to a plan hitherto thought to have been introduced about sixty-five years later, at the end of the third century. These are the so-called 'chalet' barracks. A row of separate buildings replaced the earlier single barrack-block. In the process the number of rooms was reduced from eight, nine or ten to, usually, six. At about the same time, *c.* 235, new barrack-blocks at South Shields contained only five *contubernia*: their earlier third-century predecessors appear to have contained only four *contubernia*. These new-style barrack-blocks suggest a reduction in the size of military units, but caution is needed. At Housesteads, for example, additional buildings were erected in the space achieved by removing the rampart backing to the fort walls, which may have been for accommodation, so there need be no overall loss on this. These new-style 'chalet' barracks were built at several forts on the Wall during the following decades: Wallsend, Great Chesters and possibly Chesters, at Risingham and High Rochester to the north and Ebchester to the south.

In the early third century the conditions of the army were improved in a more tangible way, by increasing pay. Previously pay had been increased at widely spaced intervals of a hundred years and more – under Caesar, Domitian and Septimius Severus. Now pay was raised again by Caracalla after just a few years. Severus, according to Herodian, about 197 also allowed the soldiers to marry. The passage stating this is not unambiguous, since the Greek word for a wife also means a woman; if true the action was probably no more than another step in recognizing that soldiers had unofficial wives and children. It does not mean that wives and families were formally introduced into the forts, nor that soldiers moved out into married quarters. Centurions had always been allowed to marry but there is no evidence where their wives and families lived. An inscription at Westerwood on the Antonine Wall does show that a centurion of legion VI Victrix had brought his wife and family with him from York.

It has been considered that Severus Alexander went beyond Septimius Severus in his treatment of the army by giving land captured from the enemy to the frontier soldiers, the *limitanei*, to cultivate as long as their sons entered the army. The statement comes from the *Historia Augusta*; it is unlikely to be true, for the whole life of Severus Alexander in the *Historia Augusta* is fictional. It has been suggested that the passage is not a reflection of the current practice when the *Historia Augusta* was written (now commonly thought to be the late fourth century), but a veiled recommendation on policy to the emperor of the day. In the third and fourth centuries there is no evidence for soldiers holding land while they were serving – in fact there is some evidence to the contrary – though veterans were apparently entitled to an allotment or a cash bonus when they retired. It is not until the fifth century, after the end of Roman Britain, that there is a reference to serving soldiers cultivating land.

NATIVE AND CIVIL SETTLEMENTS
IN THE THIRD CENTURY

We can say little about native settlements in the north in the third century owing to the fact that few excavations have taken place and to the paucity of Roman artefacts on native sites. An inscription erected at Walldürn in Germania Superior in 232 may imply recruitment from north Britain in the early third century and this has been linked with a Caledonian chieftain,

Lossio Veda, being at Colchester during the reign of Severus Alexander (222–35). Lossio Veda dedicated a bronze tablet to the Victory of the emperor, and to Mars and a native war god, and this has been taken as support for a military reason for his presence. However, the Caledonian could have been at Colchester for any one of several reasons, while the Walldürn inscription in referring to *Brittones dediticii Alexandriani* implies that the Britons were not volunteers but conscripted men, possibly joining the army as a result of the campaigns of Severus and Caracalla.

The villages outside the forts also flourished in the third century. That at Housesteads moved north from its earlier centre on Chapel Hill a quarter of a mile south of the fort, encroached on the Vallum and eventually surrounded the fort on its three southern sides. At nearby Vindolanda the settlement extended to 10 acres (4 hectares), three times the size of the fort. The villages at both these sites gained some degree of self-government in these years, if not before, for the civil settlement outside the fort at Carriden on the Antonine Wall was self-governing in the mid second century. At Corbridge, an army base from the first century, a town of some 30 acres (12 hectares) surrounded by a rampart grew up round the legionary base depot on the site of the old fort. Carlisle, probably founded at the same time as Corbridge, and where the army also appears to have retained a presence into the fourth century, occupied perhaps 80 acres (33 hectares) and was also enclosed by walls. Here the town survived the end of Roman Britain and there is a description of St Cuthbert's visit to it in 685.

Either Carlisle or Kirkby Thore became the *civitas*, the city, of the Carvetii. If Kirkby Thore became the city of the Carvetii, it is virtually certain that Carlisle also became self-governing. The *civitas Carvetiorum*, which was apparently centred on the Eden valley, has only recently been recognized. The Carvetii were probably a subdivision of the Brigantes, a tribe which extended from the south boundary of the Pennines to the rivers Tyne and Solway. The main part of the tribe was formed into the *civitas Brigantum*, whose seat of government was Isurium Brigantum, modern Aldborough. Another subdivision of the tribe was the Setantii in Lancashire and the Textoverdi of South Tyndale may have been a third. These subdivisions, together with other outlying parts of the tribe, were apparently administered by the military. The establishment of a new *civitas* in the third century – it was in existence by 260 or shortly afterwards – points to a relaxing of the army's hold on the Pennines.

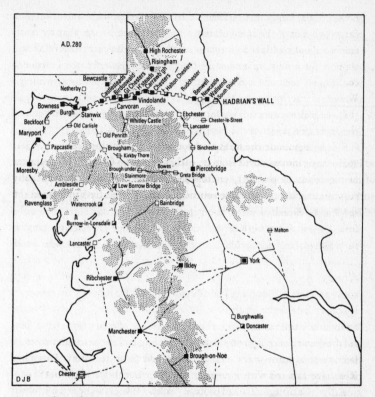

Fig. 32 Military dispositions in north England about 280. Open squares crossed through indicate forts considered to have been abandoned during the previous forty years; open squares, forts possibly occupied at this time; and half-open squares, forts probably occupied.

This is demonstrated in another, equally practical way. Some time in the late third century the units stationed in several hinterland forts were withdrawn. Units are attested at Lanchester in the 240s and at Lancaster twenty years later so the withdrawals presumably took place after that, perhaps over a period of years. Not every fort was abandoned; seven old-style auxiliary units remained in the hinterland of Hadrian's Wall and are mentioned in the *Notitia Dignitatum*, while archaeological evidence suggests that other forts may have been occupied during some of this period. On the other hand every fort where a new-style unit is recorded in the *Notitia Dignitatum* – fourteen in all – was probably abandoned in the second half of the third century. This both emphasizes that the units were no longer required to reinforce the troops on Hadrian's Wall and in the outpost forts, and that the Pennines were peaceful. Their removal also implies that they were needed elsewhere, not necessarily in the province.

There is also some evidence for new forts being built in northern England in the late third century. At Piercebridge an 11-acre (4.4-hectare) defended enclosure was constructed, probably in the 270s. Although no barrack-blocks have yet been found here there is some evidence to suggest that this is a fort. Its position, on Dere Street, beside a crossing of the river Tees, may be significant. Towards the end of the third century, or perhaps early in the fourth century, another new, large fort was built at Newton Kyme, a few miles west of the legionary base and provincial capital at York. The dating and significance of these sites are not clearly understood.

THE LATER THIRD CENTURY

If the later third century saw the abandonment of many hinterland forts and the growth of civil government in north England the peaceful conditions had other, in many ways less beneficial, effects on the army. Discipline must have suffered with no enemy to fight, though we know nothing of this. The size of the units had probably fallen well below the establishment strengths of earlier centuries (see p. 210). But the effect went beyond this, for after all the building activity at the beginning of the third century parts of some forts fell into disrepair towards its end. From his excavations at Halton Chesters and Rudchester J. P. Gillam concluded that many of the buildings in these forts lay in ruins in the later years of the third century and for much of the fourth. The third-century buildings had fallen down and become covered with earth before those of the next structural phase were erected. Halton Chesters, however, does not seem to have been abandoned entirely for the unit based there in the early third century was still there at the time of the *Notitia Dignitatum*. The third-century unit at Rudchester is not known, but the *Notitia* lists an old-style unit, which suggests that here too the same regiment remained throughout two centuries. These units could have shrunk to very low numbers. It is not unknown for commanding officers to allow this to happen in the third and fourth centuries and draw dead men's pay and allowances. Some of the *numeri* recorded at Wall forts earlier in the third century, however, may also have been withdrawn. Certainly only the *numerus Maurorum Aurelianorum* stationed at Burgh-by-Sands is mentioned in the fourth century, though that may be due to the inadequacies of our sources.

A similar pattern is emerging at Birdoswald. The series of official annual dedications by the regiment continues down to the reign of the emperor Probus (276–82), but an inscription erected here in the decade commencing in 296 states baldly that the commander's house, which had fallen down and become covered with earth, was rebuilt and the headquarters building and bath-house repaired. This extensive rebuilding suggests that the unit was in a bad way, possibly without a permanent commanding officer for some time. Recent excavations indicate that in the second half of the third century the west fort ditch was allowed to silt up and flood the berm, which in turn blocked the outflow from the fort drains. The end of one phase of activity in the west gate and an adjacent building is dated by two coins of 270–84. It has been suggested that this evidence may indicate a period of abandonment, perhaps ten to twenty years. However, as at Halton Chesters, the early third-century regiment at Birdoswald, *cohors I Dacorum*, is also listed at the fort in the *Notitia Dignitatum*, suggesting continuity of occupation. There is an additional factor. The third century witnessed a change in the sort of men who commanded army units. The commanders of auxiliary units were unlikely to be members of the municipal aristocracies as in the two previous centuries, but were more probably soldiers risen from the ranks. Indeed the rebuilding or repair of the three buildings at Birdoswald was carried out under the supervision not of a tribune but of a centurion acting as commander of the unit. This new type of commanding officer did not have the large household of his predecessor and therefore did not require a large building. Very possibly at Birdoswald he did not reside in the commander's house at all and the building was allowed to fall into ruin. This was only part of the story, however, for two other major buildings in the fort needed repair at the end of the third century.

This neglect also extended to the curtain wall itself. Some years ago the curtain wall just west of Birdoswald was found to have been rebuilt from its foundations and to contain late third-century pottery. This suggests that the wall lay in ruins and also that the fort of Birdoswald stood detached from the wall for a time.

The reduced size of the army units on the Wall in the later third century may have had an impact on the associated civil settlements. It may be no coincidence that the civil settlement at Vindolanda appears to have ended soon after 270, as dated by a coin hoard.

CONSTANTIUS IN BRITAIN

The occasion for the repair work at Birdoswald and other sites on the Wall is usually taken to be the visit of the Caesar Constantius Chlorus in 296. From 286 or 287 Britain was under the rule of the usurper Carausius and his successor Allectus. A campaign launched by the central government to regain the island resulted in a victory in 296 near Silchester for Asclepi-odotus, Constantius' praetorian prefect. If the Wall units formed part of the army of Allectus — as they probably did — they are unlikely to have taken part in the fighting, for Allectus was unable to deploy his whole force and the brunt of the fighting was borne by his barbarian mercenaries.

It is usually assumed that the Picts took the opportunity of the absence of the Wall units, which we have seen is not certain, to attack and destroy Hadrian's Wall. Signs of burning and destruction have been noted at several sites on the Wall, forts, milecastles and turrets, but no attack is recorded in the ancient sources. The burning and masonry debris could have several causes. Some sites may have been allowed to fall into decay towards the end of the third century, while the burning may simply be the build-up of fires and hearths inside the turret or milecastle during many years of occupation. There is moreover no pattern to the 'destruction' deposits; for example, in the Birdoswald area masonry debris has been found below the fourth-century floors at certain sites — 48, 48a and 49b — but not at others — 48b and 52. It is more probable that a complete overhaul of the northern defences was ordered at this time. The wide-ranging reforms which had affected the continental army, but not Britain's, was another reason to remodel accommodation. There is no necessary connection with hostile action by the Picts, as a contemporary panegyric implies Constantius did not wage war on them until his second visit to Britain in 306.

Inscriptions inform us that two of the forts renovated at this time were

Plate 37 The east gate at Birdoswald, looking north-east. Successive modifications to the
gate, which included moving the position of the entrance to the north tower, are
visible. None of these changes are dated.

Birdoswald and Housesteads. At Birdoswald the ruined commander's house
was completely rebuilt and the headquarters building and the bath-house
repaired. It is probable that the drainage problem was dealt with at this
time, and other buildings in the fort were also reconstructed. The former
storehouse and barrack-block lying immediately north of the *via principalis*
in the east half of the *praetentura* were demolished and replaced by a building
of a completely different plan. Only part of the building has been examined
but the excavated section seems to have been a suite for a junior officer
with a cook-house attached. In the south part of the fort the rebuilding
did not follow the earlier alignment, while the new barrack-blocks appear
to be of the 'chalet' type. The barracks rebuilt about this time at Housesteads are also in this style. Two of the barrack-blocks there have been
excavated and their history traced through several building phases. In both
cases in the late third or early fourth century the barrack-block, 160 feet
(49 m) long, was demolished and replaced by a series of 'chalets'. In one
building ten *contubernia* of the normal pattern gave way to six separate
barrack units measuring about 34 by 12 feet (10.3 by 3.6 m) internally. In

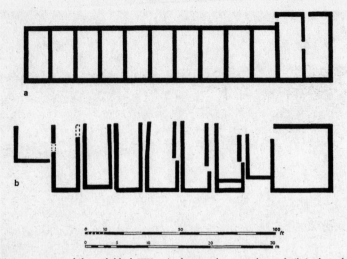

Fig. 33 Housesteads barrack-block XIV. a. in the second century; b. as rebuilt in the early fourth century. Scale 1 in. = 54 ft (1:648).

the other the *contubernia* were replaced by ten 'chalets' of differing sizes. The restyling of the barrack-blocks suggests a corresponding change in organization of the century.

At an unknown date in the late third or early fourth century a large part of the fort at South Shields was destroyed or badly damaged by fire and subsequently rebuilt. The best dating evidence is a coin of either Carausius (287–93) or Allectus (293–6) from a demolition layer in the headquarters building: this may suggest that the subsequent rebuilding took place under Constantius Chlorus (296–306). The fort was apparently set alight in systematic fashion and this has been interpreted as evidence for enemy action, though it seems more likely that the demolition was undertaken in preparation for the arrival of a new unit, the *numerus barcarorium Tigrisiensium*, the regiment listed there in the *Notitia Dignitatum*. Remodelling of the southern part of the fort appears to have been based upon a cross-pattern with a new headquarters building facing down one of the two intersecting streets. Some of the existing granaries were converted into barracks, two new barrack-blocks were erected, and a new, large house built in the south-east corner of the fort.

Some of the smaller structures on the Wall may have been repaired at

Plate 38 The fourth-century barrack-blocks at Housesteads, looking south-east.

this time. At a number of the milecastles and turrets on either side of the river Irthing modifications, which are usually dated to about 300, have been noted. New floors laid over masonry debris suggest repair to the superstructure while at one milecastle, 50, the accommodation was modified. At two other milecastles in this area more unusual changes took place. The normal round-arched south gateways of milecastles 50 and 52 were replaced, apparently by monolithic masonry doorposts which would presumably have carried a flat arch. New post-holes were cut through the masonry of the earlier gate so that the new passage was only slightly smaller than its predecessor, and presumably still passable for wheeled traffic – unlike the north gate of milecastle 52 – while a new stone threshold cutting through the earlier road surfaces was let into the floor. The first dated appearance of this type of gate in the Empire is in the Aurelian Walls at Rome constructed about 275. The remodelling of these two gateways on Hadrian's Wall must be later than 275, and possibly was part of Constantius' restoration of the frontier.

Other milecastles and turrets continued in use into the fourth century though they have produced no evidence for structural modifications. At turret 7b and milecastle 9 at the east end of the Wall fourth-century pottery has been found; at the west end of the Wall one sherd of a fourth-century cooking pot was discovered in milecastle 79, though this may be evidence for transient rather than permanent occupation. In the central sector of the Wall, however, several milecastles and turrets continued in use: milecastles 35, 37, 38, 40, 48, 50, 51, 52 and 54 and turrets 44b, 48a, 48b and 49b, though the evidence is not always very clear. Slight structural modifications simply noted in the excavation reports as later than the early third century may also date to this time, though they could have taken place in the preceding century. The picture is of continuing occupation of a relatively small number of milecastles and turrets held for the sake of convenience, not as an integrated system of observation towers and control points. No milecastle or turret can be proved to have been abandoned as a result of reappraisal at the beginning of the fourth century. The structures which were repaired a hundred years before but did not survive into the fourth century were probably abandoned piecemeal during the intervening years, or allowed to run down in the same way as some of the forts.

It seems probable that the early fourth century saw the insertion of a new gate through the Wall, at Housesteads. The gate lies just to the north-east of the fort beside the Knag Burn. It consists of a single passage gateway flanked by guard-chambers with gates to front and rear. This would allow a party to enter the gate-passage to be searched and pay their dues before admittance to the province. It has been suggested that the gate may have been to allow beasts and vehicles easier movement through the Wall when the continuing rise of the threshold of the gate made the ramp out of the north gate of the fort too steep. Whatever the reason it made life a little easier for the people of Housesteads whether they lived in the fort or the civil settlement. The possibility of traffic through this gateway that came from a greater distance cannot be excluded, though the lands to the north of the fort appear to be empty of settlement.

Two forts on the Wall exhibit no trace of reconstruction during these years, Halton Chesters and Rudchester. The military establishments of both forts seem to have been run down in the later third century, but there was no rebuilding at the end of that century. It was not until much later in the fourth century that the forts saw a resurgence of military activity. Halton and Rudchester may have been ignored for so long because they were well protected by the screen of outpost forts and patrols. This may simply have been carrying the policy of the abandonment of the hinterland forts in the late third century one step further. The difference between the permitted decay of forts like Halton and Rudchester and the abandonment of forts in the hinterland is that the units in the hinterland forts are likely to have been moved elsewhere to perform a more useful function. Only this would disturb the force of inertia.

If some sites on the Wall were left to deteriorate, the army was not inactive further north. At Risingham and High Rochester at least part of the barrack accommodation was rebuilt in the new style. At High Rochester the rebuilding apparently included the complete restoration of the head-quarters. At both sites, however, the work included the repair and remodelling of the defences: the fine west gate still visible at High Rochester was built then.

One important aspect of the northern forts in the fourth century is that they contain none of the changes in defensive architecture of the contemporary Saxon Shore forts: thick, high walls, well-defended entrances and broad ditches. However, a fort of Saxon Shore type was built at Lancaster in the early fourth century, as part of a series of new or rebuilt stations along the west coast of England and Wales – the largest was built at Cardiff – designed to protect the west coast from the marauding Scots from Ireland. The legionary fortress at York received a river front incorporating the bastions characteristic of the Saxon Shore type, but it was not continued round the whole perimeter. It seems ornamental rather than functional, befitting the dignity of the *dux*. There is no reason to date the rebuilding to Constantius; it appears to be later than 335.

Many of the repairs to Hadrian's Wall, its forts and other northern forts described above are difficult to date. They are usually assigned to the Constantian restoration more for convenience than as the result of the discovery of solid dating evidence. Thus the repairs, renovations and rebuildings at several sites could have occurred some years before the decade 296–306, the period of Constantian activity demonstrated by the inscriptions of Birdoswald and Housesteads, or more likely at a later period.

THE EARLY FOURTH CENTURY

The fourth century saw important changes in the composition of the army in Britain and the organization of the structure of command. At some date or dates many of the forts in northern England were reoccupied. They had been abandoned apparently in the later third century – perhaps during the third quarter of that century. The evidence for this survives in the army lists of the *Notitia Dignitatum*. Here are recorded in these forts new units of the type first created in the early fourth century. Chester-le-Street was occupied by the *numerus vigilum*, Binchester (if that was the Morbio of the *Notitia*) by the *equites cataphractarii*, Brough-under-Stainmore by a *numerus directorum* and other forts by a *numerus Solensium*, a *numerus Pacensium* and a *numerus supervenientium Petueriensium*. South Shields was the base of the *numerus barcariorum Tigrisiensium*. This was a military unit and the title does not indicate that the members acted as bargemen on the river Tyne, as has often been suggested. One of these new units, the *equites Crispiani*, was named after Constantine's eldest son, Crispus, Caesar from 317 to 326, while an older unit was renamed the *ala I Herculea* in honour of the emperor Maximian, Diocletian's colleague (286–305). The new units could have been assigned to their stations any time after they were raised but the retention of the title honouring Crispus, whose name was erased from many public inscriptions after his execution in 326, suggests that the *equites Crispiani* at least were in existence before that date and retained their title through neglect.

Whatever the date of the reoccupation of these forts, the purpose is clear: to give protection against the new enemies of Rome, not against a local threat such as the Brigantes, who now appeared to be peaceful members of the Empire. Nor were the units to defend their immediate locality from attack. They were clearly organized with an eye to communication. Many of the units lay beside the roads leading north, Dere Street and the Stainmore route which led both to the west end of the Wall and to Cumbria. At some time in the fourth century the Cumbrian coast defences were strengthened by the occupation of Burrow Walls, possibly other forts and some of the milefortlets (12 and 20 have both produced a small amount of ceramic evidence, while milefortlet 5 continued in occupation). The new disposition was directed against invasion not from across the Solway but from Ireland.

These new units were the successors of the older auxiliary regiments, though they were not called *cohortes* and *alae* but *vexillationes* and *auxilia*. Although they might still combine together in the field to form an army they were not technically field army troops. In the fourth century new field armies were created and a distinction introduced between them and the frontier troops (*limitanei*), who were reduced to the level of second-grade soldiers: even some legions were classed as *limitanei*. Constantine created this distinction between field armies (*comitatenses*) and frontier troops (*limitanei*) which marks an important step in the long process of the fossilization of the army on the frontiers of the Empire. It was the only way to restore the mobility lost by too-close identification of units with the forts on the frontier lines and by local recruiting. The *limitanei* guarded the frontiers of the Empire while the field army would be brought into action in the event of invasion – or civil war. Two hundred years before, this field army would have been formed from the auxiliary units on the Wall and in the hinterland forts. Now these units had a more limited function: a new field army had to be created to replace them. Although the soldiers of the field army enjoyed a higher status than the frontier troops there was no radical difference between them; the *limitanei*, as we have seen, were not a peasant militia cultivating their lands in return for military service. The soldiers of the field army and the frontier army were recruited from the same area and the same type of person. It was possible for units of *limitanei* to be upgraded into regiments of the field army as was legion II Augusta, and right through into the fifth century they remained organized fighting troops, though their efficiency sadly declined.

Documentary evidence suggests that the units of the fourth century were smaller than their predecessors – regiments 100 and 200 strong are recorded – and this has been linked with the construction of 'chalet'-style barracks and the abandonment of civil settlements, the proposal being that the 'chalets' were now occupied by soldiers and their families. However, excavations have now demonstrated that this style of barracks was introduced to the Wall forts in the mid third century. Possibly the reduction in unit numbers came earlier in the third century, though reduced numbers in the barrack-blocks may have been balanced by the construction of additional buildings. Yet the real problem is that we do not understand the 'chalet' barrack-blocks and how they were occupied. Women's and children's shoes have been found in the late first-century fort at Vindolanda and in second-century Bar Hill on the Antonine Wall, but a recent study has indicated that there are no more female artefacts in fourth-century levels in forts than in earlier periods.

The *limitanei* were commanded by a new imperial official, the *dux* (duke). This officer, who took over the military duties of the old provincial governor, was an invention of Diocletian, but under him *duces* were only appointed to certain frontiers of the Empire. Now Constantine extended the institution to virtually all the military provinces. A hundred years later the *Notitia Dignitatum* records that the *dux Britanniarum* commanded the units on Hadrian's Wall and in the Pennine forts. The detachment of the field army stationed in Britain at that time was under the command of the *comes Britanniarum*, while the Saxon Shore forts came under the authority of the *comes litoris Saxonici*. The rank of *comes* (count) was a creation of Constantine. The *comes Britanniarum* was not a permanent post until after 368. These new officials were responsible to the *magister peditum* (master of the infantry) and the *magister equitum* (master of the cavalry), the joint commanders of the central field army, by the 360s and possibly from their inception. The *duces* – but not the *comites* and the *magistri* – were selected from the prefects and tribunes commanding the auxiliary regiments; they had military backgrounds, never having wielded civil authority. They were usually uneducated, and often barbarians rather than Romans. Barbarians, or free Germans, were used increasingly in the army, and in command, from the time of Diocletian. A king of the Alamanni, Crocus, commanding a contingent of his tribe in Britain, played an important part in the elevation of Constantine to Augustus at York in 306. The two army leaders, Fullofaudes and Nectaridus, caught up in the débâcle of 367, clearly were barbarians. The provinces of Britain were governed by *praesides*, who having lost all military duties to the *duces* and *comites* were now purely civil officials. These men were often lawyers by profession, certainly educated, unlike the *duces*.

Britain had been divided into two provinces by Severus after the defeat of Albinus in 197, essentially to restrict the activities and power of the governor of the island, to prevent the establishment of an independent power-base across the Channel by dividing the three-legion province, eventually into a two-legion southern command and a northern province containing one legion and most of the auxiliary troops. Two other three-legion provinces were so treated: Pannonia Superior and Syria. A century after the division of Britain by Severus the two provinces were themselves divided by Constantine. Britannia Superior, the province of southern England and Wales, was divided into Maxima Caesariensis with its capital at London and Britannia Prima, governed probably from Cirencester. The two provinces carved out of Britannia Inferior were Flavia Caesariensis, believed to have been formed from the territory of the old tribes of the Iceni and the Coritani, and Britannia Secunda, roughly corresponding to the lands of the Brigantes and the Parisi, north England. York, home of VI Victrix and capital of Britannia Inferior, became the seat of the *praeses* of Britannia Secunda, the civilian governor of the north, and probably also of the *dux*, the military commander of Hadrian's Wall. The four provinces of Britain were organized into a diocese headed by a *vicarius* with his headquarters at London. The *vicarius* was the deputy of the praetorian prefect of Gaul based at Trier. Not only therefore was the authority enjoyed by the governors of Britain in the first and second centuries now fragmented into five or more separate commands, civilian and military, but the *vicarius* and the praetorian prefect were now interposed between the *praeses* and the emperor, while the *magistri militum* intervened between the *dux* and the emperor. The old governor of Roman Britain had reported direct to the emperor. The division of the provinces and the separation of civilian and military commands was for administrative convenience and to relieve the burden of work on the senior officials of the Empire. These changes in command reflected far-reaching reorganization in the Empire generally, but were designed to meet the new military needs of Britain. The Count of the Saxon Shore and his command were to deal with the relatively new threat to the south and east coasts, while the Duke of the Britains could concentrate on his northern military command, without having the distraction of civil responsibilities which the governors of undivided Britain and later of Britannia Inferior and Superior had experienced.

Diocletian was the author of another reform which had an effect on the troops of Hadrian's Wall. After many years of declining recruiting figures, and increasing state control, he institutionalized the long-standing traditions of the army by making military service hereditary and compulsory. Henceforth the veterans' sons living in the civil settlements who by habit had entered their fathers' units now were compelled to by law. The law was not strongly enforced, but in any case it cannot have had much effect on the young men of the north of England – there was little else with similar pay and prospects to attract the men of the civil settlements and farmsteads of the north, especially when warfare was apparently so unusual in the north.

THE PICTS

At the same time a shadow was being cast across the peace of the northern frontier by the rise of a new nation, the Picts, who were to give the Roman army much trouble in the later fourth century. This nation resulted from a unification of the many tribes north of the Forth–Clyde isthmus mentioned by Ptolemy. The four or more tribes of the central Highlands, Strathmore and the north-east by the time of Severus had become two, the Caledonians and the Maeatae. The Picts are first mentioned in a Panegyric referring to the events of 297 addressed to Constantius Chlorus. They are clearly a fusion of the Caledonians and the Maeatae, perhaps incomplete, for there is mention in 310 of the Caledones and other Picts while the Verona List of 313 lists the Picts and the Caledonians separately. This is the last reference to the Caledonians, at least in ancient sources, and thereafter all the people north of the Forth are known as the Picts, though they remained divided into different groups such as the Dicalydones and the Verturiones which Ammianus Marcellinus recorded in 367, the former obviously retaining the old tribal name in their new title.

Nine years after the first mention of the Picts in 297, Constantius Chlorus was in the field campaigning against them and, according to a contemporary writer, reached the end of the island. This was no doubt exaggerated but it does suggest serious activity on the part of the emperor. The Picts may have attacked Hadrian's Wall at the beginning of the century. The burning of a wattle-and-daub barrack-block at High Rochester and signs of destruction at Risingham may have been the work of the Picts, though this is not proved. The isolated outpost forts were peculiarly susceptible to attack. Shortly after his victory, like Severus a hundred years before, Constantius died at York and the imperial career of his more famous son, Constantine, began.

Although a son of an emperor, Constantine was not eligible to succeed his father, according to the complicated arrangements made by Diocletian. Nevertheless he was proclaimed emperor by his troops at York in 306 and immediately set out to claim the Empire. It took Constantine twenty years to become sole emperor, but during that time he seems to have visited Britain twice. The first occasion is inferred from a special coin issue in 312 and the second from his assumption of the title *Britannicus Maximus* in 314. The adoption of this title suggests campaigning in Britain, and the most likely enemy is the Picts. The former visit, it has been suggested, was in order to remove troops from Britain for the field army being assembled for the attack on the emperor Maxentius which culminated in his victory at the battle of the Milvian Bridge. The theory is further developed to suggest that the troops withdrawn at this time included those in the outpost forts.

Thirty years later Constantine's son, the emperor Constans, came to Britain. A serious situation had clearly developed for he came to the island in the middle of winter. The trouble, which broke out late in 342, seems to have involved the northern frontier, for it was connected with the *areani*, the frontier scouts.

In 360 the Scots, who were still in Ireland, and the Picts, ignoring agreements made with Rome, laid waste the territory near the frontier. The general Lupicinus with four regiments of the field army was dispatched to Britain and although nothing is recorded in the contemporary sources he presumably succeeded in restoring the situation. A reference to the peace of the province being disturbed in 364 by the Picts, Scots, Saxons and Attacotti may simply be part of a summary of the situation facing the new emperor, as so often in *Scriptores Historiae Augustae*, but in 367 they struck in earnest. The 'barbarian conspiracy' of this year saw the combined attack of Picts, Scots, Attacotti, Franks and Saxons, against the diocese of Britain. Nectaridus, Count of the Saxon Shore, was killed and Fullofaudes, the *dux Britanniarum*, was ambushed and surrounded. The *areani*, the scouts who were supposed to give advance warning of any impending invasion, had not informed the Romans of the movements of the enemy but, led by bribes, had betrayed to the enemy the military dispositions of the Romans! In the catastrophe army discipline broke down and soldiers deserted their units while others were possibly on indefinite leave, a privilege often sold by senior officers in the fourth century. The emperor Valentinian, himself campaigning against the Alamanni, in the late summer of the same year 367, sent one of his senior commanders to Britain, Count Theodosius, with four regiments from his field army. The account of the barbarian conspiracy of 367 and the measures subsequently undertaken by Count Theodosius comes from the history of Rome written by Ammianus Marcellinus. Although he was a very good historian it must not be forgotten that he wrote during the reign of Theodosius' son, the emperor Theodosius. This accounts for the attention paid to this episode, in contrast with that in 360, for example. It makes it very difficult to assess its true importance.

THEODOSIUS AND THE REBUILDING OF THE LATE FOURTH CENTURY

Ammianus records that it took Theodosius many months to restore order in the diocese and strengthen the frontier defences. His attention no doubt turned to Hadrian's Wall; he is described as restoring the cities and strongholds which had been founded to secure a long period of peace, but had suffered repeated misfortunes, and protecting the frontiers by sentinels and outposts, but it is not easy to see precisely what he did. In the first place there is little evidence that the Wall actually suffered from the Picts. The construction of a series of observation posts along the Yorkshire coast, possibly extending as far north as the Tyne, in the late fourth century suggests that the attacks of this time came by sea. In 367 the Picts may have ignored Hadrian's Wall and simply sailed round it. This may have been how Fullofaudes was caught in a trap. It would also account for the lack of evidence for the destruction of Hadrian's Wall at this time – in fact the Wall may have been the safest place in the province.

Along the Wall various renovations and modifications at Birdoswald, Housesteads and Vindolanda are generally dated to this time. The work at the first two sites included the rebuilding or repair of barrack-blocks. At Birdoswald the rebuilding of the complex immediately north of the *via principalis* was securely dated in 1929 by a coin of Valentinian I, 364–75. One building was half-timbered, resting on walls bonded with clay, while inscriptions of Severus and Diocletian were reused as paving flags. One room of the building was used as a cook-house, another as a living-room or dormitory, while next door was a small building with a raised floor, possibly a ventilated storehouse. In the south part of the fort a building was now erected in a new alignment across the earlier *via quintana*. However, the two granaries appear to have gone out of use rather earlier in the century, perhaps about 350, with one changing its function and the other collapsing. This suggests a change in the arrangements for supply, or at least storage, and possibly a reduction in the size of the unit. At Vindolanda a new building was constructed overlying the clay rampart backing on the east wall of the fort. A coin of Constans dated to 342–8 in the core of a wall of this building provides a *terminus post quem* for its erection, which may have been at the time of Theodosius. Most modifications to forts are not as well dated as this and are usually assigned to the nearest or the next 'Wall period'. In fact, of course, the buildings within forts were no doubt repaired and modified at any stage in their history.

Another modification at Vindolanda possibly carried out at this time was the addition of another hypocaust and two latrines to the offices of the headquarters building. It is possible that these rooms were now actually used as living quarters. At Housesteads a large room had been created by the conversion of the two southern administrative rooms into one, perhaps earlier in the fourth century; it also apparently became living quarters from the evidence of the considerable quantity of cinders in the later floor levels, but perhaps after the end of Roman Britain. The northern of the administrative rooms in this building was turned into a weapons store in the late fourth century – when the fort was abandoned more than 800 arrow heads were left there still tied together in bundles.

More significant perhaps was the rebuilding at Halton Chesters and Rudchester. These two forts, which had largely lain abandoned for going on for a hundred years, now underwent complete restoration. New buildings were constructed over the considerable depth of rubbish accumulated in the years of neglect. But the new buildings were not like the old. They followed different alignments and were of a different method of construction. They were largely of timber and the uprights were set in sockets cut in large, indeed megalithic, stones.

A small number of milecastles and turrets show continuing occupation into the last thirty years of the fourth century. Late fourth-century pottery has only been found at five milecastles (9, 35, 37, 48 and 54), one turret (7b) and possibly also the Pike Hill observation tower; single unstratified coins of Valens found at turret 44b and milecastle 52 do not prove occupation for they could have been dropped by a passing soldier or civilian. Structural evidence for repairs at this time has been found at even fewer sites. The north gate of milecastle 52, whose south gate had been so drastically rebuilt earlier in the century, was apparently completely blocked. No coins or pottery date this last modification to the milecastle so it has simply been dated by reference to the Wall periods: this is the third repair or modification to the gateway, therefore it 'must' belong to Wall period IV, Theodosian. No late fourth-century pottery was discovered when the milecastle was excavated, but two cooking-pot rims of Huntcliff type dated to the second half of the fourth century were found at the adjacent Pike Hill observation tower. If this tower continued in use into the last years of the century so might the milecastle. One turret in this area, 51b, was now reoccupied after having lain abandoned for close on two centuries. The doorway was blocked up and a small hut erected within the walls of the turret using stone dug out of the ruins of the earlier structure. On the Cumbrian coast milefortlet 5 (Cardurnock) continued in occupation, while further down the coast it may have been now, if not before, that the fort of Burrow Walls was occupied.

The restoration of Hadrian's Wall by Count Theodosius may also have extended to the curtain. The fort at Birdoswald had for some time been divorced from the Wall, completely surrounded by a wide ditch. The curtain wall was rebuilt from the foundations to join up the fort and the Wall again perhaps at this time, though possibly this occurred earlier in the century. The epigraphic evidence for other repairs to the curtain cannot be assigned to a specific period. The inscriptions record work on Hadrian's Wall undertaken by the *civitates* of the province. Two stones mention the *civitas Dumnoniorum*, two the neighbouring *civitas Durotrigum Lindiniensium*, one the *civitas Catuvellaunorum* and one an unknown *civitas Bricic*. These inscriptions are undated but they have usually been assigned to one of the fourth-century restorations of Hadrian's Wall. J. C. Mann has pointed out that when this work was undertaken by the southern *civitates* they are likely to have been under the same civil authority as the Wall. This was true in the second century; after Severus, or Caracalla at the latest, the *civitates* were in a different province and unlikely to have played any part in the defence or repair of the Wall. However, in the fourth century all the provinces of the island were in the same diocese, under the overriding authority of the *vicarius*, and in time of grave crisis help may have been secured from other provinces of the island.

The strengthening of fort defences is usually considered to date to these years. Rough repairs to the fort walls of Vindolanda and Birdoswald, for example, have been assigned to the Theodosian period on no other evidence than that they are 'late' and display clumsy workmanship. No formal archaeological evidence has been forthcoming and the repairs could date to any time in the fourth century, or before, or later. At Birdoswald, however, the rampart backing was certainly strengthened in at least one place in the later fourth century. Many of the walls blocking the fort gateways have also been assigned to the late fourth century, again on very slight evidence. Most of the blocking took place fairly soon after the forts were built, for the thresholds of these gates show no signs of repair. In fact there was probably an over-provision of gates in the Wall forts and some were kept closed from the very beginning. As the gate timbers rotted they were replaced not by new gates but by stone walls. Later other gates were blocked up at various times when they were no longer required. Only a very few instances of blocking can be dated, in each case to the late second or early third century. The blocking of the south gate of Carrawburgh, however, may belong to a later period, for coins of Tetricus II, 270–74, were found lying on the road surface outside the gate, suggesting that it was still open. When the gate was built up a new, wide and shallow ditch was dug, replacing the two or three earlier smaller ditches, and running across in front of the gate. Excavation in Germany has demonstrated that this new type of ditch first appears in the late third century. The broad and shallow ditch at Carrawburgh presumably belongs to the late third century, or perhaps more probably the fourth century.

It has been suggested that the civil settlements outside the forts on the Wall were abandoned in the late fourth century, but few have been extensively excavated. Vindolanda has furnished proof of occupation in the civil settlement later than 367 after a long period of abandonment, and similar evidence may yet be found at other sites. The supposed abandonment of the civil settlements after 367 has been linked with the movement into the forts of the civilians from these settlements. The evidence for civilians inside the forts is, however, slight and difficult to date closely. At Chesters a number of infant burials were found within one of the interval towers, but these could date to any time after 367 and not necessarily to the years before 411. Late fourth-century pottery in the granaries and trinkets – bracelets and beads – in the barrack-blocks at Housesteads also may date to any time after 367; they may not even prove that civilians lived in the fort. The pottery vessels may have been containers for corn or other food, while the trinkets may have been souvenirs collected by the soldiers or

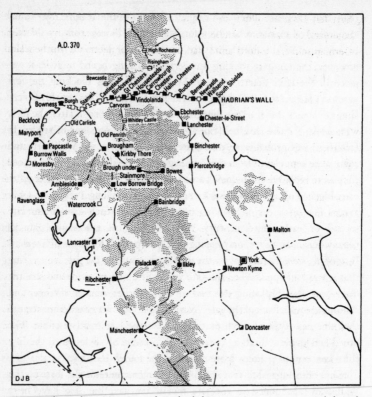

Fig. 34 Military dispositions in north England about 370. Open squares crossed through indicate forts considered to have been abandoned during the previous forty years; open squares, forts possibly occupied at this time; and half-open squares, forts probably occupied.

have resulted from the unauthorized presence of women in the barrack rooms. There is the possibility, considered above (p. 231f.), that barracks became married quarters in the late third or early fourth centuries. This must be kept quite distinct from concepts of farmer-soldiers or forts as fortified villages. We have already seen that it was not until the fifth century, after 411, that anything approaching a peasant militia came into being, and even then the men were primarily soldiers not cultivators. There is no evidence either that Theodosius introduced German barbarian troops to the Wall as has sometimes been supposed. He may, however, have left German soldiers in Britain, for in 372 Fraomar came over to take command of Alamannic soldiers stationed in the diocese, but by that time German soldiers, indeed units, had had a long connection with the island.

THE ABANDONMENT OF THE OUTPOST FORTS

Theodosius undertook one important further action: he disbanded the *areani*, the frontier scouts, following their betrayal of the Roman army in 367. The removal of this shield ought to have caused more conventional forces to be strengthened, and we have noted this as an implication of the work at Halton Chesters and Rudchester in particular. Perhaps it was at this time rather than earlier that the hinterland forts were reoccupied.

Sixty years ago it was suggested that the outpost forts continued in occupation well into the fourth century, the last being abandoned as a result of the barbarian conspiracy of 367. High Rochester was seen as being first abandoned, perhaps as a result of the events of 342/3, whatever they were, or those of 360. The situation at Netherby is not known, but Bewcastle and Risingham were considered to be abandoned in 367, the withdrawal of their units being linked to the abandonment of the *areani* by Theodosius.

More recently, however, it has been proposed that the regular units based at the outpost forts were removed much earlier, in 312. The starting-point for this suggestion is that no coins later than the early years of the fourth century have been found at any of the outpost forts. Furthermore no distinctively late fourth-century pottery has been uncovered at the forts. This was realized in 1935. Then the occupation was prolonged long into the fourth century, but, in view of the difficulties of accurately dating pottery of this period, it could equally well be argued that the occupation ended earlier. The withdrawal of the units from the outpost forts, as we have seen, has now been linked to a putative visit of the emperor Constantine to Britain in 312. In that year a visit to the island is indicated by the issue of a special coin. The reason may have been to choose troops for the army he was preparing for his impending struggle with his rival emperor Maxentius, which culminated in the famous victory at the Milvian Bridge on 28 October 312.

The abandonment of any permanent presence north of the Wall has been linked with another development of the fourth century, the creation of buffer states in the Lowlands of Scotland. The first kings of the four dynasties of these lands bear Roman names. On the Clyde the Damnonii gave way to the kingdom of Strathclyde, whose earliest kings of the dynasty of Coel Hen are called Cluim and Cinhil – Clemens and Quintilius in Latin. In the south-west the first ruler of Galloway is named Annwn (Antonius), while over the northern-part of the Votadini, the area later known as the Manau Gododdin, apparently reigned Catellius Decianus. The first three rulers of the house of Cunedda ruling over the Votadini are Tacit, Patern Pesrut and Aetern. The Roman origin of these names is obvious and the epithet *pesrut* (red cloak), may imply that this king was invested by the Romans with some kind of authority. The genealogies of these dynasties suggest that the first rulers flourished in the 370s and 380s, and the Roman names, especially *pesrut*, have led to the suggestion that the first kings were established as *praefecti gentium* appointed by the Romans to govern the tribes when they withdrew from the Lowlands. This receives some support in that three of the rulers appear to have been brought in from outside. It would make sense for the Romans to protect their interests by creating buffer states against the Picts lying further north, a device used elsewhere in the Empire at this time as before. Coroticus, the grandson of Clemens of Strathclyde, was called a Roman by St Patrick in the middle of the fifth century, as if he perpetuated the power and influence of the imperial government north of Hadrian's Wall.

Doubt has been cast on this neat explanation. The Roman names of these kings may simply show they had become Christians, their conversion being accompanied by the adoption of new names, Romanized in honour of their new religion. *Pesrut*, better translated 'red shirt' rather than 'red cloak', implies something distinctive about his dress; but purple was the Roman colour of authority, not red which was a relatively common colour at Vindolanda. Moreover, with the exception of Traprain Law, there is a complete lack of Roman pottery and other finds in the area north of the Wall. Late-Roman pottery is found abundantly on any site on Hadrian's Wall occupied at this time. If the tribes north of the Wall were philo-Roman surely some late fourth-century pottery would have been found on their territory. The difficulty with this argument is that there is very little early fourth-century, or even third-century, Roman material north of Hadrian's Wall. There seems to have been a gradual diminution in the number of

Roman artefacts drifting north into the 'barbarian' lands. At Traprain Law, considered to be the capital of the Votadini until the mid fifth century, have been found a number of late fourth-century coins, including one of Honorius. However, these do not prove trade with the Romans; they could have come to Traprain Law in the same way as the hoard of early fifth-century treasure, which originated on the continent and was probably either loot or subsidy paid to the tribe. It is therefore possible that the appearance of these kingdoms in southern Scotland owes nothing directly to Rome. They may indicate the resurgence of the pre-Roman states following the end of Roman power in the area.

THE HINTERLAND

Count Theodosius, while restoring the situation, completed the fragmentation of the island's administration started by Severus early in the third century when he created a fifth province, Valentia. J. C. Mann has suggested that the new province lay in the north of England and consisted of part of Britannia Secunda. He further pointed out that Valentia is one of the only two provinces of Britain to be governed by a senior *praeses*, a *consularis*. This should suggest that his province included York, the old capital of Britannia Inferior. One could argue that Valentia contained the greater part of the duke's command, including Hadrian's Wall, leaving only the separate group of three units at the end of the *Notitia* list in what was left of Britannia Secunda, which was now confined to the area west of the Pennines. Thus it was in the north of England, where control had been lost completely for a while, that Theodosius with judicious flattery created a new province of Valentia out of a pre-existing one. The military units of the north of England, of the provinces of Britannia Secunda and Valentia, were still commanded by the *dux Britanniarum*, whose title, Duke of the Britains, demonstrates that his authority extended over a plurality of provinces.

Another measure undertaken in the late fourth century was the construction of a series of observation posts along the Yorkshire coast, possibly extending as far north as the Tyne. Each post consists of a stone tower surrounded by a stone wall and ditch, and they thus fall into a tradition which can be traced back to the Gask Ridge watch-towers and beyond.

Pottery has demonstrated that the towers were built after 367, and they have long been associated with Theodosius and his actions in restoring the frontier outposts. Recently, however, it has been suggested that they were erected by Magnus Maximus who is known to have led a campaign against the Picts in 382, and who may therefore have taken other measures to protect his command. Unfortunately it is doubtful if it will ever be possible to determine which, if either, of these two dates is correct.

THE LAST YEARS OF ROMAN BRITAIN

These measures did not lead to peace on the frontier. In 382 Magnus Maximus conducted his campaign against the Picts and Scots before he led his abortive expedition to the continent to claim the purple. In the later 390s Stilicho, the real ruler of the Empire under the emperor Honorius, directed, presumably from Italy, a war against the Picts, Scots and Saxons, but a few years later these peoples were still causing trouble. None of these raids, or invasions, by the Picts and Scots have been recognized archaeologically, nor have the Roman campaigns, but they cannot have made life easy on the Wall. Nor can the various troop withdrawals of the late fourth and early fifth centuries have helped. In 383 the usurper Magnus Maximus led his army to the continent. In 401, after the campaign against the Picts and Scots, Stilicho withdrew more troops for the defence of Italy and in 407 Constantine III led the last British army to the continent to assert his claim to the Empire and to rescue Gaul from the invading barbarians. These armies may have included soldiers from the Wall but it is certainly clear that the Wall was not abandoned as a result of any of these possible withdrawals, though it used to be considered that Magnus Maximus milked the Wall of all its troops for his ill-fated expedition in 383.

Several pieces of evidence demonstrate continuing occupation on Hadrian's Wall after 383. Pottery, unfortunately, does not. Pottery of the late fourth century has been found in abundance on Hadrian's Wall, but it is not possible to differentiate pottery manufactured in 400 from that made in 370. Coins later than 383 have been found at several sites on the Wall and near the Wall. Coins of the house of Theodosius are rare as site finds in Britain, and rarer in the north than the south, so the scarcity of coins of this dynasty on and near the Wall is not surprising. The last coins found on the Wall are of Arcadius, 395–408, roughly contemporary with the *Notitia Dignitatum*, that enigmatic Roman army list. The Wall units listed under the heading of *item per lineam valli* are very similar to those of the early decades of the third century, though exceptions demonstrate that this section of the *Notitia* is as up to date as the rest of the document.

The last decades of Roman Britain were not necessarily years of steady decline in military strength. In fact it was probably only during the last five years of the fourth century that a new field army was established in Britain under a new commander, the *comes Britanniae*. Hitherto, during emergencies, detachments of the field army based in northern Gaul had had to be sent to the island. The British field army contained nine regiments, six certainly of cavalry, but we do not know where it was based. It had a short life, no more than fifteen years, but, so far as we know, it stayed in Britain until the end.

Much evidence is coming to light of activities within forts after about 400. At South Shields these include the excavation of a ditch at the south-west gate and the subsequent repair of the gate, while the encasing within earth banks of parts of the fort walls at Housesteads, Vindolanda and Birdoswald may also date to the fifth century. The possible churches at South Shields and Vindolanda were probably in use at the very end of Roman Britain or shortly afterwards. Presumably it was in these years that the fires were lit on the floor of the *aedes* of the Vindolanda headquarters building.

Excavations by Tony Wilmott at Birdoswald have provided valuable illuminations of these years. A substantial timber hall was erected over the site of one of the earlier granaries and a second timber building beside it. The hall's successor, probably built after 411, still respected the fort plan. Perhaps we can see here the emergence of a new social order, with the hall being the seat of a local lord, possibly even retaining the Roman system of local supply.

THE END OF THE WALL

When Roman Britain ended in 411 all that happened was that the central government ceased paying the salaries of the civil service and the army. In the mid fifth century the *cohors IX Batavorum*, which had been stationed at Passau in Raetia Secunda for 400 years, sent soldiers to Rome to collect the money due to it when the last pay chests did not arrive; the soldiers were murdered on the way by brigands. This is how the troops who survived barbarian onslaughts realized that Rome's rule was over – the pay did not arrive. The soldiers stationed on Hadrian's Wall were not withdrawn. They may well have stayed where they were, for they were local recruits, probably from the civil settlement outside the fort or a nearby farm, and many of the soldiers had families in the houses beyond the fort walls. There is some evidence for continuing occupation at several sites into the fifth century and beyond. Some more adventurous soldiers may have joined the bands of brigands which were ever a prey on settled life, others the mercenary armies which became such a feature of fifth-century life. The more home-loving, or simply the lazy, stayed where they had always lived. Not only would the pay have dried up but also supplies. Food, pottery, armour, weapons were no longer delivered to the forts of the Wall. Some of these could be, and were, made in the fort or in the civil settlement, and others, pottery for example, were replaced by other commodities. What can certainly be stated is that there is little evidence for Saxons – and none for Picts or Scots – on Hadrian's Wall, and the Wall can therefore truly be said to have successfully served its purpose.

8

CONCLUSION

The preceding chapters have put forward a particular view of the Wall. The idea of a frontier clearly marked by a running barrier was the concept of Hadrian, a concept which marked an important change in the Roman outlook, the final abandonment of the automatic expansion which would one day bring all the world under Rome's predestined sway. Although there was expansion from time to time after Hadrian, as before his reign there had been caution, his rule marks a turning-point. The artificial barriers which supplemented the rivers and the deserts so convenient for border control, though not necessarily effective military obstacles, strengthened the tendency of the Roman armies, who had won their victories through mobility, to settle down on frontier lines and do police work. Local recruiting, early adopted for administrative convenience, strengthened local links till movement of whole units, as opposed to detachments, became virtually impossible.

Hadrian's Wall ranks not as the first but as the most substantial and elaborate of these frontier barriers. It marked the abandonment of the first natural Roman ambition of eventual total conquest of Britain. From Mons Graupius, when Agricola, in his own eyes, stood on the threshold of total victory, to the inception of Hadrian's Wall no satisfactory alternative had been found. Yet the price of total conquest, the restoration of the army of Britain to a strength of four legions and vigorous support by the emperor, had been too high. Trajan seems to have accepted this; how far Domitian may have already shifted the emphasis to the Tyne–Solway line before him remains uncertain. Now Hadrian dictated the final solution, the physical separation of barbarians from Romans, to push the barbarians into virtually a different island, leaving the Romans in an artificial island of their own – what Tacitus had said a Forth–Clyde line might do.

The advance under Pius, possibly to win easy military prestige, involved abandoning Hadrian's Wall but the need for a barrier remained. In the end Hadrian's Wall was finally chosen, but not till an emperor, Septimius Severus, had tried in person total conquest once more, only to find like Edward I after him that he could not enforce his will on his son from the grave. If Domitian had not been hard pressed on the Danube, if Severus had not died, Scotland might have been conquered, and Ireland too. The success of the solution as applied after Severus is itself an enigma, for it seems only to have incorporated elements already invented in the 160s.

The fluctuation between Hadrian's Wall and the Antonine is not merely a fascinating exercise in reconstructing history. It also enables us to follow the development of a system of frontier control and of military defence, and see how the two, originally distinct, came to be merged, partly because the fighting troops were available on the spot, partly because military problems lost their urgency in the third century; the pressure on the troops to become immersed in frontier control became irresistible. Local recruitment tied unit, fort and fort settlement ever more closely, creating an immobilized army on the frontier, gradually degenerating under continuing peaceful conditions. In the army changes of the fourth century Wall units seem to have become simply frontier troops.

The men stationed in the forts of the Wall and their dependants, who included not only their immediate families, but the majority of the people in the civil settlements, had a life similar to that in and around forts Empire-wide. This fact has been emphasized by the Vindolanda writing tablets. Though the province did not lack individuality, the similarities far outweigh the differences, and life on the Wall was the ordinary life of the Roman frontiers.

The Wall then was an artificial frontier, the finest Roman artificial frontier in its elaboration and in the impressiveness of its remains. Its history and development mirrored that of the Roman frontier system in general, and though it shared the weaknesses of that system it had some success, for the barbarians from the north never made a lasting settlement within its range.

This study, even within its self-imposed limits, has thrown up questions which are still without answers. First, too little is known of the antecedents of the Wall, particularly its immediate predecessor in Britain, the Stanegate 'system'. The very existence of the system as it is generally described has yet to be demonstrated. On the details of the building of the Wall, it would be useful to be certain which legion built which type of milecastle, turret and curtain. When was the rest of the turf wall, beyond the section converted to narrow gauge under Hadrian, rebuilt in stone? In the later second century we need an agreed chronology, or at least an agreed order if dates cannot be agreed, for the two occupations of Hadrian's Wall and the occupation of the Antonine Wall. Linked with these is the question of the antecedents of the third-century system.

Our knowledge of Roman forts, paradoxically, is poor. No complete fort plan is available for the four types of auxiliary unit which contained cavalry. No stable has been completely excavated, though a little more is known about the possible internal arrangements. Many buildings in forts are of uncertain purpose, including the *basilica* building found at Birdoswald, and the precise reconstruction even of such familiar buildings as granaries is unclear. Some common statements rest on little evidence. However, our information is improving through recent excavations, which in particular have provided important new evidence on barracks. Similar doubts arise regarding the troops. What was the pay of the auxiliary compared with that of the legionary? How soon were soldiers recruited locally in Britain, and were they all volunteers? Who are the Germans who turn up at a number of forts? How much free time did the soldiers have? The questions are endless.

In the later centuries our ignorance deepens. How widespread were the conditions of decay in the third century known archaeologically at Halton Chesters and Rudchester, and epigraphically at Birdoswald? What was the real strength of the units on the Wall in the fourth century? How did the layout and nature of the buildings in their forts change? When were the forts behind the Wall reoccupied by the new units listed in the *Notitia*? What happened north of the Wall after 367?

There is still much to know about the civil settlements, their size, layout and composition. How quickly and how systematically did their development proceed? What was their history after 369, and indeed after 411? Most pressing of all, perhaps, is the history of the real people of the land, who lived with the Wall in their midst, who seemed little affected by Rome materially but nevertheless enjoyed or endured the *pax Romana*, with peace, communications and markets as never before.

There is thus no shortage of questions about the Wall. Answers must come through steady and methodical work in the field and in the study, careful investigation and careful evaluation of results. For the authors the Wall retains its fascination, and they hope that their readers will feel this too, like the sixteenth-century antiquarian William Camden: 'Verily I have seene the tract of it over the high pitches and steepe descents of hilles, wonderfully rising and falling.'

APPENDIX 1

ROMAN EMPERORS
AND GOVERNORS OF BRITAIN

This list is simply to elucidate references in the main text. The list of governors is based on that in A. R. Birley, *The Fasti of Roman Britain*, Oxford, 1981, with the following exceptions: governors whose names are totally unknown are omitted; -dius is rejected as a Hadrianic governor, following the doubts expressed by R. P. Wright regarding RIB 1997* and 1998 being from the same stone; M. Antius Crescens is omitted as he cannot be securely dated; the second Ulpius Marcellus is rejected, see p. 121; a number of governors who cannot be closely dated are omitted; the view is accepted here that the northern frontier remained under the control of a consular governor under Severus. The list of governors of Britannia Inferior is taken down to Nonius Philippus (A.D. 262). The list of emperors has been cut down to the bare minimum of 'legitimate' emperors in the third century, and in the fourth has been cut down even further. Where Britain is under the control of another than the 'legitimate' emperor or one only of Constantine's sons this indicated.

Like A. R. Birley we accept the earlier dates for Agricola's governorship, the consequences of which are worked out in chapter 1. It should be noted that after Agricola neither the starting nor finishing dates of any governor are known with certainty, though in the case of Statius Priscus dates for his preceding and succeeding activities tightly confine the possible length of his governorship.

---

* RIB numbers refer to the catalogue in R. G. Collingwood and R. P. Wright, *The Roman Inscriptions of Britain*, Oxford, 1965.

Date (A.D.)	Emperor	Date (A.D.)	Governor of Britain
31 B.C.	Augustus		
14	Tiberus		
37	Gaius (Caligula)		
41	Claudius		
		43	A. Plautius *succeeded by*
		47	P. Ostorius Scapula *succeeded by*
		52	A. Didius Gallus *succeeded by*
54	Nero		
		57	Q. Veranius *succeeded by*
		58	C. Suetonius Paullinus *succeeded by*
		61	P. Petronius Turpilianus *succeeded by*
		63	M. Trebellius Maximus *succeeded by*
68	Galba		
69	Otho Vitellius	69	M. Vettius Bolanus *succeeded by*
	Vespasian		
		71	Q. Petillius Cerialis *succeeded by*
		73/4	Sx. Iulius Frontinus *succeeded by*
		77	Cn. Iulius Agricola *succeeded by*
79	Titus		
81	Domitian		
		84	*Unknown* Sallustius Lucullus
96	Nerva		
		−98	P. Metilius Nepos *succeeded by*
98	Trajan	98	T. Avidius Quietus
		103	L. Neratius Marcellus
		108+	M. Appius (*or* Atilius) Bradua

Date (A.D.)	Emperor	Date (A.D.)	Governor of Britain
117	Hadrian		
		−122	Q. Pompeius Falco *succeeded by*
		122–4+	A. Platorius Nepos
		127	L. Trebius Germanus
		128/32	Sex. Iulius Severus
		135	P. Mummius Sisenna
138	Antoninus Pius		
		139–42	Q. Lollius Urbicus
		146	Cn. Papirius Aelianus
		158	Cn. Iulius Verus
		154 *or* 159?	—anus
161	Marcus Aurelius *and* Lucius Verus	161/2	M. Statius Priscus
		163	Sex. Calpurnius Agricola
169	Marcus Aurelius *alone*	*between* 169 *and* 180	Q. Antistius Adventus (Caerellius)
176	Marcus Aurelius *with* Commodus		
		178	Ulpius Marcellus
180	Commodus *alone*	*c.* 180/82	*Unknown*??
		184	Ulpius Marcellus
		185/7	P. Helvius Pertinax
192	Commodus *assassinated*	192–7	D. Clodius Albinus
193	Pertinax		
	Didius Iulianus		
	Pescennius Niger		
	Septimius Severus		
195	Albinus Caesar		
196	Caracalla Caesar		
197	Albinus *defeated and killed*	197	Virius Lupus
198	Caracalla Augustus		
		205	C. Valerius Pudens
		205/7	L. Alfenus Senecio
209	Geta Augustus		

Date (A.D.)	Emperor	Date (A.D.)	Governor of Britain
211	Caracalla *and* Geta *on death of* Severus		
212	Caracalla *alone*		BRITANNIA INFERIOR
		213	C. Iulius Marcus
		216	(M. Antonius Gor(?)) dianus
217	Macrinus		
218	Elagabalus		
		219?	Modius Iulius
		220	Ti. Claudius Paulinus
222	Severus Alexander	221–2	Marius Valerianus
		223	Claudius Xenophon
		225	Maximus
			Calvisius Rufus
			Valerius Crescens Fulvianus
235?	Maximinus	235?	Claudius Apellinus
		237	(T(?))uccianus
238	Gordian I *and* Gordian II		
	Gordian III		Maecilius Fuscus
			Egnatius Lucilianus
		242	Nonius Philippus
244	Philip I		
249	Decius Traianus		
250–	Decius II		
251	Gallus *and* Volusianus		
253	Valerian *and* Gallienus		
			GALLIC EMPIRE
		258	Postumus
259	Gallienus *alone*		
268	Claudius II	268	Victorinus
270	Aurelian	270	Tetricus
273	*recovers Gallic Empire*		
275	Tacitus		

Date (A.D.)	Emperor	Date (A.D.)	Governor of Britain
276	Probus		
282	Carus		
283	Numerian *and* Carinus		
284–305	Diocletian		
286–305	Maximian		'BRITISH' EMPERORS
		287–93	Carausius
293–306	Constantius Chlorus Caesar (Augustus 305)	293–6	Allectus
293–311	Galerius Caesar (Augustus 305)		
306–37	Constantine		EMPEROR CONTROLLING BRITAIN
317–40	Constantine II	337–40	Constantine II
333–50	Constans	340–50	Constans
324–61	Constantius II	350–61	Constantius II
		(350–3	Magnentius)
355–63	Julian Caesar (Augustus 360)		
363–4	Jovian		
364–75	Valentinian I		
367–83	Gratian		
375–92	Valentinian II	383–8	Magnus Maximus
379–95	Theodosius	392–4	Eugenius
395–408	Arcadius *East*		
395–423	Honorius *West*	407–11	Constantine III

APPENDIX 2

THE REGIMENTS OF HADRIAN'S WALL

The evidence presented here is for the forts on the Wall itself, the outpost forts, and those on the Cumbrian coast. In many cases the assignment of a unit's period of garrison to the time of a particular emperor is on grounds of inherent probability rather than on the basis of a dated inscription. Cases where the evidence is unambiguous are identified by an asterisk. In the third century, where most dated inscriptions occur and when the units seem to have taken up permanent positions, the earliest attested date for the unit's presence is given.

RIB numbers refer to the catalogue in R. G. Collingwood and R. P. Wright, *The Roman Inscriptions of Britain*, Oxford, 1965.

BY FORTS

WALLSEND

Under Hadrian: cohors quingenaria equitata (?)
Under Marcus Aurelius: cohors II Nerviorum civium Romanorum (?)
Third century: cohors IV Lingonum equitata
Notitia: cohors IV Lingonum*

The cohors II Nerviorum could have been the Hadrianic garrison, although it was not *equitata*. The inscriptions of cohors IV Lingonum from the fort (RIB 1299–1301) are not dated, but are certainly late and are probably third century. The tile of ala I Hispanorum Asturum (*Britannia* 7 (1976) 388) is insufficient evidence for its having been stationed here.

NEWCASTLE

Under Hadrian: no evidence
Under Marcus Aurelius: no evidence
Third century: cohors I Ulpia Traiana Cugernorum civium Romanorum (*213*)★
Notitia: cohors prima Cornoviorum★

It is impossible to say if cohors I Thracum (RIB 1323), attested on a building record, was ever stationed at Newcastle.

BENWELL

Under Hadrian: ala quingenaria (?)
Under Marcus Aurelius: cohors I Vangionum milliaria equitata
Under Commodus (Ulpius Marcellus governor): ala
Third century: ala I Asturum (205–8)★
Notitia: ala I Asturum★

The inscriptions by legionary centurions (RIB 1327 and 1330) do not necessarily indicate the presence of a full legionary detachment under Antoninus Pius.

RUDCHESTER

Under Hadrian: cohors quingenaria equitata (?)
Under Marcus Aurelius: no evidence
Third century: no evidence, fort run down from 270s till 370s
Notitia: cohors prima Frixagorum (*presumably* Frisiavonum)

HALTON CHESTERS

Under Hadrian: cohors quingenaria equitata (?)
Under Marcus Aurelius: no evidence
Third century: ala Sabiniana
Notitia: ala Sabiniana★

The fort was run down from the 270s till the 370s, but the unit apparently survived in name at least. There is an inscription of it from the fort (RIB 1433) which is apparently third century.

CHESTERS

Under Hadrian: ala Augusta ob virtutem appellata★
Under Pius: auxiliary regiment (*146*)★
Under Marcus Aurelius: no evidence
Under Commodus (Ulpius Marcellus governor): ala II Asturum★
Third century: ala II Asturum (*205–8*)★
Notitia: ala II Asturum★

The inscriptions under Pius of II Augusta are building inscriptions (RIB 1460–61) and do not prove that a detachment of the legion was in garrison. On the other hand the diploma of 146 found at the fort suggests strongly that there was an auxiliary regiment in garrison then. The tombstone to the daughter of a commanding officer of cohors I Vangionum (RIB 1482) is not easily explained as a death on a visit to the fort, and the wife's *nomen* Aurelia suggests a date not earlier than 161. The cohors I Delmatarum is also recorded at the fort, and must have been in garrison at some time in the second century.

CARRAWBURGH

Under Hadrian: cohors quingenaria equitata (*?*)
Under Marcus Aurelius: no evidence
Third century: cohors I Batavorum equitata (*213–17*)★
Notitia: cohors I Batavorum equitata★

There are a large number of units attested here, cohorts I Aquitanorum, I Tungrorum, I Cugernorum, I Frisiavonum and II Nerviorum. The first two are attested building, but the others were possibly merely honouring the local goddess Coventina. There is no evidence that RIB 1545 is earlier than RIB 1544, here used to give the earliest certain date that I Batavorum was at Carrawburgh.

HOUSESTEADS

Under Hadrian: cohors milliaria peditata
Under Marcus Aurelius: no evidence
Third century: cohors I Tungrorum milliaria, numerus Hnaudifridi, cuneus Frisiorum Ver. (Severus Alexander)★
Notitia: cohors I Tungrorum★

The inscriptions of cohors I Tungrorum and the numerus Hnaudifridi are undated, but a third-century date seems probable. A sculpture of an archer from Housesteads has been dated to the second century, with uncertain implications. The inscription referring to *mil(ites) leg. II Aug. agentes in praesidio* (RIB 1583) is generally taken with RIB 1582 to refer to a garrisoning of Housesteads by soldiers of that legion, though there is no evidence when this was.

VINDOLANDA

Under Hadrian: no evidence
Under Marcus Aurelius: cohors II Nerviorum civium Romanorum (*??*)
Third century: cohors IV Gallorum equitata (*213*)★
Notitia: cohors IV Gallorum★

The inscription of cohors II Nerviorum is discounted in RIB 1683 as evidence for the unit's being at Vindolanda, but it is no better and no worse than other evidence, and the alternative explanation in RIB is unsatisfactory.

GREAT CHESTERS

Under Hadrian: cohors VI Nerviorum (*?*)
Under Marcus Aurelius: cohors – Raetorum (*166–9*)★
Third century: cohors II Asturum (*225*),★ Raeti gaesati (*?*)
Notitia: cohors I Asturum (*presumably error for II Asturum*)★

CARVORAN

Under Hadrian: cohors I Hamiorum (*136–8*)★
Under Marcus Aurelius: cohors I Hamiorum (*governor Calpurnius Agricola*)★
Third century: cohors II Delmatarum equitata
Notitia: cohors II Delmatarum★

The inscription of cohors II Delmatarum (RIB 1795) is undated, but a third-century date is probable.

BIRDOSWALD

Under Hadrian: cohors I Tungrorum milliaria (*??*)
Under Antoninus Pius: no evidence
Under Marcus Aurelius: no evidence

Third century: cohors I Aelia Dacorum milliaria (*205–8*),★ venatores Bannienses

Notitia: cohors I Aelia Dacorum★

The evidence for the Hadrianic garrison is a tile stamp (*Ephemeris Epigraphica* IX 1279). For the venatores Bannienses, whose inscription is undated, but for whom a third-century date is probable, see p. 276. The question whether the cohors I Thracum civium Romanorum also mentioned on RIB 1909 was simply helping with the building rather than based on the fort cannot at present be answered. For the problem regarding the *Notitia* entry see pp.294ff.

CASTLESTEADS

Under Hadrian: cohors IV Gallorum equitata (?)
Under Marcus Aurelius: no evidence
Third century: cohors II Tungrorum equitata c. I. (*241*)★
Notitia: no entry (omitted in error, see pp. 294ff.)

STANWIX

Under Hadrian: ala Petriana (?)
Under Marcus Aurelius: no evidence
Third century: ala Augusta Petriana bis torquata civium Romanorum
Notitia: ala Petriana★

The rejection of Petriana as the name of the fort leaves open the question of the second-century garrisons, though the apparent size of the fort would suggest it was built for milliary *ala*, and the ala Petriana is the only such unit known in Britain.

BURGH-BY-SANDS

Under Hadrian: cohors quingenaria equitata/milliaria peditata (?)
Under Marcus Aurelius: no evidence
Third century: cohors I Nervana Germanorum milliaria equitata (?), numerus Maurorum Aurelianorum (*253–8*),★ cuneus Frisionum Aballavensium (*241*) (?)
Notitia: numerus Maurorum Aurelianorum★

The *numerus* was under the charge of a tribune of a cohort in 253–8, and cohors I Nervana would fit best at this time (see below p. 267).

Although the references to the *cuneus* come from Papcastle (RIB 882–3) the inscriptions seem to refer to a transfer of someone to the unit called cuneus Frisionum Aballavensium (the cavalry unit of Frisiones of Burgh) from an unnamed unit, presumably from the one in garrison at Papcastle to the unit at Burgh. It seems difficult and unnecessary to assume that the *cuneus* had been moved to Papcastle, and it is a well-attested Roman practice to set up inscriptions recording promotion on transfer at the post one is leaving. A *cohors milliaria peditata* is unlikely under Hadrian, as there are only two attested in the province, and there was presumably at the time one at Housesteads and one at Birdoswald.

DRUMBURGH

The history of this fort is uncertain; no unit is attested there by an inscription, and the *Notitia* entry for Congavata normally associated with it may in fact refer to another fort, see p. 295.

BOWNESS

Under Hadrian: cohors milliaria equitata (?)
Under Marcus Aurelius: no evidence
Third century: cohors milliaria (251–3)*
Notitia: no entry

There are too many forts with evidence for milliary cohorts in the third century for the seven milliary cohorts attested in this country unless there was transfer of units during the third century or the splitting up of units. The latter may seem more likely – most of the forts are too small to hold full-size milliary units, though Bowness is large enough.

There is another possibility. All the cohort commanders named in the *Notitia* are tribunes, although their units would have been commanded by prefects in the first two centuries A.D. Much of the evidence for milliary cohorts in the third century is the presence of tribunes, as here, but it may be that already at that time tribune was being used more generally for the commander of an auxiliary cohort, whatever its size.

BECKFOOT

Under Hadrian: cohors quingenaria peditata
The only unit attested at any time is the cohors II Pannoniorum.

MARYPORT

Under Hadrian: cohors I Hispanorum milliaria equitata
(quingenaria *during part of Hadrian's reign*)★
Under Pius: cohors I Delmatarum equitata
Under Marcus Aurelius: cohors I Baetasiorum civium Romanorum
Third century: cohors milliaria (?)

The suggestion of a milliary unit as a third-century garrison rests on the dedication by a *tribunus cohortis*, RIB 812, which has a feature, a *signum*, commonly thought not to appear before the third century. For the difficulties of too many forts for the number of milliary units known in the third century see above.

BURROW WALLS

No unit is recorded in connection with this fort, which seems to have been built for a *cohors quingenaria peditata*. J. P. Gillam has suggested that it was first built in the fourth century.

MORESBY

Under Hadrian: cohors II Lingonum equitata (??)
Notitia: cohors II Thracum equitata★

RAVENGLASS

Under Pius: cohors I Aelia classica (*158*)★

SOUTH SHIELDS

Under Hadrian: no evidence
Under Marcus Aurelius: cohors (?)
Third century: cohors V Gallorum (*213*)★
Notitia: numerus barcariorum Tigrisiensium★

The tombstone of a freedman of a trooper of the ala I Asturum (RIB 1064) still presents problems. A tile stamp (*Ephemeris Epigraphica* 3, 202) of ala I Pannoniorum Sabiana does not prove that the regiment was ever at South Shields.

BEWCASTLE

Under Hadrian: cohors I Dacorum milliaria peditata

Under Marcus Aurelius: no evidence

Third century: cohors milliaria (?)

The inscriptions of two tribunes dedicating to Cocidius (RIB 988–9) suggest a milliary cohort was stationed here in the third century; for the difficulties see p. 261, and notice also the possibility that the tribunes may have made a special journey to Bewcastle to dedicate at the shrine of Cocidius.

NETHERBY

Under Hadrian: no evidence

Under Marcus Aurelius: no evidence

Third century: cohors I Aelia Hispanorum equitata (214–16)★

The inscription of the third or early fourth century referring to a dedication to Cocidius by a commander of cohors I Nervana (RIB 966) may not belong to this fort.

BIRRENS

Under Hadrian: no evidence

Under Pius: cohors II Tungrorum milliaria equitata c. l. (158)★

Under Marcus Aurelius: no evidence

Third century: fort abandoned

Cohors I Nervana Germanorum milliaria equitata, attested at this fort, may have been in garrison either under Hadrian or early in the reign of Pius.

RISINGHAM

Under Hadrian: not yet built

Under Pius: no evidence

Under Marcus Aurelius: cohors IV Gallorum equitata★

Third century: cohors I Vangionum milliaria equitata (205–8),★ vexillatio Raetorum gaesatorum (213),★ exploratores Habitancenses (213)★

The dedication to the numina Augustorum (RIB 1227) by cohors IV Gallorum must be to joint emperors, and only Marcus and Verus or

Marcus and Commodus can come into consideration on the known
history of the cohort and the fort.

HIGH ROCHESTER

Under Hadrian: not occupied
Under Pius: cohors I Lingonum equitata*
Under Marcus Aurelius: cohors I Da— (?)
Third century: cohors I fida Vardullorum civium Romanorum milliaria
equitata (*213*),* explatores Bremenienses (*238–41*)*

RIB 1289, referring to an Aurelius of coh. I Da—, ought to be after 161,
and it is unlikely that the unit was based at High Rochester in the third
century in addition to or as replacement for those recorded. The
presence of a vexillation of cohors II Nerviorum and cohors IV Gallorum
is also attested at an unknown date.

BY UNITS

These are arranged under *alae* and *cohortes*, subdivided into milliary and
quingenary. The period covered is from Hadrian to the end of the
Roman period. Their mention on diplomas is recorded as evidence for
their presence in Britain. Lead seals bearing unit names found at forts
are not evidence for those units being stationed there and are therefore
not treated as such below. The milliary units appear to have been kept
in the Wall zone throughout the period, though direct evidence for the
ala Petriana is slight. The quingenary units on the other hand seem
rarely to have been in the zone in both the second and third centuries.
Again this is clearer for the cohorts than the *alae*. There was apparently
a massive reshuffle of units within the province in the late second or
early third century. The letters A and B distinguish respectively those
units which were in the area up to *c.* 180 and those which were in the
area in the third century, possibly from as early as 184 or thereabouts.

ALAE

Of the eighteen cavalry regiments securely attested in Britain only five are certainly attested on the Wall.

ALA AUGUSTA GALLORUM PETRIANA MILLIARIA CIVIUM ROMANORUM (ALA MILLIARIA)

Originally raised: Gaul
Diplomas: 98, 122, 124, 135
Under Hadrian: Stanwix (*presumably*)
Under Marcus Aurelius: Stanwix (*possibly*)
Third century: Stanwix (*presumably*)
Notitia: Stanwix* (*entry bungled, see p. 294ff.*)

A number of forts have been suggested for this unit, but none has been demonstrated conclusively to have housed it, apart from Stanwix, and in the first century Corbridge, when the unit was still quingenary (RIB 1172).

ALA AUGUSTA OB VIRTUTEM APPELLATA (ALA QUINGENARIA)

Originally raised: unknown
Diplomas: none
Under Hadrian: Chesters
Under Commodus: Old Carlisle
Third century: Old Carlisle

There is a full discussion in *AA*[5] 7 (1979), 116–25, giving reasons for not accepting the equation of this unit with ala Gallorum Proculeiana. The absence from diplomas remains puzzling. It is uncertain if RIB 606, from Lancaster, of the late first century, refers to this unit.

ALA I HISPANORUM ASTURUM (ALA QUINGENARIA) (B)

Originally raised: Asturia (*north-west Spain*)
Diplomas: 98, 122, 124, 135, 146
Third century: Benwell (*perhaps already under Commodus, see under Benwell*)
Notitia: Benwell

The problem of RIB 1064 is referred to above under South Shields.

ALA II ASTURUM (ALA QUINGENARIA) (B)

Originally raised: Asturia (*north-west Spain*)
Diploma: 122
Under Commodus: Chesters (*under Ulpius Marcellus*)★
Third century: Chesters★
Notitia: Chesters★

RIB 586 may attest its presence at Ribchester.

ALA I PANNONIORUM SABINIANA (ALA QUINGENARIA)

Originally raised: Pannonia (*approximately modern Hungary*)
Diplomas: 122, 146, 178
Third century: Halton Chesters
Notitia: Halton Chesters★

A tile stamp (*Ephemeris Epigraphica* (3 202) at South Shields does not prove that the regiment was ever there.

COHORTES

There are only seven *cohortes milliariae* attested in Britain, and it is important to note that they tend to be all stationed in the Wall area throughout the period whenever the Wall is occupied, compensating for the absence of the distant legions.

I AELIA DACORUM (COHORS MILLIARIA)

Originally raised: Dacia (*approximately modern Romania*) in the early second century A.D.
Diploma: 146
Under Hadrian: Bewcastle (?)
Third century: Birdoswald (*205–8*)★
Notitia: Birdoswald★

For the problem regarding the *Notitia* entry see p. 294ff.

I NERVANA GERMANORUM EQUITATA (COHORS MILLIARIA)

Originally raised: Germania (*the Rhineland*)
Diplomas: 122, 178
Third century: Burgh-by-Sands

It was at Birrens, probably before 158, either under Hadrian or under Pius during the first Antonine period in Scotland. In the third century it seems to have been at Burgh. An inscription at Netherby seems to be a stray dedication to Cocidius from Bewcastle, which need not imply that the unit was in garrison at Bewcastle or Netherby.

I AELIA HISPANORUM EQUITATA (COHORS MILLIARIA)

Originally raised: Spain (*as a quingenary cohort*)
Diplomas: 98, 103, 105, 122, 124, 146, 178
Under Hadrian: Maryport
Third century: Netherby (*214–16*)★
Notitia: Axelodunum

For the problem regarding the *Notitia* entry see pp. 294ff. For the possibility of another unit with this name and number in Britain see D. J. Breeze, 'The regiments stationed at Maryport and their commanders', in R. J. A. Wilson (ed.), *Roman Maryport and its setting*, Maryport, 1997, 70f.

I TUNGRORUM (COHORS MILLIARIA)

Originally raised: Gallia Belgica (*modern Belgium*)
Diplomas: 103 (*noted as already milliary*), 122, 124, 146
Under Hadrian: Birdoswald (*??*)
Under Pius: Castlecary★
Third century: Housesteads
Notitia: Housesteads★

I Tungrorum seems to have been at Vindolanda in the pre-Hadrianic period (Tab. Vindol. 30). A detachment of the cohort was in Noricum (modern Austria) for a period which included the years 122 and 124. The discovery of a diploma of 146 at Vindolanda may suggest that the cohort was there under Pius (first period) before moving to Castlecary, by which time at latest the detachment had returned. An inscription from Cramond (RIB 2135), now lost cannot be closely dated, and may refer to cohors II Tungrorum.

II TUNGRORUM EQUITATA C. L. (COHORS MILLIARIA)

Originally raised: Gallia Belgica (*modern Belgium*)
Diplomas: –
Under Pius (second period ?)*:* Birrens (*158*)★
Under Marcus Aurelius: Birrens (*?*)
Third century: Castlesteads (*241*)★
Notitia: omitted (*in error (?), see pp. 294ff.*)

This unit also seems to have been half-strength for a time, the detachment in this case being at Eining (Bavaria) in 121/25, 147 and 153. The expansion c(*ivium*) L(*atinorum*) is uncertain. The inscription from Cramond (RIB 2135) could refer to this unit.

I VANGIONUM EQUITATA (COHORS MILLIARIA)

Originally raised: Germania Superior (*the upper Rhineland*)
Diplomas: 103, 122, 124, 135, 178
Third century: Risingham (*205–8*)★

It was at Benwell, where it would best fit in some time between Hadrian and the governorship of Ulpius Marcellus, but an inscription from Chesters recording the death of a commanding officer's daughter cannot well be earlier than 161.

I FIDA VARDULLORUM EQUITATA (COHORS MILLIARIA)

Originally raised: north Spain
Diplomas: 98, 105, 122, 124, 135, 146, 159, 178
Under Pius: Castlecary
Under Marcus Aurelius: Corbridge (*161–3*)★; Lanchester (*175–6*)★
Third century: High Rochester (*213*)★

The restoration of this unit on RIB 1128 from Corbridge is now certain (*Britannia* 16 (1985), 331). The dedication to the mother goddesses by a detachment of this cohort from outside milecastle 19 (RIB 1421) cannot be closely dated. The inscription at Jedburgh (RIB 2118 – a carry from Cappuck?) seems to imply that the unit or part of it was on outpost duty.

About half of the almost fifty *cohortes quingenariae* attested in Britain found themselves on the Wall at one time or another, in contrast with only one quarter of the *alae*. Over thirty of the fifty were *equitatae*, and about half of these saw service in the Wall zone.

I AQUITANORUM EQUITATA (COHORS QUINGENARIA) (A)

Originally raised: south-west France
Diplomas: 114/122, 122, 124
Under Hadrian: Carrawburgh (*130–33??*)★
Under Pius: Brough-on-Noe, Derbyshire (*c.* 158)★

The reading of RIB 1550 remains uncertain as between the governors Sex. Iulius Severus and Cn. Iulius Verus; it is already attested under the latter governor at Brough-on-Noe. In the third century it was at Brancaster, a Saxon Shore fort, cf. the next but one entry.

II ASTURUM EQUITATA (COHORS QUINGENARIA) (B)

Originally raised: Asturia (*north-west Spain*)
Diplomas: 105, 122, 124
Third century: Great Chesters (*225*)★
Notitia: Great Chesters (?)

For the probability that the *Notitia* entry I Asturum is an error for II Asturum see p. 294.

I BAETASIORUM CIVIUM ROMANORUM (COHORS QUINGENARIA) (A)

Originally raised: Germania Inferior (*Holland*)
Diplomas: 103, 122, 124, 135
Under Pius: Bar Hill★
Under Marcus Aurelius: Maryport
Notitia: Reculver, Kent★

The unit is also attested at Old Kilpatrick: it is most likely to have been there under Pius.

I BATAVORUM EQUITATA (COHORS QUINGENARIA) (B)

Originally raised: Belgium
Diplomas: 122, 124, 135
Third century: Carrawburgh (*213–17*)★

Notitia: Carrawburgh★

There is also a dedication by a centurion of the unit from near milecastle 59.

I AELIA CLASSICA (COHORS QUINGENARIA) (B)

Originally raised: unknown
Diploma: 146
Under Pius: Ravenglass (*158*)
Notitia: Tunnocelum (*Moresby?*)

The question of whether Tunnocelum is Ravenglass rather than Moresby, and its implications, are discussed on p. 299.

I CORNOVIORUM (COHORS QUINGENARIA) (B)

Originally raised: Welsh Marches (*only unit known on the Wall originally raised in Britain*)
Notitia: Newcastle★

I ULPIA TRAIANA CUGERNORUM CIVIUM ROMANORUM (COHORS QUINGENARIA)

Originally raised: Germania Inferior (*north Germany*)
Diplomas: 103, 122, 124
Third century: Newcastle (*213*)★

The unit was road building near Cramond under Pius. One of its soldiers set up an altar at Carrawburgh after 161.

I DA—

See the next entry.

I DELMATARUM (COHORS QUINGENARIA)

Originally raised: Croatia
Diplomas: 122, 124, 135
Under Pius: Maryport
Under Marcus Aurelius: High Rochester (*?*)

An inscription from Chesters is difficult to fit in; perhaps the redistribution of units in the second Antonine period meant a move for this cohort. Perhaps the High Rochester inscription (RIB 1289) should be understood as I Dacorum, as Delmatarum is commoner than Dalmatarum, in which case it must be assumed either that the Aelia of I Aelia Dacorum was omitted or that there was another I Dacorum in Britain.

II DELMATARUM (COHORS QUINGENARIA) (B)

Originally raised: Croatia
Diplomas: 105, 122, 135
Third century: Carvoran
Notitia: Carvoran★

The inscription (RIB 1795) referring to the cohort at Carvoran is not dated, but the Hamians were at Carvoran under Hadrian and under Marcus Aurelius, so the third-century suggestion seems reasonable.

I FRISIAVONUM (COHORS QUINGENARIA) (B)

Originally raised: Scheldt area
Diplomas: 105, 122, 124, 178
Notitia: Rudchester

An undated altar to Coventina at Carrawburgh by an *optio* of this cohort (RIB 1523) might just be an expression of devotion by a soldier not stationed at the fort.

IV GALLORUM EQUITATA (COHORS QUINGENARIA) (A/B)

Originally raised: Gaul
Diplomas: 122, 146, 178
Under Pius: Castlehill
Under Marcus Aurelius: Risingham★
Third century: Vindolanda (*213*)★
Notitia: Vindolanda★

The two altars from Castlesteads, RIB 1979 and 1980, prove a period in garrison there, perhaps rather the second period under Pius than under Hadrian. The unit was at Templeborough (Yorks.) in the first century, and stamped tiles have also been found at Castleford (Yorks.).

V GALLORUM EQUITATA (COHORS QUINGENARIA) (B)

Originally raised: Gaul
Diplomas: 122, 135
Third century: South Shields (*213*)★

The unit was at one time stationed at Cramond (RIB 2134).

I HAMIORUM SAGITTARIORUM (COHORS QUINGENARIA) (A)

Raised: Syria
Diplomas: 122, 124, 135
Under Hadrian: Carvoran★
Under Pius: Bar Hill
Under Marcus Aurelius: Carvoran★

As cohors II Baetasiorum was building at Bar Hill, cohors I Hamiorum was presumably the second unit to occupy the fort. The return to Carvoran is the only case known of a unit which returned to its original fort on the Wall, apart from the probable but special case of the ala Petriana, which only one fort on the Wall, Stanwix, could accommodate.

I LINGONUM EQUITATA (COHORS QUINGENARIA)

Originally raised: Germania Superior (*around Langres, eastern France*)
Diplomas: 105, 122
Under Pius: High Rochester★ (under Urbicus)
Third century: Lanchester (*238–44*)★

This strictly is not a Wall unit at all, for it was at High Rochester when that fort was not part of the Wall complex.

II LINGONUM EQUITATA (COHORS QUINGENARIA)

Originally raised: Germania Superior (*around Langres, eastern France*)
Diplomas: 98, 122, 124, 178
Under Marcus Aurelius: Ilkley
Notitia: Congavata★

There is no necessity to identify Congavata as Drumburgh, cf. p. 295. II Lingonum is also attested at Moresby.

IV LINGONUM EQUITATA (COHORS QUINGENARIA) (B)

Originally raised: Germania Superior (*around Langres, eastern France*)
Diplomas: 103, 122, 146
Third century: Wallsend
Notitia: Wallsend★

II NERVIORUM CIVIUM ROMANORUM (COHORS QUINGENARIA) (A)

Originally raised: Gallia Belgica (*in area of modern Belgium*)
Diplomas: 98, 122, 124, 146
Third century: Whitley Castle (*213*)★

This unit is recorded at Wallsend, Carrawburgh (a detachment) and possibly at Vindolanda (an altar found reused two miles from the fort). All of these forts have known third-century garrisons. A detachment of this cohort is attested together with a detachment of cohors IV Gallorum at High Rochester.

VI NERVIORUM (COHORS QUINGENARIA) (A)

Originally raised: Gallia Belgica (*in area of modern Belgium*)
Diplomas: 122, 124, 135, 146
Under Pius: Rough Castle★
Third century: Bainbridge (*205*)★
Notitia: Virosidum (Bainbridge?)★

It is attested at Great Chesters, where it could have been under Hadrian, but hardly later.

I PANNONIORUM EQUITATA (COHORS QUINGENARIA)

Originally raised: Pannonia (*modern Hungary*)

This regiment is included here because of RIB 1667, a tombstone of a soldier, apparently of this unit, from milecastle 42 which might have come from Great Chesters. Perhaps the soldier was in II Pannoniorum; the stone is broken.

II PANNONIORUM EQUITATA (COHORS QUINGENARIA)

Originally raised: Pannonia (*modern Hungary*)
Diplomas: 105, 124

Attested at Beckfoot. A lead seal from Vindolanda does not prove the unit's presence, as such seals were presumably fixed on goods in transit, cf. the evidence from Brough-under-Stainmore.

? RAETORUM (COHORS QUINGENARIA)

Originally raised: Raetia (*parts of Switzerland and Germany*)
Under Marcus Aurelius: Great Chesters (*166–9*)*

I THRACUM CIVIUM ROMANORUM (COHORS QUINGENARIA)

Originally raised: Thrace (*southern Bulgaria and European Turkey*)

This regiment was helping with building at Birdoswald in the early third century (RIB 1909). It may be distinct from the I Thracum equitata recorded on the 122 diploma, which was at Bowes in the early third century, and if so it may possibly have been based at Birdoswald as an extra unit in the third century.

II THRACUM EQUITATA (COHORS QUINGENARIA)

Originally raised: Thrace (*southern Bulgaria and European Turkey*)
Diplomas: 103, 122, 178
Third century: Moresby?
Notitia: Gabrosentum (Moresby?)*

The tombstone of a soldier, Nectovelius, found near Mumrills, may be either first or second century in date.

NUMERI

A number of irregular units may conveniently be grouped under this heading. They need not necessarily have anything in common in their organization apart from the fact that they are not *alae* or *cohortes*.

NUMERUS BARCARIORUM TIGRISIENSIUM

Notitia: South Shields*

This unit is apparently distinct from the *numerus barcariorum* attested at Lancaster, see now *Britannia* 4 (1973), 206–9 and cf. B. Dobson and D. J.

Breeze, *Army of Hadrian's Wall*, Newcastle upon Tyne, 1972, 47. The name means 'lightermen'; their precise function is unknown.

EXPLORATORES BREMENIENSES

Third century: High Rochester (238–44)*

The name means 'scouts'; a similar force existed at Risingham, and presumably at Netherby, which is called Castra Exploratorum ('camp of the scouts') in the Antonine Itinerary, see p. 144, cf. 146.

EXPLORATORES HABITANCENSES

Third century: Risingham (213)*

See discussion under the previous entry.

CUNEUS FRISIONUM ABALLAVENSIUM

Originally raised: Frisia (Holland)

Although mentioned on inscriptions at Papcastle in 241 the unit clearly belongs to Burgh (Aballava) and the inscriptions need not imply its presence at Papcastle, see above p. 261. A *cuneus* was a regiment of irregular cavalry.

CUNEUS FRISIORUM VER.

Originally raised: Frisia (*Holland*)
Third century: Housesteads (*Severus Alexander*)

A *cuneus* was a regiment of irregular cavalry.

NUMERUS HNAUDIFRIDI

Originally raised: Germany, *possibly from outside the Empire*
Third century: Housesteads

The inscription (RIB 1576) referring to this unit is undated, but the Alaisiagae honoured on it were goddesses brought to the fort by one of the units in the third century.

NUMERUS MAURORUM AURELIANORUM

Originally raised: North Africa
Third century: Burgh (253–8)*
Notitia: Burgh

As its earliest attestation is earlier than the emperor Aurelian the name must be derived from one of the earlier emperors, starting with Marcus Aurelius himself, who were known officially as Marcus Aurelius.

VEXILLATIO GAESATORUM RAETORUM

Originally raised: Raetia (*Switzerland and parts of Germany*)
Third century: Great Chesters

This is probably a distinct unit from the following one, as there is no reference to a *tribunus cohortis* in overall command.

RAETI GAESATI

Originally raised: Raetia (*Switzerland and parts of Germany*)
Third century: Risingham (*213*)*

See discussion under previous entry. The altar to IOM at Jedburgh (RIB 2117 – a carry from Cappuck?) presumably refers to an outposting from Risingham, as a tribune, who can only be a tribune of the milliary cohort stationed at the latter fort, is mentioned as being in overall command.

VENATORES BANNIENSES

Third century: Birdoswald

The third-century date is suggested in conformity with the appearance of the other irregular units on the Wall. It seems clear that this is a unit rather than a collection of the men in the cohort who held the post of *venator* ('hunter'); the form of the title – a place-name added to a descriptive term – is common to a number of irregular units, and J. C. Mann has furnished us with a parallel from the *Notitia, sagittarii venatores* (*Occ.* V 45). The term 'hunters' is not inappropriate for an army unit, but no more implies that the men concerned spent their time hunting animals than the term *vigiles* for the unit at Chester-le-Street implies that they were firemen.

APPENDIX 3

THE GODS WORSHIPPED ON THE WALL

The gods worshipped on Hadrian's Wall did not differ greatly from those worshipped by soldiers all over the Empire, and hardly at all from those worshipped in the rest of the military zone in Britain. Such differences as there were arose mainly in the cults peculiar to provinces or areas within provinces. On the Wall the native cults of Coventina, Antenociticus, Belatucadrus, Cocidius and Vitiris give a local flavour to a blend of beliefs that could otherwise be easily paralleled anywhere else in the Empire. There is the occasional varied response to an Empire-wide cult from province to province; thus in Britain unofficial emperor-worship found expression in the cult to the *numina Augusti*, while in other provinces similar feelings found expression in dedications to *domus divina*, not as popular in Britain. A god might even be imported by a unit, as Mars Thincsus was apparently at Housesteads. But there were no gods of the Wall as such.

Here the dedications from the forts on the line of the Wall, the outpost forts and those of the Cumbrian coast are examined. The evidence comes from inscriptions, the easiest to interpret; some account is taken of other evidence, which though important is often difficult to use because the god honoured is uncertain. The inscriptions and some other material from Corbridge, Carlisle and South Shields are also included; presumably because Corbridge had legionary connections and all three places had larger civilian populations, some gods are represented at these sites which are not known from the forts on the Wall. With these provisos we have here the attitudes of a typical cross-section of the auxiliaries of the army in Britain, and not very different from such a cross-section anywhere in the Empire.

THE OFFICIAL RELIGIONS

The official military calendar is best attested by the *Feriale Duranum*, a fascinating document showing the religious festivals observed by a unit of the Roman army, the *cohors XX Palmyrenorum*, at Dura-Europos in the third century.

The most obvious symbol of official religious activity is the great series of altars to Jupiter Best and Greatest, represented at practically every fort and in particularly large numbers at Birdoswald and Maryport. At Maryport they were discovered in great pits, where they had been buried at intervals. It seems that one was dedicated annually. The Maryport altars, mainly from the second century, show variation in phrasing between different garrisons. Where a prefect was commander for more than a year he seems to have dedicated only his first altar on behalf of the cohort; in succeeding years he dedicated each time in his own name. Maenius Agrippa at Maryport dedicated his 'personal' altars to 'IOM,* et numen Augusti'. Interestingly enough the only altar that varies from 'IOM' to 'IOM et numen Augusti' at Birdoswald is the only example of a second altar by the same prefect that has survived there. At Housesteads the regular dedication by the cohors I Tungrorum was to 'IOM et numina Augustorum'. Of the other two gods of the Capitoline Triad who presided over the destinies of Rome Juno is only honoured once, doubtfully and unofficially (the dedicator is a woman). If a statue at Corbridge is correctly identified the legionaries stationed there included Juno in official ceremonies. Minerva, the third member, apparently has a temple at High Rochester, with three dedications, two of them by tribunes. The cohort at Birrens honoured her while the dedication to Brigantia there portrays her with the attributes of Minerva Victrix. This last-named dedication was by an *architectus*, whose patron goddess would be Minerva. Elsewhere she is honoured by individuals, including another *architectus*. The Corbridge legionaries may have honoured her also, again in the guise of Minerva Victrix. However the Birrens dedications may be regarded simply as evidence for a local cult; auxiliaries

---

* IOM was the standard abbreviation for '*Iuppiter Optimus Maximusque*', 'Jupiter Best and Greatest'.

as opposed to legionaries worshipped only IOM of the Capitoline Triad. The point is re-emphasized by a new dedication from Carlisle, to the Capitoline Triad, Mars Pater and Victory – by a legionary tribune.

Other gods and goddesses are honoured by whole units, and such worship may have had at least a semi-official character. Local gods – such as Antenociticus at Benwell, Cocidius at Birdoswald, the Matres at Housesteads, and Silvanus at Moresby – were honoured, and the soldiers' gods – Hercules at Housesteads and Burgh, Mars at Vindolanda and Birdoswald, and a god brought in by a unit, Mars Thincsus, at Housesteads. At Maryport *cohors I Baetasiorum* has left two altars to Mars Militaris, as well as one to Jupiter, and two to Victoria Augusta. Dedications by commanding officers do not necessarily have any official character, but they may betray a unit's special reverence for a god when three commanders dedicate to the same deity, such as Hercules at Risingham. Coventina at Carrawburgh is a special case. Dedications to Mithras come into a different category, as Mithraism was an international religion well represented in the army at commanding officer level.

Jupiter Best and Greatest, with some support from Mars and Victory, dominated the parade-ground, and represented the traditions of Rome. The goddess Roma herself has only one doubtful semi-official dedication, though there was clearly a temple to her at Corbridge and she also appears on linked dedications from Maryport, discussed below. In the religious calendar the gods and festivals of Rome are overshadowed by the birthdays and accession days and victories of the god-emperors. Direct emperor-worship was, however, foreign to Roman sentiment. Dedications therefore are not to the emperor, but for his safety and well-being, *pro salute*, to his Victory or his Virtue (manliness rather than moral character) and his Discipline. There was an unofficial but widely spread cult of his *numen*, a difficult concept which represents his supernatural guiding spirit, his superhuman power and wisdom. It is only twice worshipped on its own in the group under study, by the cohort at Risingham and by an unknown dedicator at Halton. Normally it or they were revered (the concept would be plural, even for a single emperor) together with other gods, the official worship of Jupiter, Mars, and the standards, the classical god Mercury, the local god Antenociticus, the god of the unit Mars Thincsus, the eastern god Dolichenus, the regional god Maponus, and Celtic gods such as Mars Ocelus and the Matres. Most but not all dedications were by prefects and cohorts. In other provinces the worship of the *numina Augusti/Augustorum* was replaced by dedications on behalf of the imperial family, *domus divina*. In this group the only example of the latter type of dedication is at Vindolanda, where the *vicus*-dwellers in fact linked it with *numen*-worship.

The third element in the official religious worship was the gods of the army itself, particularly the standards which represented in sacred form loyalty to the unit and to one's comrades. The cult of the *signa* is represented at Birdoswald, coupled with the *numen*, and at High Rochester, where it is linked with the *genius* or guardian spirit both of the cohort and of the *exploratores* stationed there.

There then were the gods of the headquarters shrine and the parade-ground, or at least gods who might be honoured in their own temples by the unit as a whole. Outside these lay a whole wealth of deities; apart from the deities already referred to and such popular local gods as Belatucadrus and the Veteres, few could command large groups of worshippers. Even fewer were honoured in elaborate shrines, for which the offerings of the faithful had to pay.

A number of gods were concerned with the fort itself or its environs. At Vindolanda there is evidence for the worship of the spirit presiding over the commander's house, the *praetorium*. Three formal inscriptions were set up, in each case by the prefect of the cohort, and in two cases linked with Jupiter Best and Greatest. In the bath-house Fortuna, protectress of man in his naked helpless state against the evil eye, reigned supreme, sometimes described as Augusta or Conservatrix (Preserver). Fortuna Redux (Fortune the Homebringer) is worshipped on three occasions, all by tribunes, and on two of them at Maryport is linked with Roma Aeterna. One of these is further linked with the Genius Loci, the spirit that presided over the place, Maryport, and Bonum Fatum, good luck. A free rendering of the thought behind this might be: 'May the gods of this place be good to me, and Fortune bring me a quick posting home.' The commanding officer was perhaps the one man in the fort who had a home away from it to go to. In yet another manifestation, Fors Fortuna may have had her festival observed by the soldiers of Vindolanda.

The cavalry had special goddesses, the *matres campestres*, who were linked with the *genius* of the *ala* in a dedication by the prefect at Benwell, and the horse goddess Epona, who was the subject of a dedication at Carvoran.

THE GODS OF GREECE AND ROME

The gods of Greece and Rome without official altars did not fare well on the whole. They did occasionally receive sacrifices during the official round of festivals, it is true, but this did not ensure them regular worship. Identification with local gods may account for a number of dedications. Thus Mercury is quite well represented, in the towns possibly because of his commercial connections as god of travel and trade, but in the forts because of similarities to native gods. Caesar fastened on Mercury as the god most like the gods of Gaul. Neptune comes out quite well on dedications, perhaps because his associations were with flowing water, rivers as well as seas. Silvanus was a woodland god, worshipped under his own name and in identification with native gods. The two dedications to Asclepius, the god of medicine, one in Greek, one from South Shields, may have been dedicated by people with professional loyalties to the doctors' god. Vulcan the smith god is honoured by the *vicus*-dwellers at Vindolanda, and at Maryport by a prefect. Apollo, unfortunate in that his identification is with a rare native god, Maponus, is not well represented, and neither is Diana. Venus does not appear on inscriptions, nor does her associate Cupid, although there is perhaps a crude representation of her on a large sculpture from High Rochester. Here the number of pipe-clay figurines found of Venus give a more balanced picture. The private religion of an individual might well be represented by figurines, and not find expression in words on stone at all. Interestingly, there are no references to religion in the Vindolanda writing tablets, apart from festivals.

THE NATIVE GODS

The native gods rather overshadow those of Greece and Rome once the official ceremonies are over, apart from the soldiers' gods Mars and Hercules. Antenociticus at Benwell had his own temple and was revered by the unit, and Coventina at Carrawburgh, whatever her origin, native or imported, was honoured at every military and social level. Three other gods stand out for the number of their dedications, Belatucadrus, Cocidius, and the god or gods known to his worshippers as Vetris, Vitiris, Veteres, Votris, Hviteres, Hviteris and Hvitris. Belatucadrus is sometimes identified with Mars, and is mainly a god of the west; his inscriptions range from Carvoran to Netherby, with an outlying dedication at Carrawburgh. His worshippers have almost as much difficulty with spelling his name as the worshippers of Vetris, and like them are relatively unimportant socially. They do not put their names on their small altars, or they give one name rather than the three of the Roman citizen. An *optio* is the only soldier of any rank attested for Belatucadrus, an *imaginifer* for the Vetris god. Dedications to the Vetris god stretch along the Wall from Benwell to Carvoran, which has no fewer than sixteen dedications, and stop there, apart from an outlier at Netherby. There are now (1999) nine dedications known from Vindolanda. He is not identified with any Roman god, but is linked with Mogons at Netherby. Mogons is honoured at Risingham by a *beneficiarius consularis*, at High Rochester by a decurion, and at Vindolanda. The third native god honoured on a large scale is Cocidius. His dedications extend from Housesteads along the Wall to the area of Stanwix, and north to Risingham, Netherby and Bewcastle, where his dedications occur on silver plaques found in the headquarters building. It has been suggested that Bewcastle was Fanum Cocidi, the shrine of Cocidius, which according to the Ravenna Cosmography was in the general area (see p. 293). Cocidius is identified with Silvanus at Housesteads and associated with him at Risingham, but at Bewcastle and in the Castlesteads–Stanwix area Cocidius is identified with Mars. Cocidius is definitely of superior social status in comparison with Belatucadrus. He was honoured by the cohort at Birdoswald, by commanding officers at Housesteads, Vindolanda, Netherby and Bewcastle, and by soldiers of all three legions of Britain in the area between Birdoswald and Stanwix.

Maponus is also possibly a god of some social standing, but dedications to him are rare on the Wall and elsewhere. There is only one inscription in stone, which has no exact provenance, set up by four Germans; otherwise there are at Corbridge inscriptions by a prefect of the camp, a tribune and a legionary centurion. However, the discovery of a silver *lunula* from Vindolanda dedicated to Maponus extends the recorded area of the cult, but without knowledge of the dedicator, clearly a man of some wealth, firm conclusions can hardly be suggested. The same is true of the figure allegedly of Maponus associated with a serpent at Birrens.

The territorial deity is presumably Brigantia, but the few scattered dedications give no coherent pattern, though presumably the places where they were erected, South Shields, Corbridge and Birrens, fell in her territory.

A god clearly introduced from overseas is Mars Thincsus, brought to Housesteads by the *cuneus Frisiorum* or the *numerus Hnaudifridi* from Germania.

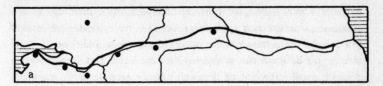

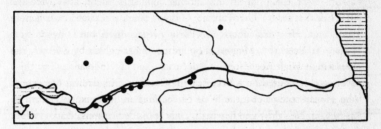

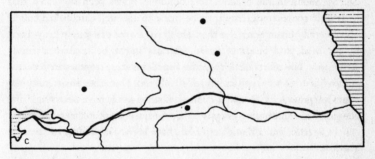

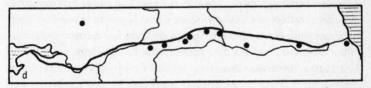

Fig. 35 Gods of the Wall. Distribution of the find-spots of altars to: a. Belatucadrus; b. Cocidius; c. Mogons; d. the Veteres.

Ricagambeda and Viradecthis were honoured by men from different districts in Germania serving in the *cohors II Tungrorum* at Birrens. The Hamians at Carvoran, originally recruited in Syria, worshipped Dea Syria, who was identified with Jupiter, Hammia and alone on the Wall IOM Heliopolitanus, the local deity of Heliopolis in Syria. Of more general appeal but also apparently first introduced from overseas was the cult of the mother goddesses, represented as a powerful triad. They have already been encountered as the protectresses of the cavalry parade-ground at Benwell. They also appear as goddesses of the overseas homeland (*tramarinae patriae*), common to all (*communes*), of all people (*omnium gentium*), of the household (*domesticae*), German, or just my mother goddesses (*suae*). They were also identified with the Fates (Parcae). Units, officers and individuals honour them, and their dedications are fairly evenly distributed. Apart from the special case of Coventina they are the most popular goddesses, not surprisingly perhaps.

The antecedents of a number of these gods are uncertain. Many gods who appear once or twice only on dedications are just names: Harimella, Iu, tres Lamiae (the three witches), Latis (twice), Matunus, Ratis (twice), Saitada and Setlocenia.

In this context reference may be made to the well-established cult of the severed human head. For the Celt all the virtue of a slain enemy dwelt in his head, and heads of noted warriors might be treated as family heirlooms. The efforts made to secure and retain these trophies are reflected in a number of scenes from Trajan's Column. This passed naturally into their religious activity, and a number of stone heads have been found and identified as cult objects – so many that the question of authenticity arises. They are nameless, although attempts have been made to identify some of them.

Before turning to those gods from the East who established themselves all over the Roman world a word may be said on the process by which different gods with similar attributes were identified as one and the same. Thus Maponus was identified with Apollo. Belatucadrus was identified with Mars. Brigantia at one stage was identified with Caelestis, and on another occasion given the attributes of Minerva Victrix. The Matres were identified with the Parcae. The two non-Roman gods, Vitiris and Mogons, are identified with each other. Most strikingly of all Cocidius appears to be identified in one area with Mars, in another with Silvanus. However, if the figure in a rock-chamber shrine near High Rochester is Cocidius, the division into geographical areas breaks down, as Cocidius here would appear identified as Mars in the 'Silvanus' area. This last example also shows the problems that might arise over identification. The Graeco-Roman gods had become specialized, dealing with some aspect of human activities, though they often retained other aspects than those we immediately associate with them. The Celtic gods were less specialized, differing in territory rather than in characteristics, so any identification with a specialist god would be an inadequate representation of the Celtic god's sphere of activity. Cocidius sometimes seemed like Mars, sometimes like Silvanus, sometimes completely different from either. It is not surprising that Mars is a frequent identification, for the warrior aspect of the tribal god is bound to be very pronounced, though it should also be remembered that Mars himself is much more than simply a warrior god: he is concerned with agriculture and fertility. A number of identifications of him with Celtic gods from other areas turn up in the towns, Mars Alator at South Shields, Mars Barrex and Mars Ocelus at Carlisle, reflecting the larger and more cosmopolitan civilian population in these places.

The identification of Jupiter with the local supreme deity was a natural one. It has already been seen in the case of IOM Heliopolitanus. In the case of Jupiter of Doliche, a town in Syria, however, the worship of the god identified with Jupiter oversprang any local boundaries. He had his own group of associated subordinate deities, Sun, Moon and Heavenly Twins, and is honoured in Britain at four Wall forts, three outpost forts and at Corbridge, where fragments of a temple survive. Corbridge seems to have harboured a community receptive to eastern influences, for Astarte and Heracles of Tyre, Phoenician deities, are honoured there. Both inscriptions are in Greek, the latter by a priestess, and here perhaps someone from the East was brought in to serve the temple, for Greek although common in the eastern Empire would have been in Britain restricted to traders and other travellers from the East, and to the well-educated. Also at Corbridge the Magna Mater, Cybele, centre of an Oriental and orgiastic cult, was worshipped.

MITHRAS

The cult that has attracted most modern attention is that of Mithras. He had his special temples (*mithraea*) at Rudchester, Carrawburgh and Housesteads, and dedications at Castlesteads and High Rochester may suggest that there are temples to be found there also. At no Wall site are both Mithras and Dolichenus recorded. Mithraism was a Roman adaptation of an ancient religion of the East, centring on the struggle between light and darkness, good and evil. A subordinate figure in the original concept,

Mithras came to be the one most invoked. Born from the rock, he pursued, caught, brought back to his cave and killed the bull, thereby releasing creative power for mankind. This bull-slaying, the act of redemption, generally formed the central scene in every *mithraeum*. *Mithraea* often recalled the cave in their form. The best-preserved one on the Wall, at Carrawburgh, was basically a nave with benches on either side, with a sanctuary at one end and at the other a narthex, an ante-room for those not yet initiated. It was dimly lit by clerestory lighting. After a farewell feast Mithras had returned to heaven to be men's guide and aide, and his votaries after initiation shared ritual meals, progressing from grade to grade by ordeals. The cult appealed to the army, officers in particular, for Mithras was the Unconquered, but it was exclusively male and did not demand unconditional and exclusive allegiance, two grave weaknesses. It bulks large in our thought, for it attracted the special hatred of Christians, largely because of what were thought to be blasphemous imitations of the Christian gospel and its rites. However, it never came near to being universal. The worshippers recorded on the Wall are senior officers, mainly commanders of auxiliary units, and the history of the Carrawburgh *mithraeum* suggests that it was often difficult to find sufficient initiates in the fort to keep services going.

OTHER TEMPLES

Mithraea are very specialized temples. Other temples tend to be either classical, rectangular on a raised platform, or Roman–Celtic, small square, polygonal or circular shrines surrounded by porticoes. Neither type was intended for congregational worship; people made individual vows. On feast days ceremonies could be held in the open air. There are no big temples on the Wall; there were too many competing cults. Temples are not always easy to recognize on excavation, and inscriptions do not necessarily demonstrate their presence, unless they appear in large numbers. There was at least one temple at Wallsend (RIB 1305) but the god is not known, and perhaps the figure of Mercury came from that or another temple. It is uncertain whether the two inscriptions of VI Victrix (RIB 1319, 1320) came from a shrine on the Tyne bridge. The temple of Antenociticus at Benwell is known, a simple apsidal building. The Campestres also had a temple there, as the dedication refers to its restoration. A *mithraeum* is known at Rudchester, and a temple to the Matres existed somewhere near milecastle 19. Carrawburgh had its *mithraeum*, the shrine of Coventina, built in the Roman–Celtic style, a shrine to the Nymphs, and perhaps another temple. At Housesteads there was a *mithraeum*, and a temple to Mars Thincsus which has been provisionally identified. At Carvoran a temple appears to have been built to a god 'M . .' At Castlesteads a temple was restored to the Matres, and apparently a temple was dedicated to the same deities at Bowness. There seems a strong case for a temple to Mercury at Birrens, where there was a guild of worshippers, and the inscriptions all come from the same building. A temple to an unknown god was restored by the cohort at Netherby. A fragmentary inscription at Netherby probably implies the existence of another temple. Three altars to Minerva in a building outside the fort at High Rochester point to a temple there, as does the existence of a guild of worshippers, and an inscription implies the construction of a *mithraeum* there. At South Shields there was a temple to an unknown goddess. A shrine is mentioned at Carlisle. At Corbridge there is a well-known group of temples, but not all are definitely temples, and none can be assigned to a particular deity. Sculptural fragments suggest a temple to Dolichenus and another to Dea Roma. The altars from Maryport may imply the presence of a temple to Jupiter there. All this shows the urgent need for a complete plan of the environs of a Wall fort, showing the temples. A minimum of three or four outside every fort ought to be allowed for. In a different category is the shrine in a rock-chamber near High Rochester to a native god, perhaps Cocidius.

OTHER RELIGIOUS OBJECTS

No attempt is made here to enter into a discussion in detail of the assemblage of religious objects other than dedications. Among famous objects may be mentioned the sculpture of the Genii Cucullati at Housesteads, a triad of cowled Celtic deities, the pots from Corbridge which display a Celtic smith god (not Dolichenus), the pottery mould also from Corbridge which shows apparently the god Taranis with his wheel and the silver lanx. The decoration of the lanx connects it with the Greek mystery religions of the East, but it is an imported object belonging to some rich individual, and does not imply any important influence of these religions in the area. On the other hand it adds to the evidence of eastern religions at Corbridge.

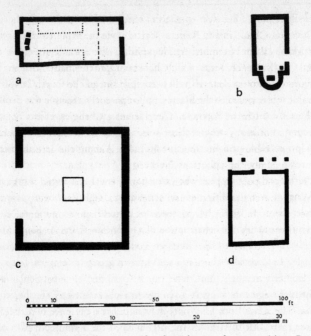

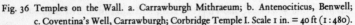

Fig. 36 Temples on the Wall. a. Carrawburgh Mithraeum; b. Antenociticus, Benwell; c. Coventina's Well, Carrawburgh; Corbridge Temple I. Scale 1 in. = 40 ft (1 : 480).

THE STRENGTH OF PAGANISM

Before turning to Christianity one more element remains to be emphasized. Paganism on the whole was not strong on theology or organization. It was strong in its ability to respond to the needs of all men. Intellectuals might need philosophical systems or mystics the mystery religions, and they got them; ordinary people were just afraid, superstitious, anxious to protect themselves against malign powers. There is therefore a goodly element of magic, amulets and charms, in the lives of the people studied here. One very clear example of this is the appearance of phallic symbols, representing fertility and good fortune, and therefore potent against the evil eye, on structures and as finds. They appear at Chesters on the lowest course of the bath-house basement, on the bridge abutment, and in the headquarters courtyard, and on the curtain wall rebuilt in stone east of Birdoswald. They remind us forcibly of the element of straightforward fear.

CHRISTIANITY

What about Christianity? There is scarcely one piece of material evidence from the Wall that has not been disputed. There are two reasons for this shortage of evidence. First of all, Christianity at this period did not leave much in the way of material relics. Inscriptions of the fourth century are rare in Britain, and the formulae on the tombstones that survive may have been used by Christians but not exclusively. Christian churches of this period are not always easy to recognize. The chi-rho sign is perhaps the only indisputable evidence, but it tells us little about the date and nothing about the number of Christians involved.

The second point is that when Constantine was converted and gave the Christian church peace from persecution in 312, Christians were a minority in the Empire. Indeed A. H. M. Jones reckoned them a tiny minority, and predominantly in the urban lower class. Although Constantine banned sacrifices and confiscated temple lands and treasures, sacrifice was tolerated from 361 to 391, and at other times the law against it was laxly enforced. It is no surprise then that Coventina's Well, for instance, continued to receive offerings. Not till the early fifth century were pagans excluded from governmental positions, and although the army must have had its official calendar modified to suit Christian beliefs, as the military oath was, the army remained a stronghold of paganism. The pagans had the advantage that unlike Christians, who had jibbed in the past over observing pagan rites, they made no difficulty over observing official Christian rites; there were few pagan martyrs. But the strength of paganism lay in its deep roots in the age-old practices of peasants, and for the educated in the traditions, literature and glory of Rome. It is therefore unlikely that Christianity on any scale came to the Wall before 312, and thereafter its main channel was probably as the official military religion. The official gods were displaced and perhaps other gods of Greece and Rome who had no strong local roots. The local gods no doubt held on as did Coventina. The temples of Mithras may have come in for harsh treatment, though if so not on any general legal basis. The first recorded official act against a *mithraeum* was the destruction of one in Rome in 377; individual temples could be destroyed on petition. Thus the most positive evidence for Christianity on the Wall may be acts of destruction, at Rudchester and Carrawburgh.

Recent work has added a little more in the way of possible evidence. A church has been suggested at Housesteads, based on an uncertain interpretation of an old excavation report. A church-like building has been uncovered at Vindolanda, apparently of an immediately post-Roman date. At South Shields it has been suggested that there was a Christian altar in the headquarters courtyard, within a building which might have been a church.

This is not the whole story; there is evidence that the Celtic kingdoms, both those that grew up in the Lowlands, Strathclyde and Manau Gododdin, and those that succeeded Roman Britain in northern England, were Christian in the fifth century. Patrick, a third-generation Christian, may have come from north-west England in the early fifth century, and Bede retains the tradition that Ninian was bishop at Whithorn early in the fifth century and apostolized the southern Picts. It is possible that Christianity made substantial progress in the north during the last decades of Roman Britain and therefore began to affect seriously the beliefs of the men on the Wall. But the evidence is still to be found.

APPENDIX 4

THE ROMAN NAMES OF THE FORTS
ON HADRIAN'S WALL

The sources for the Roman names of the forts on the Wall, the outpost forts and those on the Cumbrian coast are as follows:

The Rudge Cup and Amiens Skillet. These are a small bowl and skillet (small vessel with a long handle) respectively, with a running border around their rims representing the Wall, and carrying the names of the Wall forts in the western sector. Presumably there were matching vessels completing the series. The absolute date suggested for the Rudge Cup on the basis of its decoration is *c.* 150, but a date when the Wall was standing empty seems improbable, and the evidence does not rule out the reign of Hadrian, a more probable date.

The Antonine Itinerary. This is apparently a collection of some 225 routes used for particular journeys. The longest route has been associated with a journey taken by the emperor Caracalla, but this does not necessarily date the others. There is a discussion of the date of the route which includes Blatobulgium (Birrens) and Castra Exploratum (Netherby) above (p. 148).

The Notitia Dignitatum. An official document which gives among other things a list of army units under the command of the generals of the Empire. The date of the British section has been much discussed. Here the view is taken that this part of the document dates to the very end of the Roman period of Britain, *c.* 411. The section includes a sub-section entitled 'also, along the line of the wall' and the certain identifications show garrisons which are the same as those known in the late second and early third century.

The Ravenna Cosmography. A compilation of the late seventh century of the countries, towns and rivers of the known world. The British section seems to be based on reading off names from roadbooks or maps.

There is no debate about the names of the forts on the Wall reading east to west from Wallsend to Great Chesters. The difficulty lies in fitting names to the known forts west of Great Chesters, as the sources disagree among themselves. No satisfactory solution has yet been offered. The suggestions here, which are not original, differ from the present conventional solution for reasons which will be explained.

THE RUDGE CUP AND THE AMIENS SKILLET

A start may be made with the Rudge Cup and Amiens Skillet. These differ only in that the latter has an extra name, that of Aesica, Great Chesters. As has been noted, all the forts from Great Chesters eastwards have agreed names, so the cup and skillet must cover the forts to the west. They give the same five names in the same order:

A MAIS   ABALLAVA   UXELODUM   CAMBOGLANS   BANNA

Seven forts are known between Bowness and Great Chesters inclusive: Bowness, Drumburgh, Stanwix, Castlesteads, Birdoswald, Carvoran and Great Chesters. The formula is A MAIS i.e. starting from Maiae, so it seems reasonable to conclude that the starting-point is Bowness and the direction west to east, a conclusion confirmed by the addition of Esica (Great Chesters) on the end of the Amiens Skillet. The next fort to Bowness, Drumburgh, is very small, and may be discounted, particularly as there is strong evidence that Burgh-by-Sands is Aballava. It would seem logical to continue westwards and identify Stanwix as Uxelodum, Castlesteads as Camboglans, and Birdoswald as Banna. Opportunely an inscription from Birdoswald refers to a unit called the *venatores Bannienses*; normally this would be sufficient to establish that Birdoswald was Banna. The omission of Carvoran on the Amiens Skillet may be explained by its location south of the Wall line, beyond the Vallum; Castlesteads though south of the Wall

Fort	Rudge Cup, Amiens Skillet	Ravenna	Notitia Dignitatum	Other
South Shields			Arbeia	
Wallsend		Serduno	Segeduno	
Newcastle			Ponte Aeli	
Benwell		Condecor	Conderco	
Rudchester		Vindovala	Vindobala	
Halton Chesters		Onno	Hunno	
Chesters		Celuno	Cilurno	
Carrawburgh		Brocoliti	Procolitia	
Housesteads		Velurtion	Borcovicio	Ver-*
Vindolanda		Vindolande	Vindolana	Vindolandess -es*
Great Chesters	Esica	Esica	Aesica	
Carvoran		Magnis	Magnis	
Birdoswald	Banna	Banna		Bannienses*
Castlestead	Camboglans	Gabaglanda	Amboglanna	
Stanwix	Uxelodum	Uxelludamo	Petrianis	
Burgh-by-Sands	Aballava	Avalana	Aballaba	
Drumburgh				
Bowness	Mais	Maia		
Beckfoot (??)		Bribra		
Maryport (?)		Alauna		
Burrow Walls				
Moresby (??)		Gabrocentio	Gabrosenti	
(St Bees ??)		Iuliocenon	Tunnocelo	
Birrens				Blatobulgium†
Netherby				Castra exploratum†
Bewcastle (?)		Fanocodi		
Risingham				Habitanci*
High Rochester				Brem–* Bremenium†

* From an inscription.
† From the Antonine Itinerary.

line is included by the Vallum and was one of the primary forts. Sir Ian Richmond long ago pointed out that the Ravenna list also omitted Magnae (Carvoran), and concluded that the cup and skillet were based on itineraries. This is not necessarily so; no road linked the Wall forts till the Military Way was built, well after the latest date proposed for the cup, and if the cup and skillet were to refer to the Wall, as their decoration suggests, there need be no direct reference to an itinerary. The correspondence may show only that Carvoran was not felt to belong to the Wall by the designers of the cup and skillet, and that Carvoran was classed as part of the Stanegate itinerary by the compilers of Ravenna.

THE NOTITIA DIGNITATUM

The difficulty in accepting these identifications lies in reconciling them with the *Notitia* list. This follows the line of forts westwards from Wallsend, giving wherever it can be checked the third-century garrison still in place, except at Great Chesters, where I Asturum replaces II Asturum, but this surely is a scribal error. The relevant section following Great Chesters reads:

tribunus cohortis secundae Dalmatarum, Magnis
tribunus cohortis primae Aeliae Dacorum, Amboglanna
praefectus alae Petrianae, Petrianis
praefectus numeri Maurorum Aurelianorum, Aballaba
tribunus cohortis secundae Lingonum, Congavata
tribunus cohortis primae Hispanorum, Axeloduno
tribunus cohortis secundae Thracum, Gabrosenti
tribunus cohortis primae Aeliae classicae, Tunnocelo
tribunus cohortis primae Morinorum, Glannibanta
tribunus cohortis tertiae Nerviorum, Alione

If the list of identifications proposed for the Rudge Cup and Amiens Skillet is compared with this:

Banna	*Birdoswald*
Camboglanna	*Castlesteads*
Uxellodunum	*Stanwix*
Aballava	*Burgh*
Maiae	*Bowness*

it will be noted that neither Banna nor Maiae appears in the *Notitia* list; Axelodunum if the same as Uxellodunum is not placed between Aballava and Camboglanna; Birdoswald, the home of *cohors I Aelia Dacorum* on incontrovertible inscriptional evidence, is called Camboglanna; Stanwix, the home of the *ala Petriana*, is called Petriana. One solution is to suppose that Banna on the Rudge Cup and Amiens Skillet is Bewcastle, an outpost fort evacuated by the time that the *Notitia* was compiled. This, however, supposes that the omission of Stanwix results from the list being taken from an itinerary, on which Stanwix was replaced by Carlisle. However, this is hardly satisfactory; the cup and skillet represent the Wall, not a road, and to include one and only one outpost fort instead of a major Wall fort would seem a remarkable error. Moreover this explanation is only acceptable on the assumption that the one inscription mentioning Banna, of the *venatores Bannienses* at Birdoswald, was set up there by troops garrisoned at Bewcastle or carried there from that fort. The alternative view that Banna is Carvoran has the same difficulties, and involves the further assumption that Magnis in the *Notitia* is a corruption of Banna.

There is a way out of these difficulties following a suggestion by M. Hassall that on the *Notitia* list the name Banna and the unit at Camboglanna have been omitted in later copying. We may add that it is likely that the name of the unit, Petriana (otherwise unattested as a place-name), has been repeated by mistake, displacing Axeloduno (Uxellodunum), which has then been attached, equally mistakenly, to *cohors I Hispanorum*. (A suggestion in a previous edition that Axelduno might be another name for Netherby is to be rejected, following A. L. F. Rivet and C. Smith.) The following result is obtained:

tribunus cohortis secundae Dalmatarum, Magnis [*Carvoran*]
tribunus cohortis primae Aeliae Dacorum, *Banna* [*Birdoswald*]
tribunus cohortis secundae Tungrorum, Amboglanna [*Castlesteads*]
praefectus alae Petrianae, *Uxelloduno* [*Stanwix*]
praefectus numeri Maurorum Aurelianorum, Aballaba [*Burgh*]
tribunus cohortis secundae Lingonum, Congavata
tribunus cohortis primae Hispanorum, Axeloduno

It is tempting to identify Congavata as Drumburgh, and assume that the missing fort for *cohors I Hispanorum* is Maiae (Bowness), but there is no reference to Bribra and Alauna, mentioned in the Ravenna Cosmography and generally identified with the next two forts down the Cumbrian coast, Beckfoot and Maryport respectively. It is possible that after Aballava the *Notitia* simply lists the forts held in the north-west.

The modifications may seem outrageous but they are preferable to assuming the omission of Stanwix on the Rudge Cup and Amiens Skillet; the inclusion of Bewcastle and no other outpost fort on them; the setting-up of a stone by a unit stationed at Bewcastle at Birdoswald or that stone's transport there; the name of Stanwix to be the otherwise unattested Petriana – every other fort name on the Wall is attested twice with the significant exception of Congavata.

THE RAVENNA COSMOGRAPHY

The evidence of the Ravenna Cosmography must now be examined. It is important to keep to the order of the relevant sections, since if a site has already appeared in the lists it is passed over in silence:

Ravenna	Antonine Itinerary	Notitia	Modern name
Aluna			
Camuloduno			
Calunio	Galacum		Burrow-in-Lonsdale (?)
Gallunio	Galava		Ambleside
Mediobogdo			Hardknott
Cantiventi	Clanoventa	Glannibanta	Ravenglass
Iuliocenon		Tunnocelo	
Gabrocentio		Gabrosenti	
Alauna			
Bribra			
Maio			
Derventione			
Bravoniaco	Brovonacis		Kirkby Thore

If Maio is Maia the four forts lying between it and Clanoventa (Ravenglass) in the Ravenna list may be Cumbrian coast forts, and two of those names appear in the *Notitia*. However, it is most unusual for a name to appear twice in the Ravenna list, and the possibility cannot be excluded that Maio represents another fort. There could perhaps be a fort between Beckfoot and Bowness, for the gap between them is 14⅔ miles (23.5 km) two-fifths of the total distance from Bowness to Moresby. The list continues below.

Ravenna	Itinerary	Notitia	Modern name
Valteris	Verteris	Verteris	Brough-under-Stainmore
Bereda	Voreda		Old Penrith
Lagubalumi	Luguvallo		Carlisle
Magnis		Magnis	Carvoran
Gabaglanda		[C]amboglanna	Castlesteads (?)
Vindolanda		Vindolana	Chesterholm

The road to Carlisle is now followed through Brough-under-Stainmore, Old Penrith and Carlisle, then the writer moves his finger up the Maiden Way from Kirkby Thore, already mentioned so not repeated, to the fort near the junction with the Stanegate, Carvoran. He then lists the fort immediately to the west, Camboglanna, and the fort immediately to the east, Vindolanda. On the interpretation adopted here Camboglanna would be Castlesteads. As that fort probably preceded Hadrian's Wall, though it was carefully incorporated into it by the Vallum, it may well have had a road link with the Stanegate. The conventional identification with Birdoswald has to find a road link, and explain why the writer did not then naturally follow up the road which ran from Birdoswald to Bewcastle, Banna on the conventional interpretation. Instead he moves to the line of the Wall as shown on the next page:

Newcastle is omitted by Ravenna, curiously, but then we know little of its history. The next omission is of Magnis, already mentioned in Ravenna, and not apparently regarded as belonging to the Wall on the Amiens Skillet. Camboglanna is also omitted by the Ravenna but not by the Rudge Cup and Amiens Skillet, so they are not working from the same source. Ravenna omitted it because it had been mentioned already. The omission of Banna from the *Notitia* is startling; Banna cannot be identical with Magnis for in Ravenna both names appear. There follows the entries for the fort Uxellodunum; clearly Stanwix must either be omitted altogether

Ravenna	Rudge Cup, Amiens Skillet	Notitia	Modern name
Serduno		Segeduna	Wallsend
		Ponte Aeli[o]	Newcastle
Condecor		Conderco	Benwell
Vindovala		Vindobala	Rudchester
Onno		Hunno	Halton Chesters
Celuno		Cilurno	Chesters
Brocoliti		Procolitia	Carrawburgh
Velurtion		Borcovicio	Housesteads
Esica	Esica	Aesica	Great Chesters
		Magnis	Carvoran
Banna	Banna		Birdoswald (?)
	Camboglans	[C]amboglanna	Castlesteads (?)
Uxelludamo	Uxelodum	Petrianis	Stanwix
Avalana	Aballava	Aballaba	Burgh-by-Sands
Maia	Mais		Bowness

from Ravenna, the Rudge Cup and the Amiens Skillet or be Uxellodunum. The argument that an itinerary would only mention Carlisle and omit Stanwix is invalid. The list in Ravenna is following either the Wall or the Military Way; in either case the list must have come to Stanwix, and there is no warrant to suppose Stanwix was subsumed in Carlisle. The Rudge Cup and Amiens Skillet had nothing but the Wall to follow.

SUMMARY

Ravenna, the cup and the skillet agree that there were three forts between Aesica = Great Chesters and Aballava = Burgh-by-Sands. It seems to solve more problems to assume that Banna = Birdoswald, confirmed by an inscription, Camboglanna = Castlesteads and Uxellodunum = Stanwix. This interpretation seems better to explain the Rudge Cup and Amiens Skillet, take proper account of the inscription of the *venatores Bannienses*, and is at least as easy to reconcile with the Ravenna Cosmography as the traditional explanation that Banna = Bewcastle or Carvoran, Camboglanna = Birdoswald and Uxellodunum = Castlesteads. It supposes, following M. Hassall, a bad blunder in the *Notitia* list as we have it, but on any interpretation so far offered there is a blunder; the point at issue is its nature and magnitude.

ADDITIONAL NOTE

Recent discoveries at Ravenglass suggest the *cohors I Aelia classica* was stationed there, certainly in A.D. 158. This could mean that Ravenglass is the *Notitia*'s Tunnocelum (correct form Itunocelum) in which case a new identification for Glannibanta must be sought. Equally the unit may have changed location between 158 and the early years of the fifth century.

APPENDIX 5

THE EVIDENCE ON
THE GROUND

The list is not exhaustive, but it contains the best places to see the visible
evidence relating to the building and history of Hadrian's Wall.

GENERAL

Stone curtain: East of 39, Thorny Doors (41a–b: highest standing stretch),
    Walltown Crags, Willowford–Birdoswald

Turf wall: 49b–51

  Section: Appletree

Ditch: Chesters–Sewingshields, Carvoran, Willowford–Appletree

  End of a ditch at crags: Sewingshields (34)

  Uncompleted ditch: Limestone Corner (30)

Turrets: 7b (Denton, 48a (Willowford east), 52a (Banks east), Peel Gap

Milecastles: 37 (Housesteads), 48 (Poltross Burn), 39 (Castle Nick)

Forts

  General: Wallsend, Chesters, Housesteads, Great Chesters, Birdoswald,
    South Shields

  Defences: Carrawburgh (fort platform)

  Walls: Housesteads, Vindolanda, Birdoswald

  Ditches: Great Chesters, Carrawburgh

  Gates: Chesters east (both) and west (iron collars for door pivots),
    Housesteads west (bar holes), Birdoswald east (both), South Shields
    (reconstruction)

  Wall towers: Chesters, Birdoswald

Headquarters buildings: Chesters, Housesteads, Vindolanda, South Shields
Strong rooms: Chesters, Great Chesters, South Shields (note window sill)
Commanding officer's house: Housesteads, Vindolanda
Granaries: Housesteads, South Shields
Hospital: Housesteads (?)
Barracks: Chesters, Housesteads, South Shields
Latrine: Housesteads, Vindolanda, South Shields
Water tanks: Housesteads
Aqueduct: Great Chesters, South Shields
Bath-houses: Chesters, Vindolanda
Bridges: Chesters, Willowford
Vallum: Cawfields, Limestone Corner
Crossing: Benwell

THE BUILDING OF THE WALL

Milecastles
   Legion A: 37 (Housesteads), 42 (Cawfields)
   Legion B: 35 (Sewingshields), 39 (Castle Nick) (both gates later modified)
   Legion C: 48 (Poltross Burn)
Turrets
   Legion A: 41a (Caw Gap)
   Legion B: 7b (Denton), 26b (Brunton)
   Legion C: 48a and b (Willowford)
Curtain
   Broad wall standard A: 7b (Denton), Heddon (11b–12)
   Broad wall standard B: Willowford (48a–Bridge) (the broad wall standard
     B has the later narrow wall standard A on top)
   Narrow wall standard A: Shield-on-the-Wall (41a)
   Narrow wall standard C: Walltown (45a–b), Birdoswald sector (49–49a)
Narrow wall turret
   legion uncertain: 44b (Mucklebank)
Points of reduction from broad wall to narrow wall
   Curtain: Planetrees (26a)
   Milecastles: 42 (Cawfields), 48 (Poltross Burn)
   Turrets: 26b (Brunton), 29a (Blackcarts), 48a and b (Willowford)
   Narrow wall on broad wall: 49–Willowford Bridge, Chesters Bridge
   Narrow wall on broad foundation: Shield-on-the-Wall (41a)

Relationship between forts and curtain

    Turret demolished and replaced by fort: Housesteads (36b)

    Narrow wall and fort walls bonding: Chesters, Housesteads north-west corner, Great Chesters

    Narrow wall abutting fort wall: Housesteads north-east corner, Birdoswald

Turf wall

    Turrets: 51a (Piper Syke), 51b (Lea Hill), 52a (Banks east)

    Realignment of wall: Birdoswald north-west corner

    New stone milecastle: 49 (Harrow's Scar)

    New stone turret: 49b (Birdoswald)

HISTORY OF THE WALL

Turrets

    Raising of threshold: 33b (Coesike)

    Blocking of recess: 33b (Coesike), 35a (Sewingshields Crag), 41b (Caw Gap)

Milecastles

    Narrowing of gates: 37 (Housesteads), 48 (Poltross Burn), 49 (Harrow's Scar)

    Rebuilding of gate: 39 (Castle Nick)

    Rebuilding of accommodation: 35 (Sewingshields), 48 (Poltross Burn)

Gate through wall: Knag Burn (Housesteads)

Forts

    Severan supply base: South Shields

    Blocking of gates: Great Chesters west gate, Birdoswald east gate, Housesteads east gate, Chesters south gate

    Headquarters buildings: Housesteads (remodelling of rear rooms, partitioning of verandah), Vindolanda (storerooms in courtyard, hypocaust in rear room), South Shields (hypocausts in rear rooms)

    Commanding officer's house: Chesters, Vindolanda

    Barracks: Housesteads and Great Chesters (rebuilt in early fourth century)

    Civil settlements: Vindolanda (houses, shops, *mansio*), Housesteads (houses and shops), Carrawburgh (temples of Mithras and Coventina), Benwell (temple of Antenociticus)

RECONSTRUCTIONS

Stone wall: Wallsend, Vindolanda

Turf wall: Vindolanda

Turf wall milecastle: Vindolanda

Stone turret: Vindolanda

Fort gate: South Shields

Bath-house: Wallsend

Civil settlement buildings: Vindolanda

MUSEUMS

Main collections: Newcastle upon Tyne (Museum of Antiquities), Carlisle (Tullie House), South Shields (Roman Remains Park), Corbridge, Chesters, Housesteads, Vindolanda; Birdoswald; Carvoran (Roman Army Museum), Maryport (Senhouse Roman Museum)

SELECT BIBLIOGRAPHY

LIST OF ABBREVIATIONS

AA[2-5]	*Archaeologia Aeliana*, series 2–5
Birley	Eric Birley, *The Roman Army: Papers 1929–1986*, Amsterdam, 1988.
Breeze/Dobson	David J. Breeze and Brian Dobson, *Roman Officers and Frontiers*, Stuttgart, 1993.
CIL	*Corpus Inscriptionum Latinarum*
Handbook	J. C. Bruce, *Handbook to the Roman Wall* (13th edn by Charles Daniels), Newcastle upon Tyne, 1978
ILS	H. Dessau, *Inscriptiones Latinae Selectae*, Berlin, 1893–1916
JRS	*Journal of Roman Studies*
Mann	J. C. Mann (ed.), *The Northern Frontier in Britain from Hadrian to Honorius: Literary and Epigraphic Sources*, Newcastle upon Tyne, n.d. [1971]
PSAS	*Proceedings of the Society of Antiquaries of Scotland*
RIB	R. G. Collingwood and R. P. Wright, *The Roman Inscriptions of Britain*, Oxford, 1965
TAASDN	*Transactions of the Architectural and Archaeological Society of Durham and Northumberland*
Tab. Vindol. II	Alan K. Bowman and J. David Thomas, *The Vindolanda Writing-Tablets (Tabulae Vindolandenses II)*, London, 1994
TCWAAS	*Transactions of the Cumberland and Westmorland Antiquarian and Archaeological Society*

TSSAHS	*Transactions of the South Shields Archaeological and Historical Society*
ZPE	*Zeitschrift für Papyrologie und Epigraphik*

GENERAL WORKS

P. Bidwell, *Hadrian's Wall 1989–99*, South Shields, 1999.

A. R. Birley, *The Fasti of Roman Britain*, Oxford, 1981.

E. Birley, *Research on Hadrian's Wall*, Kendal, 1961.

R. E. Birley, *Vindolanda, a Roman Frontier Fort on Hadrian's Wall*, London, 1977.

D. J. Breeze, *The Northern Frontiers of Roman Britain*, London, 1982.

D. J. Breeze and B. Dobson, 'Hadrian's Wall: some problems', *Britannia*, 3 (1972), 182–208.

D. J. Breeze and B. Dobson, 'Roman military deployment in North Britain', *Britannia*, 16 (1985), 1–19.

J. C. Bruce, *Handbook to the Roman Wall* (13th edn by Charles Daniels), Newcastle upon Tyne, 1978.

R. G. Collingwood and I. A. Richmond, *The Archaeology of Roman Britain*, London, 1969.

C. M. Daniels, 'Problems of the Roman northern frontier', *Scottish Archaeological Forum*, 2 (1970), 91–101.

C. M. Daniels, *The Eleventh Pilgrimage of Hadrian's Wall 26 August–1 September 1989*, Newcastle upon Tyne, 1989.

B. Dobson, 'The function of Hadrian's Wall', *AA*⁵ 14 (1986), 1–30.

S. S. Frere, *Britannia* (3rd edn), London, 1987.

J. P. Gillam, 'The frontier after Hadrian – a history of the problem', *AA*⁵ 2 (1974), 1–15.

J. P. Gillam and J. C. Mann, 'The northern British frontier from Antoninus Pius to Caracalla', *AA*⁴ 48 (1970), 1–44.

B. R. Hartley, 'The Roman occupation of Scotland: the evidence of samian ware', *Britannia*, 3 (1972), 1–55.

M. G. Jarrett and J. C. Mann, 'Britain from Agricola to Gallienus', *Bonner Jahrbücher*, 170 (1970), 178–210.

J. C. Mann (ed.), *The Northern Frontier in Britain from Hadrian to Honorius: Literary and Epigraphic Sources*, Newcastle upon Tyne, n.d. [1971].

J. C. Mann, 'The northern frontier after A.D. 369', *Glasgow Archaeological Journal*, 3 (1974), 34–42.

G. S. Maxwell, *The Romans in Scotland*, Edinburgh, 1989.

Ordnance Survey, *Map of Hadrian's Wall* (2nd edn, 1972).

T. W. Potter, *Romans in North-West England*, Kendal, 1979.

I. A. Richmond (ed.), *Roman and Native in Roman Britain*, Edinburgh, 1958.

P. Salway, *Roman Britain*, Oxford, 1981.

F. G. Simpson, *Watermills and Military Works on Hadrian's Wall: Excavations in Northumberland, 1907–1913* (ed. G. Simpson), Kendal, 1977.

H. Welfare and V. Swan, *Roman Camps in England, The Field Archaeology*, London, 1995.

1

THE CONCEPT OF A FRONTIER

ROMAN IMPERIALISM IN GENERAL (pp. 1ff.)

A. R. Birley, 'Roman frontiers and Roman frontier policy: some reflections on Roman imperialism', *TAASDN*, n.s., 3 (1974), 13–25.

P. A. Brunt, review of H. D. Meyer, *Die Aussenpolitik des Augustus und die Augusteische Dichtung*, *JRS*, 53 (1963), 170–76.

B. Isaac, *The Limits of Empire: the Roman army in the East*, Oxford, 1990.

Edward N. Luttwak, *The Grand Strategy of the Roman Empire*, Baltimore and London, 1976.

J. C. Mann, 'The frontiers of the Roman principate', *Aufstieg und Niedergang der römischen Welt II Principat 1* (ed. H. Temporini), Berlin, 1974, 508–33; the quotation is from 509.

J. C. Mann, review of Luttwak, *JRS*, 69 (1979), 175–83.

F. Millar, 'Emperors, frontiers and foreign relations, 31 B.C. to A.D. 378', *Britannia* 13 (1982), 1–23.

G. Webster, *The Roman Imperial Army*, London, 3rd edn, 1985, chapter 2, 'The frontier systems'.

C. M. Wells, *The German Policy of Augustus*, Oxford, 1972, especially chapter 1, 'Augustus in the tradition of Roman imperialism'.

V. A. Maxfield, 'The frontiers – mainland Europe', in *The Roman World* (ed. J. Wacher), London, 1987, 139–93.

C. R. Whittaker, *Frontiers of the Roman Empire*, Baltimore, 1994.

JULIUS CAESAR IN BRITAIN (pp. 5f.)

C. E. Stevens, 'Britain and the Lex Pompeia Licinia', *Latomus* 12 (1953), 14–21.

J. Sabben-Clare, *Caesar and Roman Politics 60–50 B.C.*, Oxford, 1971; on the return in 54 B.C. and the possibility that Caesar heard of Julia's death in Britain see 119 and cf. 121.

Christopher Hawkes, 'Britain and Julius Caesar', *Proceedings of the British Academy* 63 (1977), 125–92.

BRITAIN FROM CAESAR TO CLAUDIUS (p. 6)

C. E. Stevens, 'Britain between the invasions', in *Aspects of Archaeology in Britain and Beyond* (ed. W. F. Grimes), London, 1951, 332–44.

BRITAIN FROM CLAUDIUS TO THE FLAVIANS (pp. 6ff.)

G. Webster, *The Roman Invasion of Britain*, London, 1980, 112; *Rome against Caractacus*, London, 1981; *Boudica*, London, 1978, 92; do not show linear dispositions.

V. A. Maxfield, 'Pre Flavian forts and their garrisons', *Britannia* 17 (1986), 59–72.

W. S. Hanson and D. B. Campbell, 'The Brigantes: from Clientage to Conquest', *Britannia*, 17 (1986), 73–89.

BRITAIN UNDER AGRICOLA (pp. 9ff.)

R. M. Ogilvie and I. A. Richmond (eds), *Cornelii Taciti de Vita Agricolae*, Oxford, 1967; cf. review by J. C. Mann, *AA*[4] 46 (1968), 306–8.

Agricola's Campaigns in Scotland, *Scottish Archaeological Forum* 12, Edinburgh, 1981, especially Brian Dobson, 'Agricola's life and career', 1–13, and S. S. Frere, 'The Flavian frontier in Scotland', 89–97, for different viewpoints.

W. S. Hanson, *Agricola and the Conquest of the North*, London, 1987.

BRITAIN AFTER AGRICOLA (pp. 11ff.)

B. R. Hartley, 'The Roman occupation of Scotland: the evidence of samian ware', *Britannia* 3 (1972), 4–15.

E. Birley, 'Britain after Agricola and the end of the Ninth Legion', *Roman Britain and the Roman Army*, Kendal, 1953, 20–30.

A. S. Hobley, 'The Numismatic Evidence for the Post-Agricolan Abandonment of the Roman Frontier in Northern Scotland', *Britannia* 20 (1989), 69–74.

GERMANY (pp. 15f., 22f.)

H. Schönberger, 'The Roman frontier in Germany: an archaeological survey', *JRS* 59 (1969), 144–97, especially 155–64. The quotation is from 160. (A new edition in German appeared as 'Die römischen Truppenlager der frühen und mittleren Kaiserzeit zwischen Nordsee und Inn', *Bericht der Römisch-Germanischen Kommission*, 66 (1985), 322–495, especially 366–91.)

Dietwulf Baatz, *Der römische Limes*, Berlin, 1974; review of Breeze and Dobson, *Hadrian's Wall*, *Bonner Jahrbücher*, 177 (1977), 775.

Dietwulf Baatz, *Der römische Limes*, 3. überarbeitete Auflage, Berlin, 1993.

TENCTERI AND HERMUNDURI (p. 16)

Tacitus, *Histories*, 4, 64 (Tencteri); *Germania* 41 (Hermunduri).

THE STANEGATE SYSTEM (pp. 16ff.)

E. Birley, *Research on Hadrian's Wall*, Kendal, 1961, 132–50 is the most detailed description; for comments cf.

C. M. Daniels, *Scottish Archaeological Forum* 2 (1970), 94f.

B. Dobson, 'The function of Hadrian's Wall', *AA*[5] 14 (1986), 2–5.

G. D. B. Jones, 'The Solway frontier: interim report 1976–81', *Britannia* 13 (1982), 283–5.

G. D. B. Jones, 'The emergence of the Tyne–Solway frontier', in *Roman Frontier Studies 1989*, ed. Valerie A. Maxwell and Michael J. Dobson, Exeter, 1991, 98–107.

Washing Well: N. McCord and G. Jobey, *AA*[4] 49 (1971), 120.

J. Poulter, 'The date of the Stanegate, and a Hypothesis about the Manner and Timing of the Construction of Roman Roads in Britain', *AA*[5] 26 (1998), 49–56.

SIGNALLING (p. 20)

G. H. Donaldson, 'Roman military signalling on the North British frontiers', *AA*[5] 13 (1986), 19–24.

LEGIONARY FORTRESSES (pp. 23f.)

RIB, 330, 464, 665.

VINDOLANDA INSCRIPTION (pp. 14, 26)

A. R. Birley, *Britannia* 29 (1998), 299–306, cf. 435f. n. 7.

FORT REBUILDING *c.* 105 (p. 23)

Carlisle: I. D. Caruana, *Britannia* 23 (1992), 104.

Corbridge: J. P. Gillam, *AA*[5] 5 (1997), 60.

Vindolanda: Either R. E. Birley, *Vind. Research Reports* III, 1103 or I, Bardon Mill, 1994, 89.

2

THE BUILDING OF HADRIAN'S WALL

HADRIAN (p. 25)

Scriptores Historiae Augustae, Hadrian.
Cassius Dio, 69.
ILS, 308.

BRITAIN IN 117 (pp. 25f.)

Scriptores Historiae Augustae, Hadrian, 5 (Mann 1).
Cornelius Fronto, p. 218 Naber (Loeb edn, ii 22, Mann 2).
H. Mattingly and E. A. Sydenham, *The Roman Imperial Coinage*, 577a (Mann 3).

NINTH LEGION (p. 26)

E. Birley, 'The fate of the Ninth Legion', in *Soldier and Civilian in Roman Yorkshire* (ed. R. M. Butler), Leicester, 1971, 71–80.
W. Eck, 'Zum Ende der *legio IX Hispana*', *Chiron* 2 (1972), 459–62.
A. R. Birley, *The Fasti of Roman Britain*, Oxford, 1981, 220–2.

HADRIAN IN BRITAIN (p. 26)

Scriptores Historiae Augustae, Hadrian, 10–11 (Mann 4–5).

DESCRIPTION OF THE WALL (pp. 26ff.)

See the articles listed in *Handbook*, and E. Birley, *Research on Hadrian's Wall*, Kendal, 1961. Most subsequent work on Hadrian's Wall has been published in *AA*, *TCWAAS* or *Britannia*.
P. R. Hill and B. Dobson, 'The Design of Hadrian's Wall and its Implications', *AA*[5] 20 (1992), 27–52.

THE STONE WALL (pp. 30ff.)

P. R. Hill, 'Stonework and the archaeologist: including a stonemason's view of Hadrian's Wall', *AA*[5] 8 (1981), 1–22; note correction of p. 3, 'squared rubble, not coursed', *AA*[5] 25, 47 fn. 20.
P. R. Hill, 'Hadrian's Wall: Some aspects of its execution', *AA*[5] 19 (1991), 33–9.
P. T. Bidwell and M. Watson, 'Excavations on Hadrian's Wall at Denton, Newcastle upon Tyne 1986–89', *AA*[5] 24 (1996), 1–56.

THE TURF WALL (pp. 31f.)

F. G. Simpson and I. A. Richmond, 'The turf wall of Hadrian, 1895–1935',
  TCWAAS[2] 35 (1935), 1–18.

J. C. Mann, 'Hadrian's Wall west of the Irthing', *Britannia* 21 (1990), 289–92.

TURRETS (pp. 34ff.)

Dorothy Charlesworth, 'The Turrets on Hadrian's Wall', in M. R. Apted,
  R. Gilyard-Beer and A. D. Saunders, *Ancient Monuments and their Interpretation*,
  London, 1977, 13–26.

P. R. Hill, 'The Stone Wall Turrets of Hadrian's Wall', *AA*[5] 25 (1997), 27–49.

Charmian Woodfield, 'Six Turrets on Hadrian's Wall', *AA*[4] 43 (1965), 87–200.

THE TOP OF THE WALL (pp. 41ff.)

R. L. Bellhouse, 'Roman sites on the Cumberland coast, 1967–68', *TCWAAS*[2]
  68 (1969), 79–93.

J. D. Cowen and I. A. Richmond, 'The Rudge Cup', *AA*[4] 12 (1935), 310–42.

J. Heurgon, 'The Amiens Patera', *JRS* 41 (1951), 22–4.

D. Charlesworth, 'Recent work on Hadrian's Wall, Cawfields', *AA*[4] 46 (1968),
  73–4.

P. T. Bidwell and N. Holbrook, *Hadrian's Wall Bridges*, London, 1989.

J. G. Crow, 'A Review of Current Research on the Turrets and Curtain of
  Hadrian's Wall', *Britannia* 22 (1991), 51–63.

THE PURPOSE OF HADRIAN'S WALL (pp. 39ff.)

E. Birley, 'Hadrianic frontier policy', *Carnuntina* 3 (1956), 25–33.

R. G. Collingwood, 'The purpose of the Roman Wall', *Vasculum* 8 (1921).

B. Dobson, 'The function of Hadrian's Wall', *AA*[5] 14 (1986), 5–30.

J. C. Mann, 'The Function of Hadrian's Wall', *AA*[5] 18 (1990), 51–4.

D. J. Woolliscroft, 'Signalling and the design of Hadrian's Wall', *AA*[5] 17 (1989),
  5–19.

THE RHINE AND THE DANUBE FRONTIERS (p. 40)

Tacitus, *Histories*, 4, 64; *Germania*, 41.

THE USE OF TROOPS IN DETACHMENTS (p. 43)

D. J. Breeze, 'The Roman fortlet at Barburgh Mill, Dumfriesshire', *Britannia* 5
  (1974), 145–7.

C. Bradford Welles, R. O. Fink and J. F. Gillam, *The Excavations at Dura-Europos,
  Final Report V, part I: The Parchments and Papyri*, New Haven, 1959, 100, 101.

Pliny, *Letters*, 10, 20.

FINDS FROM MILECASTLES AND TURRETS (p. 43)

E. Birley, *Research on Hadrian's Wall*, Kendal, 1961, 271.

J. R. Dockerill, 'Pottery from the milecastles and turrets on Hadrian's Wall' (unpublished M.A. thesis), University of Durham, 1969, 394.

L. Allason-Jones, ' "Small finds" from turrets on Hadrian's Wall', in J. C. Coulson (ed.), *Military Equipment and the Identity of Roman Soldiers, Proceedings of the Fourth Roman Military Equipment Conference*, Oxford, 1988, 197–233.

THE CUMBRIAN COAST (pp. 44ff.)

G. D. B. Jones, 'The western extension of Hadrian's Wall: Bowness to Cardurnock', *Britannia* 7 (1976), 236–43.

R. L. Bellhouse, 'Hadrian's Wall: the limiting ditches in the Cardurnock peninsula', *Britannia* 12 (1981), 135–42.

R. L. Bellhouse, *Roman Sites on the Cumberland Coast*, Kendal, 1989.

G. D. B. Jones, 'The Solway frontier: interim report, 1976–81', *Britannia* 13 (1982), 283–97.

T. W. Potter, 'The Biglands Milefortlet and the Cumberland Coast Defences', *Britannia* 8 (1977), 149–83.

T. W. Potter, 'The Roman frontier in Cumbria', in *Roman Frontier Studies 1979* (= BAR International Series 71) (ed. W. S. Hanson and L. J. F. Keppie), Oxford, 1980, 195–200.

P. Turnbull, 'Excavations at Milefortlet 21', *TCWAAS²* 98 (1998), 61–106.

R. J. A. Wilson, *Roman Maryport and its Setting*, Kendal, 1998.

D. J. Woolliscroft, 'Signalling and the Design of the Cumberland Coast System', *TCWAAS²* 94 (1994), 54–64.

THE SOUTH BANK OF THE TYNE (p. 46)

E. Birley, *Research on Hadrian's Wall*, Kendal, 1961, 157–9.

THE OUTPOST FORTS (p. 46f.)

RIB, 974, 995.

Transactions of the Dumfriesshire and Galloway Natural History and Archaeological Society 38 (1959–60), 143f.

RIB, 2091.

F. G. Simpson, I. A. Richmond and J. K. St Joseph, 'The turf-wall milecastle at High House', *TCWAAS²* 35 (1935), 220–9.

A. S. Robertson, *Birrens* (Blatobulgium), Edinburgh, 1975.

P. Austen, *Bewcastle and Old Penrith, A Roman Outpost Fort and a Frontier Vicus*, Kendal, 1991.

J. P. Gillam, I. M. Jobey and D. Welsby, *The Roman Bath-House at Bewcastle, Cumbria*, Kendal, 1993.

D. J. Woolliscroft, 'The Outpost System of Hadrian's Wall', *TCWAAS*² 88 (1988), 23–8.

THE NEW FORTS ON THE WALL (pp. 47ff.)

B. Swinbank and J. E. H. Spaul, 'The spacing of the forts on Hadrian's Wall', *AA*⁴ 29 (1951), 221–38.

D. J. Breeze and B. Dobson, 'Fort types on Hadrian's Wall', *AA*⁴ 47 (1969), 15–32.

P. S. Austen and D. J. Breeze, 'A new inscription from Chesters on Hadrian's Wall', *AA*⁵ 7 (1979), 115–26.

THE VALLUM (pp. 56ff.)

B. Heywood, 'The Vallum – its problems restated', in *Britain and Rome* (ed. M. G. Jarrett and B. Dobson), Kendal, 1996, 85–94.

F. G. Simpson and I. A. Richmond, 'The Vallum at milecastles 51, Wall Bowers, and 50 TW, High House', *TCWAAS*² 37 (1937), 157–77.

SALLYPORTS (pp. 62)

Handbook, 26.

Frontinus, *Strategemata*, 2, 6.

Vegetius, *de re militari*, 3, 21.

THE BUILDING OF HADRIAN'S WALL (pp. 63ff.)

C. E. Stevens, *The Building of Hadrian's Wall*, Kendal, 1966.

J. Hooley and D. J. Breeze, 'The building of Hadrian's Wall: a reconsideration', *AA*⁴ 46 (1968), 97–114.

D. J. Breeze and B. Dobson, 'Hadrian's Wall: some problems', *Britannia* 3 (1972), 182–208.

R. L. Bellhouse, 'Roman sites on the Cumberland coast 1967–68', *TCWAAS*² 69 (1969), 93–101.

R. Hunneysett, 'The milecastles of Hadrian's Wall: an alternative explanation', *AA*⁵ 8 (1980), 95–107.

V. A. Maxfield and R. Miket, 'The excavation of turret 33b (Coesike)', *AA*⁴ 50 (1972), 158.

P. R. Hill and B. Dobson, 'The Design of Hadrian's Wall and its Implications', *AA*⁵ 20 (1992), 27–52.

R. Kendal, 'Transport Logistics Associated with the Building of Hadrian's Wall', *Britannia* 27 (1998), 129–52.

HADRIAN'S OTHER FRONTIERS (pp. 64f.)

E. Birley, 'Hadrianic Frontier Policy', *Carnuntina* 3 (1956), 25–33.

H. Schönberger, 'The Roman frontier in Germany: an archaeological survey', *JRS* 59 (1969), 144–97.

D. Baatz, *Der römische Limes*, Berlin, 1973.

J. Baradez, *Fossatum Africae*, Paris, 1949.

V. A. Maxfield, 'Hadrian's Wall in its Imperial Setting', *AA*⁵ 18 (1990), 1–27.

THE COST OF HADRIAN'S WALL (pp. 82f.)

Robert Rawlinson's figures are quoted in:

J. C. Bruce, *The Roman Wall*, Newcastle upon Tyne, 1851, 94–5.

Hunter Davies, *A Walk Along the Wall*, London, 1974, 286f.

'A Quote for Hadrian's Wall', *Concrete*, January 1985, 26–7.

3

THE ANTONINE WALL

THE MOVE NORTH (pp. 88ff.)

Pausanias, *Description of Greece*, 8, 43 (= Mann 40).

Scriptores Historiae Augustae, Antoninus Pius, 5 (= Mann 39).

A. R. Birley, 'Roman frontiers and Roman frontier policy: some reflections on Roman imperialism', *TAASDN*, n.s., 3 (1974), 17f.

D. J. Breeze, 'The abandonment of the Antonine Wall: its date and implications', *Scottish Archaeological Forum*, 7 (1975), 67–80.

B. Swinbank, 'The activities of Lollius Urbicus as evidenced by inscriptions', *TAASDN*, 10 pt 4 (1953), 382–403.

THE ABANDONMENT OF HADRIAN'S WALL (p. 90ff.)

Cockmount Hill: *JRS* 30 (1940), 132.

RIB, 1460.

RIB, 1330.

M. G. Jarrett and J. C. Mann, 'Britain from Agricola to Gallienus', *Bonner Jahrbücher*, 170 (1970), 188.

M. C. Bishop and J. N. Dore, *Corbridge, Excavations of the Roman Fort and Town, 1947–80*, London, 1989.

P. Bidwell, *The Roman Fort of Vindolanda*, London, 1985.

THE OCCUPATION OF SCOTLAND (pp. 92ff.)

G. Jobey, 'Notes on some population problems in the area between the two Roman Walls, I', *AA*[5] 2 (1974), 17–26.

K. A. Steer, 'John Horsley and the Antonine Wall', *AA*[4] 43 (1964), 1–21.

D. Baatz, *Kastell Hesselbach* (*Limesforschungen* 12), Berlin, 1973.

S. N. Miller (ed.), *The Roman Occupation of South-western Scotland*, Glasgow, 1952.

D. J. Breeze, 'The Roman fortlet at Barburgh Mill, Dumfriesshire', *Britannia*, 5 (1974), 130–62.

G. S. Maxwell, 'The excavation of the Roman fort at Crawford, Lanarkshire', *PSAS* 104 (1971–2), 147–200.

THE ANTONINE WALL (pp. 91ff.)

W. S. Hanson and G. S. Maxwell, *Rome's North-West Frontier, the Antonine Wall* (paperback edn), Edinburgh, 1986.

L. J. F. Keppie, 'The Antonine Wall 1960–1980', *Britannia* 13 (1982), 91–111.

G. Macdonald, *The Roman Wall in Scotland* (2nd edn), Oxford 1934.

A. S. Robertson, *The Antonine Wall*, 4th edn revised and ed. by L. Keppie, Glasgow, 1979.

THE BUILDERS (pp. 98f.)

L. J. F. Keppie, *Roman Slabs from the Antonine Wall*, Glasgow, 1979.

R. W. Feachem, 'Six Roman camps near the Antonine Wall', *PSAS* 89 (1955–6), 329–39.

G. S. Maxwell, 'The building of the Antonine Wall', *Actes du IXe Congrès international d'études sur les frontières Romaines*, Bucharest, 1974, 327–32.

FORTS AND FORTLETS (pp. 99ff.)

L. J. F. Keppie and J. J. Walker, 'Fortlets on the Antonine Wall at Seabegs Wood, Kinneil and Cleddans', *Britainia* 12 (1981), 143–62.

K. A. Steer, 'The nature and purpose of the expansions on the Antonine Wall', *PSAS* 90 (1956–7), 161–9.

W. S. Hanson and G. S. Maxwell, 'Minor enclosures on the Antonine Wall at Wilderness Plantation', *Britannia* 14 (1983), 227–43.

J. P. Gillam, 'Possible changes in plan in the course of the construction of the Antonine Wall', *Scottish Arachaeological Forum* 7 (1976), 51–6.

THE UNITS ON THE WALL (pp. 110ff.)

D. J. Breeze, 'Roman forces and native populations', *PSAS* 115 (1985), 65–70.

THE BUILDING OF THE ANTONINE WALL (pp. 114ff.)

L. J. F. Keppie, 'The building of the Antonine Wall: archaeological and epigraphic evidence', *PSAS* 105 (1972–4), 151–65.

G. S. Maxwell, 'Fortlets and distance slabs on the Antonine Wall', *Britannia* 16 (1985), 25–8.

G. S. Maxwell, 'The building of the Antonine Wall', *Actes du IXe Congrès international d'études sur les frontières Romaines*, Bucharest, 1974, 327–32.

G. B. Bailey, 'The provision of fort-annexes on the Antonine Wall', *PSAS* 124 (1994), 299–314.

G. B. Bailey and J. Cannel, 'Excavations at Kinneil fortlet on the Antonine Wall, 1980–1', *PSAS* 126 (1996), 303–46.

A. Dunwell and I. Ralston, 'Excavations at Inveravon on the Antonine Wall, 1991', *PSAS* 125 (1995), 521–76.

L. Keppie, *Roman Inscribed and Sculptured Stones in the Hunterian Museum, University of Glasgow*, London, 1998.

J. C. Mann, 'The construction of the Antonine Wall', *PSAS* 116 (1986), 191–3.

D. J. Woolliscroft, 'Signalling and the design of the Antonine Wall', *Britannia* 27 (1996), 153–77.

4

THE TWO WALLS

LITERARY AND EPIGRAPHIC EVIDENCE (pp. 120f.)

J. C. Mann, 'The history of the Antonine Wall', *PSAS* 118 (1988), 131–7.

BRITAIN ON THE ACCESSION OF MARCUS (p. 120)

Scriptores Historiae Augustae, Marcus Aurelius, 8.

For comparison see: *Scriptores Historiae Augustae, Hadrian*, 5; *Antoninus Pius*, 5; Cassius Dio, 72, 8.

GOVERNORS OF BRITAIN (p. 120)

A. R. Birley, *The Fasti of Roman Britain*, Oxford, 1981.

E. Birley, 'Senators in the emperors' service', *Proceedings of the British Academy*, 39 (1953), 197–214.

Severus and Verus: O. Salomies, *Adoptive and Polyonymous Nomenclature in the Roman Empire*, Helsinki, 1992, 126ff.

TROUBLE IN THE 170S AND 180S (p. 121f.)

Scriptores Historiae Augustae, Marcus Aurelius, 22 (= Mann 78).

Cassius Dio, 71, 16 (= Mann 79).

Cassius Dio, 72, 8 (= Mann 83).

Scriptores Historiae Augustae, Pertinax, 3; Cassius Dio, 73, 4.

THE EVENTS OF THE 190S AND 200S (pp. 122f.)

Cassius Dio, 75, 5, 4; 67, 11; 76, 12, 1; 76, 13, 1; Herodian, 3, 14 (= Mann 97, 112, 113, 118, 123, 128–31, 133).

STRUCTURAL EVIDENCE (pp. 124ff.)

J. P. Gillam and J. C. Mann, 'The northern British frontier from Antoninus Pius to Caracalla', *AA*[4] 48 (1970), 1–44.

M. G. Jarrett and J. C. Mann, 'Britain from Agricola to Gallienus', *Bonner Jahrbücher* 170 (1970), 185–205.

K. A. Steer, 'John Horsley and the Antonine Wall', *AA*[4] 43 (1964), 21–40.

K. A. Steer, 'Excavations at Mumrills Roman fort', *PSAS* 94 (1960–61), 97–9.

S. N. Miller, *The Roman Fort at Balmuildy*, Glasgow, 1922, 54f.

D. J. Breeze, *The Roman Fort at Bearsden, 1973 Excavations: An Interim Report*, Edinburgh, 1974, 12–19.

I. A. Richmond, 'Excavations at the Roman fort of Newstead, 1947', *PSAS* 84 (1949–50), 14.

G. S. Maxwell, 'Excavations at the Roman fort at Crawford, Lanarkshire', *PSAS* 104 (1971–2), 147–80.

S. S. Frere and J. J. Wilkes, *Strageath, Excavations within the Roman Fort, 1973–86*, London, 1989.

N. Hodgson, 'Were there two Antonine Occupations of Scotland?', *Britannia* 26 (1995), 29–49.

NUMISMATIC EVIDENCE (pp. 123f.)

A. S. Robertson, 'Roman coins found in Scotland, 1971–82', *PSAS* 113 (1983), 424–6.

A. S. Robertson, 'A hoard of Roman silver coins from Briglands, Rumbling Bridge, Kinross-shire', *PSAS* 90 (1956–7), 241–6.

D. C. A. Shotter, 'Coin evidence and the northern frontiers in the second century A.D.', *PSAS* 107 (1975–6), 81–91.

POTTERY (pp. 125)

B. R. Hartley, 'The Roman occupation of Scotland: the evidence of samian ware', *Britannia* 3 (1972), 15–42.

J. P. Gillam, 'Sources of pottery on northern military sites', in *Current Research in Romano-British Coarse Pottery* (ed. A. Detsicas), London, 1973, 55–62.

J. P. Gillam and J. C. Mann, 'The northern British frontier from Antoninus Pius to Caracalla', *AA*⁴ 48 (1970), 1–44.

THE ABANDONMENT OF THE ANTONINE WALL (pp. 128ff.)

J. P. Gillam, 'Calpurnius Agricola and the northern frontier', *TAASDN*, 10 pt 4 (1953), 359–75.

J. P. Gillam, 'The Frontier after Hadrian – a history of the problem', *AA*⁵ 2 (1974), 1–12.

D. J. Breeze, 'The abandonment of the Antonine Wall: its date and implications', *Scottish Archaeological Forum* 7 (1975), 67–80.

CASTLECARY (pp. 129f.)

B. R. Hartley, 'The Roman occupation of Scotland: the evidence of samian ware', *Britannia* 3 (1972), 28, fig. 2A.

RIB, 2138; M. G. Jarrett and J. C. Mann, 'Britain from Agricola to Gallienus', *Bonner Jahrbücher* 170 (1970), 194.

THE REBUILDING OF THE TURF WALL (p. 131)

I. A. Richmond and J. P. Gillam, 'Milecastle 79 (Solway)', *TCWAAS*² 52 (1952), 17–40.

G. Simpson, 'The close of period 1A on Hadrian's Wall and some Gaulish potters', *AA*⁴, 49 (1971), 109–18.

REBUILDING IN THE PENNINES (p. 132)

J. P. Gillam and J. C. Mann, 'The northern British frontier from Antoninus Pius to Caracalla', *AA*⁴ 48 (1970), 25.

THE INVASION OF THE EARLY 180s (pp. 133f.)

D. J. Breeze and B. Dobson, 'Hadrian's Wall: some problems', *Britannia* 3 (1972), 200–6.

RIB, 2034 (= Mann 82) from Kirksteads.

RIB, 1234 (= Mann 99) from Risingham.

RIB, 1465 (= Mann 170) from Chesters.

Cassius Dio, 75, 5, 4 (= Mann 97)

RIB, 1463 and 1464 (= Mann 85 and 86) from Chesters record work under Ulpius Marcellus.

Ulpius Marcellus diploma, M. M. Roxan, *Roman Military Diplomas 1985–1993*, London, 1994, no. 184, pp. 308–10.

THE MODIFICATIONS TO HADRIAN'S WALL
IN THE 180S (pp. 135ff.)

V. A. Maxfield and R. Miket, 'The excavation of turret 33b (Coesike)', *AA*⁴ 50 (1972), 158f.

D. J. Breeze and B. Dobson, 'Hadrian's Wall: some problems', *Britannia* 3 (1972), 203, note 121.

THE SEVERAN PERIOD (pp. 139ff.)

A. R. Birley, *Septimius Severus*, London, 1971.

A. R. Birley, 'Virius Lupus', *AA*⁴ 50 (1973), 179–89.

M. G. Jarrett and J. C. Mann, 'Britain from Agricola to Gallienus', *Bonner Jahrbücher* 170 (1970), 195–205.

J. P. Gillam and J. C. Mann, 'The northern British frontier from Antoninus Pius to Caracalla', *AA*⁴ 48 (1970), 39–44.

J. D. Leach and J. J. Wilkes, 'The Roman military base at Carpow, Perthshire, Scotland: summary of recent investigations (1964–70, 1975)', in *Limes: Akten des XI International Limeskongressus* (ed. J. Fitz), Budapest, 1977, 47–62.

J. K. St Joseph, 'Air reconnaissance in Britain, 1969–1972', *JRS* 63 (1973), 230–33.

J. K. St Joseph, 'Air reconnaissance in Britain, 1973–76', *JRS*, 67 (1977), 125–61.

R. P. Wright, 'Carpow and Caracalla', *Britannia*, 5 (1974), 289–92.

P. Bidwell and S. Speak, *Excavations at South Shields Roman Fort, Volume I*, Newcastle upon Tyne, 1994.

J. C. Mann, 'Loca', *AA*⁵, 20 (1992), 53–5.

M. P. Speidel, 'The Risingham *Praetensio*', *Britannia*, 29 (1998), 356–9.

M. Todd, 'The Falkirk hoard of denarii: trade or subsidy?', *PSAS*, 115 (1985), 229–32.

THE THIRD-CENTURY REORGANIZATION (pp. 142ff.)

D. J. Breeze, 'Cavalry on frontiers: Hadrian to Honorius', in *The Later Roman Empire Today, Papers given in honour of Professor John Mann* (ed. D. F. Clark, M. M. Roxan and J. J. Wilkes), London, 1993, 19–35.

I. A. Richmond, 'The Romans in Redesdale', *Northumberland County History*, 15 (1940), 82–106.

K. A. Steer, 'The Severan reorganisation', in *Roman and Native in North Britain* (ed. I. A. Richmond), Edinburgh, 1961, 91–111.

THE DEVELOPMENT OF THE FRONTIER (pp. 148ff.)

D. J. Breeze and B. Dobson, 'The development of the mural frontier in Britain from Hadrian to Caracalla', *PSAS*, 102 (1969–70), 109–21.

D. J. Breeze and B. Dobson, 'The development of the northern frontier in Britain from Hadrian to Caracalla', *Actes du IXe Congrès international d'études sur les frontières Romaines*, Bucharest, 1974, 321–6.

5

THE ARMY OF THE WALL

G. Webster, *The Roman Imperial Army* (3rd edn), London, 1985.

H. M. D. Parker, *The Roman Legions*, Oxford, 1928.

G. L. Cheesman, *The Auxilia of the Roman Imperial Army*, Oxford, 1914.

P. A. Holder, *The Roman Army in Britain*, London, 1982; reviews in *Britannia*, 14 (1983), 362–4, and in *Antiquaries Journal*, 62 (1983), 434–6.

Peter Connolly, *Greece and Rome at War*, London, 1981.

ORIGINS OF LEGIONS (p. 153)

Lawrence Keppie, *The Making of the Roman Army*, London, 1984.

RECRUITING OF LEGIONS (p. 154)

B. Dobson and J. C. Mann, 'The Roman army in Britain and Britons in the Roman army', *Britannia* 4 (1973), 191–205 = *Breeze/Dobson*, 511–25.

J. C. Mann, *Legionary Recruitment and Veteran Settlement during the Principate*, London, 1983.

ORGANIZATION OF FIRST COHORT OF LEGION (p. 154)

D. J. Breeze, 'The organization of the legion: the first cohort and the *equites legionis*', *JRS* 59 (1969), 50–55 = *Breeze/Dobson*, 65–70.

S. S. Frere, 'Hyginus and the First Cohort', *Britannia* 11 (1980), 51–60.

OFFICERS OF LEGION (pp. 154f.)

E. Birley, 'Senators in the emperors' service', *Proceedings of the British Academy*, 39 (1954), 197–214 = *Birley*, 75–92.

A. R. Birley, 'The senatorial career under the principate', *The Fasti of Roman Britain*, Oxford, 1981, 1–35.

E. Birley, 'The equestrian officers of the Roman army', *Roman Britain and the Roman Army*, Kendal, 1953, 133–53 = *Birley*, 147–64.

H. Devijver, *Prosopographia militiarum equestrium*, Louvain, 1976–87.

B. Dobson, 'The significance of the centurion and "primipilaris" in the Roman army and administration', *Aufstieg und Niedergang der römischen Welt II Principat 1* (ed. H. Temporini), Berlin, 1974, 393–434 = *Breeze/Dobson*, 143–85.

ORIGINS OF AUXILIA (pp. 156f.)

P. A. Holder, *The Auxilia from Augustus to Trajan*, Oxford, 1980.

D. B. Saddington, *The Development of the Roman Auxiliary Forces from Caesar to Vespasian (49 B.C.–A.D. 79)*, Harare, 1982.

TRAJAN'S COLUMN (pp. 157f.)

I. A. Richmond, 'Trajan's army on Trajan's Column', *Papers of the British School at Rome*, 13 (1935), 1–40; reprinted by the British School at Rome, London, 1982.

F. Lepper and S. Frere, *Trajan's Column*, Gloucester/Wolfboro, 1988.

AUXILIARIES' TECHNICAL SKILLS (pp. 157)

Tab. Vindol. II, no. 155.

ROMAN ARMY ORGANIZATION (p. 159ff.)

D. J. Breeze and B. Dobson, 'Fort types on Hadrian's Wall', *AA*[4] 47 (1969), 15–32 = *Breeze/Dobson*, 461–78.

R. W. Davies, 'A note on a recently discovered inscription from Carrawburgh', *Epigraphische Studien* 4 (1967), 108–11.

I. A. Richmond, 'Roman Britain and Roman military antiquities', *Proceedings of the British Academy* 41 (1955), 297–315.

Mark Hassall, 'The internal planning of Roman auxiliary forts', in *Rome and her Northern Provinces* (ed. Brian Hartley and John Wacher), London, 1983, 96–131.

SOURCES FOR UNIT SIZE (pp. 159ff.)

Hyginus, *liber de metatione castrorum* (ed. A. Grillone), Leipzig, 1977.

Arrian, *Tactica*, 18.

R. O. Fink, *Roman Military Records on Papyri*, New Haven, 1971.

J. D. Thomas and R. W. Davies, 'A new military strength report on papyrus', *JRS* 67 (1977), 50–61.

COHORTES EQUITATAE (pp. 159ff.)

R. W. Davies, 'Cohortes equitatae', *Historia* 20 (1971), 751–63.

MILLIARY UNITS (pp. 160ff.)

E. Birley, '*Alae* and *cohortes milliariae*', *Corolla Memoriae Erich Swoboda Dedicata*, Graz, 1966, 54–67.

D. Kennedy, 'Military Cohorts: the evidence of Josephus, BJ, III, 4. 2 (67) and of epigraphy', *ZPE* 50 (1983), 253–63.

Tab. Vindol. II, no. 154.

NUMERI (p. 163)

H. Callies, 'Die fremden Truppen im römischen Heer des Prinzipats und die sogenannten nationalen Numeri. Beiträge zur Geschichte des römischen Heeres', *Bericht der Römisch-Germanisclen Kommission 1964*, 45 (1965), 130–227.

J. C. Mann, 'A note on the numeri', *Hermes* 82 (1954), 501–6.

M. P. Speidel, 'The rise of the ethnic units in the Roman Imperial Army', *Aufstieg und Niedergang der römischeu Welt II* 3, Berlin/New York, 1975.

P. Southern, 'The numeri of the Roman Imperial Army', *Britannia* 20 (1989), 81–140.

D. Baatz, 'Keeping watch over the *Limes*', *AA*[5] 25 (1997), 7–9 (on the *numerus* fort at Hesselbach).

THE ROMAN FORT (pp. 163ff.)

R. G. Collingwood and I. A. Richmond, *The Archaeology of Roman Britain*, London, 1969.

V. E. Nash-Williams, *The Roman Frontier in Wales* (2nd edn revised by M. G. Jarrett), Cardiff, 1969.

Anne Johnson, *Roman Forts*, London, 1983.

P. Bidwell, *Roman Forts in Britain*, London, 1997.

D. J. Breeze, *The Roman Fort in Britain*, Princes Risborough, 1994.

GATES (pp. 164ff.)

P. Bidwell, R. Miket and B. Ford (eds), *Portae cum Turribus: Studies of Roman Fort Gateways*, BAR British series, 206 (1988).

ARCHAEOMAGNETIC SURVEYS (p. 168)

P. J. Casey, M. Noel and J. Wright, 'The Roman fort at Lanchester, Co. Durham: a geophysical survey and discussion of garrisons', *Arch. Journ.* 149 (1992), 69–81.

HEADQUARTERS BUILDING (pp. 168ff.)

H. von Petrikovits, 'Die Spezialgebäude römischer Legionslager', *Legion VII Gemina*, Leon, 1970, 238.

GOVERNOR'S VISITS (p. 171)

A. K. Bowman and J. David Thomas, 'New writing-tablets from Vindolanda', *Britannia* 27 (1996), no. 2, 307–23.

GRANARIES (p. 171)

F. Haverfield and R. G. Collingwood, 'The provisioning of Roman forts', *TCWAAS*[2] 20 (1920), 127–42.

W. Bulmer, 'The provisioning of Roman forts: a reappraisal of ration storage', *AA*[4] 47 (1969), 7–13.

G. E. Rickman, *Roman Granaries and Store Buildings*, Cambridge, 1971.

W. H. Manning, 'Roman military timber granaries in Britain', *Saalburger Jahrbuch* 32 (1975), 105–29.

Anne P. Gentry, *Roman Military Stone-Built Granaries in Britain*, BAR, 32, 1976.

STABLES (pp. 174ff.)

D. J. Breeze and B. Dobson, 'Fort types on Hadrian's Wall', *AA*[4] 47 (1969), 15–32 = *Breeze/Dobson*, 461–78.

D. J. Breeze and B. Dobson, 'Fort types as a guide to garrisons: a reconsideration', in *Roman Frontier Studies 1969* (ed. E. Birley, B. Dobson, M. G. Jarrett), Cardiff, 1974, 13–19.

I. A. Richmond, 'Roman Britain and Roman military antiquities', *Proceedings of the British Academy*, 41 (1955), 297–315.

C. M. Wells, 'Where did they put the horses? Cavalry stables in the early Empire', in *Limes: Akten des XI International Limeskongressus* (ed. J. Fitz), Budapest, 1977, 659–65.

K. R. Dixon and P. Southern, *The Roman Cavalry from the 1st to 3rd Centuries A.D.*, London, 1992 (ch. 4 on stables).

6

LIFE ON THE WALL

G. R. Watson, *The Roman Soldier*, London, 1969.

R. W. Davies (ed. D. J. Breeze and V. A. Maxfield), *Service in the Roman Army*, Edinburgh, 1989.

RECRUITMENT (pp. 181ff.)

B. Dobson and J. C. Mann, 'The Roman army in Britain and Britons in the Roman army', *Britannia*, 4 (1973), 191–205.

P. A. Brunt, 'Conscription and volunteering in the Roman army', *Israel Exploration Journal* 1 (1974), 90–115.

BURNSWARK (p. 182)

G. Jobey, 'Burnswark Hill', *Transactions of the Dumfriesshire and Galloway Natural History and Archaeological Society* 53 (1977–8), 57–104.

HADRIAN'S SPEECH (p. 183)

CIL, VIII 2532 = 18042 = *ILS*, 2487.

SWIMMING OF DANUBE (p. 183)

ILS, 2558.

PAY (pp. 183ff.)

G. R. Watson, *The Roman Soldier*, London, 1969, 99ff. M. Speidel (the Elder), 'The pay of the auxilia', *JRS* 63 (1973), 141–7; M. A. Speidel (the Younger), 'Roman Army Pay Scales', *JRS* 82 (1992), 87–106. R. Alston, 'Roman Military Pay from Caesar to Diocletian', *JRS* 84 (1994), 113–23, carries less conviction and is not taken up here.

LETTERS FROM SOLDIERS (p. 183)

There is no convenient collection, as R. O. Fink, *Roman Military Records on Papyri*, New Haven, 1971, gives only official documents. G. R. Watson, *The Roman Soldier*, London, 1969, and R. W. Davies quote them extensively, and the former gives a hand-list of military documents, including letters.

PROMOTION (pp. 185ff.)

D. J. Breeze, 'Pay grades and ranks below the centurionate', *JRS* 61 (1971), 130–35 = *Breeze/Dobson*, 59–64.

D. J. Breeze, 'The organization of the career structure of the *immunes* and *principales* of the Roman army', *Bonner Jahrbücher* 174 (1974), 245–92 = *Breeze/Dobson*, 11–58.

J. F. Gillam, 'The appointment of auxiliary centurions', *Transactions of the American Philological Association* 88 (1958), 155–68.

THREE DECURIONS TO A TURMA (p. 186)

Polybius, VI, 25, 1–2.

EQUITES SINGULARES AUGUSTI (p. 186)

M. Speidel, *Riding for Caesar*, London, 1994.

DOCUMENTATION (pp. 187f.)

R. O. Fink, *Roman Military Records on Papyri*, New Haven, 1971.

G. R. Watson, 'Documentation in the Roman army', *Aufstieg und Niedergang der römischen Welt II Principat 1* (ed. H. Temporini), Berlin, 1974, 493–507.

A. K. Bowman and J. David Thomas, *The Vindolanda Writing Tablets (Tabulae Vindolandenses II)*, London, 1984. The strength report appears as no. 154, pp. 90–98.

A. K. Bowman and J. D. Thomas, 'New writing-tablets from Vindolanda', *Britannia* 27 (1996), 299–328.

E. Birley, R. Birley and A. Birley, *Vindolanda Research Reports II: Reports on the Auxiliaries, the Writing-Tablets, Inscriptions, Brands and Graffiti*, Bardon Mill, 1993.

A. R. and R. E. Birley, 'Four new writing-tablets from Vindolanda', *ZPE* 100 (1994), 431–46.

R. S. O. Tomlin, 'Roman Manuscripts from Carlisle: the Ink Writing-Tablets', *Britannia* 29 (1998), 31–85.

TRAJAN (pp. 187)

The desire, Pliny, *Letters*, 10, 20; the reality, R. O. Fink, *Roman Military Records on Papyri*, New Haven, 1971, no. 63.

ARMS AND ARMOUR (pp. 190ff.)

H. Russell Robinson, *The Armour of Imperial Rome*, London, 1975.

M. C. Bishop and J. C. N. Coulston, *Roman Military Equipment from the Punic Wars to the Fall of Rome*, London, 1993.

WOMEN IN BARRACKS (p. 190)

C. van Driel-Murray, *Vindolanda III*, Hexham, 1993, 1–75.

SADDLES (pp. 191f.)

P. Connolly and C. van Driel-Murray, 'The Roman Cavalry Saddle', *Britannia* 22 (1991), 33–50.

C. van Driel-Murray, 'The Leatherwork', in *Vindolanda III, the Early Wooden Forts*, Bardon Mill, 1993, 31–47.

SPORTS HELMETS (p. 192)

F. Kiechle, 'Die "Taktik" des Flavius Arrianus', *Bericht der Römisch-Germanischen Kommission 1964*, 45 (1965), 87–129.

HORSES (p. 192)

J. Curle, *A Roman Frontier Post and its People*, Glasgow, 1911, 362–71 (by J. C. Ewart).

Ann Hyland, *Equus: the Horse in the Roman World*, London, 1990.

ARTILLERY (pp. 192f.)

E. W. Marsden, *Greek and Roman Artillery, Historical Development*, Oxford, 1969, 191.

D. Baatz, 'Recent finds of ancient artillery', *Britannia* 9 (1978), 1–17.

D. B. Campbell, 'Ballistaria in first to mid-third century Britain: a reappraisal', *Britannia* 15 (1984), 75–84.

G. H. Donaldson, 'A Reinterpretation of *RIB* 1912 from Birdoswald', *Britannia* 21 (1990), 207–14.

LEAVE (p. 194)

Tab. Vindol. II, nos. 166–77.

RELIGION (pp. 194ff.)

See notes to Appendix 3, pp. 277ff.

I. P. Haynes, *Britannia*, 24 (1993), 145 and fn. 35 cites an unpublished D.Phil. thesis of D. L. Kennedy against recruitment of Syrian units from the homelands.

SURVIVAL (p. 198)

A. R. Burn, 'Hic breve vivitur', *Past and Present* 4 (1953), 2–31.

P. A. Brunt, *Italian Manpower 225 B.C.–A.D. 14*, Oxford, 1979, 339; suggests 40 per cent mortality during service. K. Hopkins's much higher estimate (*JRS* 70, 1980, 124) is difficult to reconcile with known numbers being discharged on completion of service.

FOOD (pp. 198f.)

R. W. Davies, 'The Roman military diet', *Britannia* 2 (1971), 122-42.

B. A. Knights, C. A. Dickson, J. H. Dickson and D. J. Breeze, 'Evidence concerning the Roman military diet at Bearsden, Scotland, in the 2nd century A.D.', *Journal of Archaeological Science* 10 (1983), 139–52.

R. S. O. Tomlin, 'Roman Manuscripts from Carlisle: the Ink Writing-Tablets', *Britannia* 29 (1998), 31–85, especially 36–51.

CLOTHING (p. 199)

E. Sander, 'Die Kleidung des römischen Soldaten', *Historia*, 12 (1963), 144–66.

MILITARY MEDICAL SERVICE (pp. 199f.)

R. W. Davies, 'The Roman military medical service', *Saalburger Jahrbuch* 27 (1970), 84–104.

R. W. Davies, 'The medici of the Roman armed forces', *Epigraphische Studien* 8 (1969), 83–99.

MISSIO CAUSARIA (p. 200)

G. R. Watson, *The Roman Soldier*, London, 1969, 123f.

DEATH (pp. 200f.)

Royal Commission on Historical Monuments (England), *Eboracum, Roman York*, London, 1962.

L. P. Wenham, *The Romano-British Cemetery at Trentholme Drive, York*, London, 1968.

D. B. Charlton and M. Mitcheson, 'The Roman cemetery at Petty Knowes, Rochester, Northumberland', *AA*[5] 12 (1984), 1–31.

M. E. Snape, 'An excavation in the Roman cemetery at South Shields', *AA*[5] 22 (1994), 43–66.

DIPLOMAS (pp. 201f.)

G. Alföldy, 'Zur Beurteilung der Militärdiplome der Auxiliarsoldaten', *Historia* 17 (1968), 215–27.

M. Roxan, 'The distribution of Roman military diplomas', *Epigraphische Studien* 12 (1981), 265–86.

M. M. Roxan, 'Observations on the Reasons for Changes in Formula in Diplomas circa A.D. 140', in *Heer und Integrationspolitik*, ed. W. Eck and H. Wolff, Cologne/Vienna, 1996, 265–92.

WOMEN ON THE FRONTIER (pp. 201f.)

Lindsay Allason-Jones, *Women in Roman Britain*, London, 1989.

M. Roxan, 'Women on the Frontiers', in Valerie A. Maxfield and Michael J. Dobson (eds), *Roman Frontier Studies 1989*, Exeter, 1991, 462–5.

THE CIVIL SETTLEMENTS (pp. 203ff.)

P. Salway, *The Frontier People of Roman Britain*, Cambridge, 1965.

R. E. Birley, *Civilians on the Roman Frontier*, Newcastle upon Tyne, 1973.

C. Sebastian Sommer, *The Military Vici in Roman Britain, etc.* (= BAR British Series 129), 1984.

R. E. Birley, *Vindolanda, a Roman frontier fort on Hadrian's Wall*, London, 1977.

M. E. Snape, 'Roman and native: vici on the north British frontier', *Roman*

Frontier Studies 1989, in Valerie A. Maxfield and Michael J. Dobson (eds), *Roman Frontier Studies 1989*, Exeter, 1991, 468–71.

THE COMMANDING OFFICERS (pp. 207ff.)

E. Birley, 'The equestrian officers of the Roman army', *Roman Britain and the Roman Army*, Kendal, 1953 = *Birley*, 147–64.

E. Birley, '*Alae* and *cohortes milliariae*', *Corolla Memoriae Erich Swoboda Dedicata*, Graz, 1966, 54–67 = *Birley*, 349–64.

THE LATE ROMAN ARMY (pp. 209ff.)

A. H. M. Jones, *The Decline of the Ancient World*, London, 1966.

Roger Tomlin, 'The mobile army', in *Greece and Rome at War* (ed. Peter Connolly), London, 1981, 249–59.

S. T. James, 'Britain and the Late Roman Army', in *Military and Civilian in Roman Britain* (ed. T. F. C. Blagg and A. C. King), Oxford, 1984, 161–86.

THE LOCAL POPULATION (pp. 212ff.)

G. Jobey, 'Homesteads and settlements of the frontier area', in *Rural Settlement in Roman Britain* (ed. C. Thomas), London, 1966, 1–14, with detailed bibliography.

7

THE THIRD AND FOURTH CENTURIES

MODIFICATIONS TO FORTS (pp. 216ff.)

M. G. Jarrett and J. C. Mann, 'Britain from Agricola to Gallienus', *Bonner Jahrbücher* 170 (1970), 202–10.

R. F. J. Jones, 'Change on the frontier: northern Britain in the third century', in *The Roman West in the Third Century, Contributions from Archaeology and History* (= BAR International Series 109) (ed. A. King and M. Henig), Oxford, 1981, 393–414.

ARMY REFORMS (pp. 218f.)

E. Birley, 'Septimius Severus and the Roman army', *Epigraphische Studien* 8 (1969), 63–82.

R. E. Smith, 'The army reforms of Septimius Severus', *Historia* 21 (1972), 481–500.

SOLDIERS' WIVES (pp. 219f.)

Scriptores Historiae Augustae, Severus Alexander, 58, 4–5.

R. Macmullen, *Soldier and Civilian in the Later Roman Empire,* Cambridge (Mass.), 1963, 13.

A. H. M. Jones, *The Later Roman Empire,* Oxford, 1964, 649f.

R. P. Wright, 'A Roman altar from Westerwood on the Antonine Wall', *PSAS* 100 (1967–8), 192f.

Brian Campbell, 'The marriage of soldiers under the Empire', *JRS* 68 (1978), 153–66, repeated in his *The Emperor and the Roman Army,* Oxford, 1984, does not carry conviction.

NATIVE AND CIVIL SETTLEMENTS IN THE THIRD CENTURY (pp. 219f.)

P. Salway, *The Frontier People of Roman Britain,* Cambridge, 1965, 192–7.

G. Jobey, 'Homesteads and settlements of the frontier area', in *Rural Settlement in Roman Britain* (ed. C. Thomas), London, 1966, 6–13.

I. A. Richmond, *Roman Art and Archaeology,* London, 1969, 25 (Walldürn inscription).

I. A. Richmond and K. A. Steer, 'Castellum Veluniate and civilians on a Roman frontier', *PSAS* 90 (1956–7), 1–6.

R. E. Birley, *Vindolanda,* Newcastle upon Tyne, 1973.

E. Birley, 'Hadrian's Wall and its neighbourhood', *Studien zu den Militärgrenzen Roms,* Berlin, 1967, 11–13 (the Carvetii).

THE WITHDRAWAL OF ARMY UNITS (pp. 221f.)

J. C. Mann, 'The northern frontier after A.D. 369', *Glasgow Archaeological Journal,* 3 (1974), 37–40.

Notitia Dignitatum Occ. XL, 51–3.

THE LATER THIRD CENTURY (pp. 222ff.)

J. P. Gillam, R. M. Harrison and T. G. Newman, 'Interim report on excavations at the Roman fort of Rudchester 1972', *AA*[5] 1 (1973), 82.

J. P. Gillam, 'The Frontier after Hadrian – a history of the problem', *AA*[5] 2 (1974), 12–15.

J. N. Dove and J. P. Gillam, *The Roman Fort at South Shields,* Newcastle upon Tyne, 1979, 68–9.

J. P. Gillam, 'Excavations at Halton Chesters, 1961', *University of Durham Gazette,* n.s., 9, no. 2.

I. A. Richmond, 'Excavations on Hadrian's Wall in the Birdoswald–Pike Hill Sector, I Birdoswald Fort', *TCWAAS*[2] 30 (1930), 171f.

CONSTANTIUS IN BRITAIN (pp. 224ff.)

J. J. Wilkes, 'Early fourth century rebuilding in Hadrian's Wall forts', in *Britain and Rome* (ed. M. G. Jarrett and B. Dobson), Kendal, 1966, 114–38.

C. M. Daniels, 'Excavations at Wallsend and the fourth-century barracks on Hadrian's Wall', in *Roman Frontier Studies 1979* (= BAR International Series 71) (ed. W. S. Hanson and L. J. F. Keppie), Oxford, 1980, 173–93.

D. J. Breeze and B. Dobson, 'Hadrian's Wall: some problems', *Britannia* 3 (1972), 200–6.

F. G. Simpson and I. A. Richmond, 'Bankshead milecastle, 52', *TCWAAS*² 35 (1935), 245–56.

I. A. Richmond, 'The Romans in Redesdale', *Northumberland County History* 15 (1940), 106–12.

G. H. Donaldson, 'A Reinterpretation of *RIB* 1912 from Birdoswald', *Britannia* 21 (1990), 207–14.

THE CAMPAIGNS AGAINST THE PICTS (p. 224)

Pan. Constantio Caes. = *Pan. Lat. Vet.* VIII (V) 11, 4 (= Mann 185).
Pan. Constantino Aug. = *Pan. Lat. Vet.* VI (VII) 7, 1–2 (= Mann 188).
Anonymus Valesianus, 2, 4 (= Mann 189).

ARMY REFORMS (pp. 230ff.)

A. H. M. Jones, *The Later Roman Empire*, Oxford, 1964, 607–16 *passim*.

WOMEN IN BARRACKS (pp. 231f.)

C. van Driel-Murray, 'The Leatherwork', *Vindolanda III*, Hexham, 1993, 1–75.

THE PICTS (pp. 234ff.)

F. Wainwright, 'The Picts and the problem', in *The Problem of the Picts* (ed. F. Wainwright), Edinburgh, 1955, 1–53.

J. C. Mann, 'The northern frontier after A.D. 369', *Glasgow Archaeological Journal* 3 (1974), 40–42.

Ammianus, 20, 1, 1; 28, 3, 8; 26, 4, 5; 27, 8 (Mann 193–7).

THEODOSIUS AND THE REBUILDING OF THE LATE FOURTH CENTURY (pp. 236ff.)

For individual sites see notes to 'The later third century', pp. 328f.

R. S. O. Tomlin, 'The Date of the Barbarian Conspiracy', *Britannia* 5 (1974), 302–9.

I. A. Richmond, 'Roman and native in the fourth century A.D. and after', in

Roman and Native in North Britain (ed. I. A. Richmond), Edinburgh, 1958, 112–30.

J. C. Mann, 'The northern frontier after A.D. 369', *Glasgow Archaeological Journal* 3 (1974), 34–42.

H. von Petrikovits, 'Fortifications in the north-western Roman Empire from the third to the fifth century A.D.', *JRS* 61 (1971), 197.

RIB, 1672, 1673, 1843, 1844, 1962 (*civitates*).

BLOCKING OF FORT GATES (p. 239.)

D. J. Breeze and B. Dobson, 'Hadrian's Wall: some problems', *Britannia* 3 (1972), 193–7.

THE ABANDONMENT OF THE OUTPOST FORTS (pp. 241f.)

P. J. Casey, 'Constantine the Great in Britain – the evidence of the coinage of the London mint, A.D. 312–14', in *Collectanea Londiniensia* (ed. J. Bird *et al.*), London, 1978, 181–93.

P. J. Casey and M. Savage, 'The coins from the excavations at High Rochester in 1852 and 1855', *AA*[5] 8 (1980), 75–87.

THE LATE FOURTH CENTURY (pp. 242ff.)

I. A. Richmond, 'The Romans in Redesdale', *Northumberland County History* 15 (1940), 112–16.

J. C. Mann, 'The northern frontier after A.D. 369', *Glasgow Archaeological Journal* 3 (1974), 34–42.

L. Alcock, *Arthur's Britain*, London, 1971.

J. Morris, *The Age of Arthur*, London, 1973.

J. P. C. Kent, 'Coin evidence and the evacuation of Hadrian's Wall', *TCWAAS*[2] 51 (1951), 4–15.

D. J. Breeze, 'The Imperial Legacy – Rome and her Neighbours', in B. Crawford (ed.), *Scotland in Dark Age Europe*, St Andrews, 1994, 13–19.

THE YORKSHIRE WATCH-TOWERS (pp. 243f.)

P. J. Casey, 'Magnus Maximus in Britain: a reappraisal', in *The End of Roman Britain* (= BAR British Series 71) (ed. P. J. Casey), Oxford, 1979, 66–79.

VICI AFTER 369 (pp. 244f.)

R. E. Birley, *Civilians on the Roman Frontier*, Newcastle upon Tyne, 1973.

P. Bidwell and S. Speak, *Excavations at South Shields Roman Fort Volume I*, Newcastle upon Tyne, 1994, 103–5.

APPENDIX 1

ROMAN EMPERORS AND GOVERNORS OF BRITAIN

A. R. Birley, *The Fasti of Roman Britain*, Oxford, 1981.

L. Trebius Germanus, *ZPE* 117 (1997), 269–76.

Ulpius Marcellus, M. M. Roxan, *Roman Military Diplomas 1985–1993*, London, 1994, no. 184, pp. 308–10.

APPENDIX 2

THE REGIMENTS OF HADRIAN'S WALL

E. Birley, 'The Beaumont inscription, the Notitia Dignitatum and the garrison of Hadrian's Wall', *TCWAAS*[2] 39 (1939), 190–226.

P. A. Holder, *The Roman Army in Britain*, London, 1982, 'Appendix: The garrison of Britain, 107–33', to be used with caution.

M. G. Jarrett, 'The garrison of Maryport and the Roman army in Britain', in *Britain and Rome* (ed. M. G. Jarrett and B. Dobson), Kendal, n.d. [1966].

M. G. Jarrett, 'Non-Legionary Troops in Roman Britain: the Units', *Britannia* 25 (1994), 35–77.

APPENDIX 3

THE GODS WORSHIPPED ON THE WALL

C. M. Daniels, *Mithras and his Temples on the Wall* (2nd edn), Newcastle upon Tyne, 1967.

A. von Domaszewski, 'Die Religion des römischen Heeres', *Westdeutsche Zeitschrift für Geschichte und Kunst* 14 (1895), 1–121.

E. and J. R. Harris, *The Oriental Cults in Roman Britain*, Leiden, 1965.

M. J. T. Lewis, *Temples in Roman Britain*, Cambridge, 1966.

I. A. Richmond, 'Roman legionaries at Corbridge, their supply-base, temples and cults', *AA*[4] 21 (1943), 127–224.

A. Ross, *Pagan Celtic Britain*, London, 1967.

M. Henig, *Religion in Roman Britain*, London, 1984.

E. Birley, 'The Religion of the Roman Army 1895–1977', *Aufstieg und Niedergang der römischen Welt*, ii, 16, 2 (1978), 1606–41 = *Birley*, 397–432; 'The Deities of Roman Britain', *ANRW*, ii, 18, 1 (1986), 3–112.

I. P. Haynes, 'The Romanization of Religion in the *Auxilia* of the Roman Imperial Army from Augustus to Septimius Severus', *Britannia* 24 (1993), 141–57.

MARYPORT ALTARS (p. 278)

D. J. Breeze, 'The regiments stationed at Maryport and their commanders', in *Roman Maryport and its setting, essays in memory of Michael G. Jarrett* (ed. R. J. A. Wilson), Kendal, 1997; 67–89, especially 67–70.

OFFICIAL MILITARY CALENDAR (pp. 278f.)

R. O. Fink, *Roman Military Records on Papyri*, New Haven, 1971, no. 117; the major study is R. O. Fink, A. S. Hoey and W. F. Snyder, 'The *Feriale Duranum*', *Yale Classical Studies*, 7 (1940), 1–222.

REFERENCES TO INDIVIDUAL INSCRIPTIONS (pp. 278ff.)

These may be traced in the indexes of *RIB* 9. Inscriptions not in *RIB* are identified.

CAPITOLINE TRIAD (p. 278f.)

I. A. Richmond, 'Roman legionaries at Corbridge, their supply-base, temples and cults', *AA*[4] 21 (1943), 154–8, 173–6.

Britannia 20 (1989), 331ff. n. 5.

COVENTINA (p. 279)

L. Allason-Jones and B. McKay, *Coventina's Well*, Chesters, 1985.

FESTIVALS (p. 281)

A. K. Bowman and J. D. Thomas, *Vindolanda: the Latin writing-tablets*, London, 1983, 86.

Tab. Vindol. II 190 festivals of Fors Fortuna? and of an unknown goddess; 301 Saturnalia.

MERCURY (p. 281)

Caesar, *de bello Gallico*, 6, 17.

VENUS AT HIGH ROCHESTER (p. 281)

A. Ross, *Pagan Celtic Britain*, London, 1967, 207 identifies the sculpture simply as a trio of nymph goddesses.

VETRIS (pp. 281f.)

To the examples in *RIB* add *Britannia* 4 (1973), 329, n. 11, 12; 6 (1975), 285f., n. 6, n. 7; 8 (1977), 432, no. 22; 10 (1979), 346, n. 8 (Vindolanda); 18 (1987), 368, n. 7 (South Shields).

MAPONUS (p. 282)

To the examples in *RIB* add *Britannia* 2 (1971), 291, n. 12 (*lunula*, Vindolanda). Birrens figure, *JRS* 58 (1968), 209, n. 28.

MOGONS (p. 284)

To the examples in *RIB* add *Britannia* 4 (1973), 329, n. 10 (Vindolanda).

COCIDIUS (pp. 284f.)

D. B. Charlton and M. M. Mitcheson, 'Yardhope, a shrine to Cocidius?', *Britannia*, 14 (1983), 143–53.

MATRES (p. 284)

To the examples in *RIB* add *Britannia* 1 (1970), 309, n. 16; 440, n. 31 ring, Matres Parcae (Vindolanda).

SEVERED HEAD (p. 284)

A. Ross, *Pagan Celtic Britain*, London, 1967, 61–126.
Trajan's Column, XXIV (58, 60), CXIII (303).

MARS ALATOR (p. 285)

Ephemeris Epigraphica, VII, 399.

IOM DOLICHENUS AT CORBRIDGE (p. 285)

I. A. Richmond, 'Roman legionaries at Corbridge, their supply-base, temples and cults', *AA*[4] 21 (1943), 179–96.

TEMPLES AT CORBRIDGE (pp. 287f.)

I. A. Richmond, 'Roman legionaries at Corbridge, their supply-base, temples and cults', *AA*[4] 21 (1943), 136–46. Temples IV and V did not exist, III is doubtful as a temple.

CHRISTIANITY (pp. 289f.)

J. Crow, *Housesteads*, London, 1995, 95–8.
A. H. M. Jones, *The Later Roman Empire*, Oxford, 1964, chapter 23.
G. R. Watson, 'Christianity in the Roman army in Britain', in *Christianity in*

Britain 300–700 (ed. M. W. Barley and R. P. C. Hanson), Leicester, 1968, 51–4.

Charles Thomas, *Christianity in Roman Britain to A.D. 500*, London, 1981.

P. Bidwell and S. Speak, *Excavations at South Shields Roman Fort Volume I*, Newcastle upon Tyne, 1994, 103–5.

APPENDIX 4

THE ROMAN NAMES OF THE FORTS ON HADRIAN'S WALL

J. D. Cowen and I. A. Richmond, 'The Rudge Cup', *AA*[4] 12 (1935), 310–42.

J. Heurgon, 'The Amiens Patera', *JRS* 41 (1951), 22–4.

J. C. Mann, 'Birdoswald to Ravenglass', *Britannia* 20 (1989), 75–9.

I. A. Richmond and O. G. S. Crawford, 'The British section of the Ravenna Cosmography', *Archaeologia* 93 (1949), 1–50.

A. L. F. Rivet and Colin Smith, *The Place-Names of Roman Britain*, London, 1979.

INDEX

335

Fraomar, king of the
Alamanni 241
frontier army (*limitanei*) 210,
219, 231
frontier control 14, 16, 18,
20–21, 22, 23, 24, 26,
39–40
frontiers
in Britain 9, 10, *11*, 12,
13–14, 15, 16, 17, *19*,
24, 26
concept of 1, 2–4, 8–9,
15, 22–4, 90
development of 102,
148–50, *151*, 152
in Germany 15, 16, 21,
64, 66
natural 26
rivers as 3, 8, 9, 15–16,
22, 23, 26, 39, 158, 163
roads as 16, 17, 23
timber palisades as 64, 66
types 64, 95
see also Antonine Wall;
Hadrian's Wall
Frontinus, Iulius, governor
of Britain 8, 252
Fronto, Cornelius 25–6, 90
Fullofaudes, *dux
Britanniarum* 232, 235,
236
funerals *see* death/burial
furnaces 177

Gallia Narbonensis 5, 154,
181
Galloway, kingdom of 242
Gallus, Didius 7
Gask frontier, Perthshire
forts on 16
towers on 21, 64, 244
see also Scotland

gates
in fortlets 102
in forts 78–9, 81, 100,
102, 164–6, *165*, *167*,
168
in Hadrian's Wall 34,
40–41, 53
in turrets 135–6, *137*
see also milecastles
Gaul
army recruits from 157
barbarian invasion, AD
407 244
praetorian prefect of 233
Roman conquest 3, 5
sack of Rome by, 390 BC
2
under Severus 138
see also Gallia Narbonensis
Genii Cucullati (the gods)
287
genius (guardian spirit) 280
Genius Loci (the god) 290
Genouian 'district' 88–9
Germanicus 195
Germany 14, 118, 119
barbarians (free
Germans) 232, 240–41
forts 22–3, 31, 64, 173
frontiers 15, 16, 21;
timber palisades as 64,
66
governors of 120
Hadrian in 64
Lower 15, 26, 64
Raetia province 89, 144,
249
Roman invasion 3, 6,
12–13, 15–16
towers 64
under Trajan 64
troops in 22, 92–4, 163

Upper 15, 15, 22, 23–4,
92–4, 219–20
see also Danube river;
Rhine river
Geta, emperor 139, 140,
141, 142
Gillam, J. P. xv, xvii, 99,
222
Gloucester 11, 14
Roman colony 154
gods 196
attributes of 284–5
native 196, 277, 279, 284,
285
see also individual gods;
religion
governors *see* provincial
governors
granaries (*horrea*)
built by British fleet
66–7, 78
in forts 18, *53*, 66–7,
107, 140, *141*, 166,
167, 171, *171*, *172*,
178
Great Chesters fort
under Hadrian 29, 51, 54;
under Marcus 121;
third century 217
building/s 121, 139,
217
dating 78, 81, 102, 121,
133, fig. 23
design *52*, 61
gates 102
granary 217
Roman name 292, 293,
294, 298
size 54
units at 53, 54, 147,
259
water supplies 203